John Alexander Dowie

American First-Fruits

Being a brief Record of eight Months' Divine Healing Missions in the State of

California

John Alexander Dowie

American First-Fruits

Being a brief Record of eight Months' Divine Healing Missions in the State of California

ISBN/EAN: 9783337187590

Printed in Europe, USA, Canada, Australia, Japan

Cover: Foto ©ninafisch / pixelio.de

More available books at **www.hansebooks.com**

American First-Fruits

BEING A

Brief Record of Eight Months'

Divine Healing Missions

IN THE

STATE OF CALIFORNIA

CONDUCTED BY THE

Rev. John Alex. Dowie  Mrs. Dowie

FROM MELBOURNE, AUSTRALIA,

WITH AN APPENDIX CONTAINING

Two Addresses on Divine Healing

DELIVERED BEFORE THE

CONGREGATIONAL MINISTERS' CLUB OF SAN FRANCISCO.

PUBLISHED AT "LEAVES OF HEALING" OFFICE,
320 SANSOME STREET,
SAN FRANCISCO.
1889.

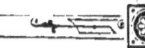

[SECOND, AND ENLARGED, EDITION]

American

✤ First-Fruits

——BEING A——

Brief Record of Eight Months'

Divine Healing Missions

IN THE

STATE OF CALIFORNIA

CONDUCTED BY THE

Rev. John Alex. Dowie ✤ Mrs. Dowie

FROM MELBOURNE, AUSTRALIA,

WITH AN APPENDIX CONTAINING

Two Addresses on Divine Healing

DELIVERED BEFORE THE

CONGREGATIONAL MINISTERS' CLUB OF SAN FRANCISCO.

PUBLISHED AT "LEAVES OF HEALING" OFFICE,
320 SANSOME STREET,
SAN FRANCISCO.
1889.

INTRODUCTION.

With joyous songs and grateful hearts, the people of God in ancient days obeyed His command, "Thou shalt not delay to offer the first of thy ripe fruits, . . . the FIRST-FRUITS of thy labors which thou hast sown in the field." (Exodus 21 : 29 ; 23 : 16.) We, therefore, giving all the praise to our God and Father, who has, by the Holy Spirit, so gloriously blessed our first eight months work for His dear Son in this land, send forth these "First-Fruits" of our labors in America in the cause of Christ our Lord, especially in the ministry of Divine Healing. We do this on the eve of going forth again for a second and longer period of service to our Lord on this Pacific Coast.

We begin, on Lord's Day, April 28th, a mission in the city of Los Angeles, Southern California, and, God willing, we shall visit other cities in that portion of this State, and proceed from thence to Oregon, Washington and British Columbia, where we intend to conduct missions until the Fall, in which labors we ask the prayers and sympathies of all our Christian readers.

The following pages are, for the most part, simply extracts from our shorthand writer's reports of the words of testimony uttered by those who have been healed through faith in Jesus, as given by themselves before a multitude of witnesses in the Praise and Testimony Meetings which have been held at the close of each of our missions, ten of which have been conducted by us in this State. Concerning the genuineness of these statements there can be no righteous dispute, but we deeply regret (although we cannot be surprised) that we have been under the necessity of defending the truthfulness of these witnesses against the false and malicious attacks, not of the world, but of some who profess to be ministers within the Church of God. "No strange thing has happened to us" in our being compelled to discharge this painful duty, but it is none the less to be regretted, although we trust such conduct will never be repeated. One good result is that it has given us an opportunity, and laid upon us the necessity, of again and again bringing forward these witnesses, who, before hundreds and even thousands of persons, have reaffirmed their testimony without challenge. In this matter, remembering the words of the great apostle, we say to our Christian friends, "Pray for us, that the word of the Lord may have free course and be glorified, and that we may be delivered from unreasonable [margin, Gr. "absurd"] and wicked men, for all men have not faith." 2 Thessalonians 3 : 2.

In only two, or possibly three, cases do we know of any of the witnesses whose testimonies are herein reported having gone back to former conditions, and the cause of their declension in every case is to be found in a return to sin, largely through evil and ungodly surroundings which the persons concerned have yielded to instead of overcoming through the grace of God. In this connection, we desire to remind all who read, that what is received through faith in Jesus may be lost through unbelief and other sins. Our Lord's warning in John 5 : 14 sufficiently proves this assertion. He said to one whom he had healed, "Behold, thou art made whole. Sin no more, lest a worse thing come unto thee."

We have added to this new and enlarged edition of "First-Fruits" two addresses which we delivered before the Congregational Ministers' Club of San Francisco. These contain brief, and necessarily incomplete, outlines of our doctrinal teaching, which forms by far the greatest portion of our ministry; but we think it well to add these pages, since there is a widespread desire that we should publish our TEACHING. We reserve, however, the full publication of that in book form until we have opportunity to write our intended work on the whole subject, which we trust will be during next Fall and Winter. Meanwhile, we shall publish articles on various aspects of Divine Healing truth in our monthly magazine. Our constant experience is that Teaching is of the first importance. Our Lord's example in His earthly ministry, as shown in Matt. 4 : 23 and 9 : 35, makes this clear. There we see that Jesus went about, firstly Teaching, secondarily Preaching, and thirdly Healing, and, so far as He enables us, we follow in his footsteps. The greater part of our work is Teaching. Preaching is simply the proclamation of the results of the Teaching, and the Healing always follows where the truth is fully received.

We have been led to establish in this country our little magazine entitled "Leaves of Healing," which we established last June in New Zealand on our way to this country. We have transplanted it to this coast, and the first number of the new issue will be ready early next month, God willing.

In connection with this matter, we have established an office at 320 Sansome Street, San Francisco, where subscriptions will be received ($1.00 per annum) for this monthly magazine, and where copies of various pamphlets which we have written on this subject can be obtained. We are asking our Lord to enable us to print *with our own press*, as soon as possible, our various publications, and we trust soon to be in a position to supply tracts and Divine Healing Literature to those who desire it throughout this coast.

One important outcome of this work has been the formation, in San Francisco, on Lord's Day, Nov. 11th, of the American Divine Healing Association, of which I have accepted the office of President *pro tem*. Three Branches have now been formed in the cities of San Francisco, Oakland and San Jose respectively, numbering about seven hundred members, which are steadily growing and maintaining most interesting weekly meetings, and conducting a widespread visitation. It is our intention, at the close of our missions, to establish Branches of this Association in each of the places that we are led of God to visit.

In answer to many inquiries, we desire to inform Christian readers who are interested that we purpose, if the Lord permit, leaving this coast next spring. Proceeding eastward, we trust to hold missions in a number of central positions in the United States. Thereafter, we intend to visit Canada and Great Britain and Ireland. But we can fix no program, for our absolute duty is to follow God's plan, and we simply make these announcements in answer to many inquiries. At the same time, we shall be glad to communicate with friends in many of the centers of population in this and other countries, and help by correspondence, and otherwise, in the extension of this beautiful gospel and ministry of Divine Healing. All who desire to communicate with us will please address their letters to the office of "Leaves of Healing," 320 Sansome Street, San Francisco, from whence they will be forwarded to us should we not be in that city.

We desire to record our gratitude to God that He is raising up able and devoted servants and handmaidens, to whom we shall be able to leave this work next year with perfect confidence. Already, the presidents and officers of the variou Branches of the Association are justifying our choice, and hundreds of the members are engaging much more actively than before in the work of God in connection with their various churches, besides promoting this work.

Our ministry is to the whole "Household of Faith," irrespective of all sects or parties. We know only Christ, and desire to preach only His atoning sacrifice, and to declare the blessings which flow therefrom. From the Covenant of Jehovah-Ropphi, in Ex. 15:23-26, and throughout the whole Shining Way of the Promises of God in all the Scriptures, we see the stars of Divine Love forming in the Heavens above us the beautiful covenant name, "I am the Lord that healeth thee," and the Stripes of that universal banner seem to become more glorious every day, as we see more fully the meaning of the prophetic words, "With His Stripes we are Healed." Beneath the Banner of the Cross we march on to certain ultimate Triumph, and, although the way may sometimes be drear, and the foe we know is ever near, yet we can follow, calm and fearless, if we are guided by His hand.

So we send forth this little book on its way, praying that our "American First-Fruits" may be sweet to the taste of many sick and weary Pilgrims Zionward, leading them to see in Jesus the Tree of Life whose fruits are always ready for their need, and whose words are "Leaves of Healing for the nations," which are now groaning beneath the oppression of Satan and Sin and Disease and Death and Hell, but which, through the "Saving Health" the Gospel brings, shall yet be brought, though dark days lie between, to see in Christ their Saviour, their Healer, and their all.

Asking once more for the prayers of every brother and sister in Christ who reads these lines, that we may in all things be led of the Spirit of God, and sustained amidst the toils and trials of this most blessed ministry, we are

Your brother and sister in Jesus,   JOHN ALEX. DOWIE,
                                     JEANIE DOWIE.

Borden, Fresno Co., Cal., April 21, 1889.

American First-Fruits,

—BEING A—

Brief Record of Nearly Eight Months'

DIVINE HEALING MISSIONS

IN THE

STATE OF CALIFORNIA,

CONDUCTED BY THE

Rev. John Alex. Dowie & Mrs. Dowie.

[Extract from Record of our Travels and Missions in August number of "Leaves of Healing," pp. 63–67.]

On the morning of Saturday, 16th of June, the seats of the corridor in the hotel near my room were crowded with persons desiring interviews with me. Amongst these was an aged woman from Sacramento, who came in leaning upon a crutch, and in great pain. She was accompanied by her daughter. After a few words of prayer I found she was a most interesting character. She was a tall, gaunt-visaged, weird-looking person, abrupt in manner, without imagination, conscious of her ignorance, and doubtful of her standing in Christ. She presented a most peculiar study as the conversation proceeded. She said, "Doctor" (most persons here call me doctor), "I am a hard case, very poor, and very ignorant. My husband read about you yesterday in Sacramento, the capital of this State, about 100 miles distant from this city. He said, 'That is the old-time religion, or else it is all a lie; go down and see if the doctor is what they say he is, and if he is,

You Will Come Back Cured.'

I stared at him in astonishment. But he was very pressing, and said, 'Go!' So I have come."

"But are you a Christian?" I said.

"I don't know," she said; "I want to know; I do not believe in saying I am, unless I am sure."

And then in a few minutes she burst out, "O Doctor I want to be sure of salvation; you do not know how ignorant I am; I can't read or write; I don't know a B from a bull's foot; I am *poor white trash;* do you know what that means?"

I said, "Yes, you were born in the South, were you not?"

She said, "Yes, they talk of slaves—black slaves—but I have been a white slave all my life, and I am a slave now as regards work. They sent me out when I was only four years old to gather sticks in the woods; I was beaten, half starved and cruelly treated by a drunken step-father; I grew up ignorant; I do not know how to talk even now to such a gentleman as you; oh! tell me how I can be sure of salvation."

I was deeply moved, for she was speaking with a natural, or perhaps I should say a supernatural, eloquence that was irresistible. I gladly responded to her cry, and it was not long before I had the joy of seeing her led into a simple trust in Christ as her Saviour; the Holy Spirit had already wrought in her conviction of sin, and a fervent love for Christ the Righteous, and she was ready to yield her heart to him. I realized that Satan was condemned, and she was set free. She looked at me with tears in her stony face, and when I said, "Now will you just trust Jesus as your healer?" she again replied, "Show me how."

I said, "If Jesus were to enter this room now and to present himself to you, would you ask him to heal you, believing that he would?"

"Oh, yes, Doctor," she said, "and I believe he would."

"Then," I replied, "he is present."

She looked around. I said, "Invisibly present, for he has said, 'Lo, I am with you alway.' If that is true he is here now in spirit and in power."

"Doctor," she said, "I believe he is."

Without another word I knelt at her feet, and asked her to put the diseased foot in my hand. She did so. I took off her slipper, and, holding the foot in my hand, I prayed that God would use me by the Holy Spirit in Jesus' name, and for his sake, in her healing. When I had finished praying, I looked up and saw that she was softly crying. I think my attitude at her feet had deeply touched her; but she was looking upward lost in reverent prayer. I rose and said, "In Jesus' name, rise and walk!" She looked for the crutch, which I had placed beyond her reach. I repeated the words, "In Jesus' name, rise and walk!" She arose, and walked several times across the room.

I Said, "You Are Healed!"

She could not speak for emotion, which she tried hard to restrain, but at last gave way, and falling on Mrs. Dowie's neck, kissed her warmly, and also embraced her daughter, whom she had told me she had not kissed for many years. It was a very affecting scene. The daughter was a backslider, but ere she left the room she was restored to God. As they were going away, I said to the old lady, "You have left something which belongs to you."

She said, "What?"

I said, "Your crutch."

"Oh," she said, "I don't need it any more; I am healed."

I said, "What do you intend to do with it then?" holding it in my hand.

She said, "O Doctor, if you would like to take it, I will leave it with you."

I said, "Very well; put it in the corner." And in the corner it remains, in the room where this is now being written.

In two days, on Monday, the 19th of June, she came back rejoicing, saying she had walked about quite well. She told me that she had not for two and a half years rested upon that foot without a crutch, and that for ten months she thought she had not slept one "solid hour." I asked her how she slept now, and she said, "like a baby." And then she told me she was going home. I said, "What are you going to do when you get home?"

"I will tell all," she said, "that

Jesus Saved and Healed Even Me."

This incident I have thus narrated in detail, because it is the first case of divine healing which I have been permitted to witness, and to be instrumental in, on this great continent. I could not have desired a better. Ignorant, almost without hope, she was one of those common people who, in the days of Jesus' earthly ministry, heard him gladly, and received him fully, not only as their Saviour, but as their Healer. I pray that she may be the representative of multitudes who shall thus, like the poor of old, have this gospel preached unto them, and who shall receive all its saving, cleansing, healing, and uplifting power.

But let me give

Another Illustration of This Work.

Applying to a very opposite class of American society. This to me is also intensely interesting, and I pray it may be profitable to you.

On the forenoon of Wednesday, 20th of June, there was a knock at the door of the room in which I am now sitting, and a visitor was announced by the attendant, a tall, finely-proportioned, elegantly-dressed lady, who at a glance I could see was one accustomed to move in what is called "society." Bowing very respectfully, she said, with her voice trembling with emotion, "Doctor, will you grant me a conversation?" Holding the keys of her room in her hand, she slowly extended it and said, "I also am a guest in this hotel."

Having introduced her to Mrs. Dowie, she sat down and told us her story. It was one which I can never forget. She said, as nearly as I can recollect her words, "Doctor, I have come, although I knew it not, from New York to see you."

I asked her to explain. She said: "Six weeks ago I was, as I have been for many years, a worldly, frivolous, vain lady in society, neither worse nor better than my mother before me, and like many in my own station of life about me. It has pleased God (I would not have used his name six weeks ago) to give to myself and husband much wealth; but we never used it except for to gratify ourselves and to entertain people like ourselves. I used to go to church occasionally, sometimes quite frequently; but it was a part of society duty, of society life. I never remember realizing God's presence once in any part of the worship, or in any of the many discourses I heard. But six weeks ago I was reading a new book, to which my attention had been directed. I am fond of reading and of discussing in society the literature of the day. It was just because it was a book being talked about that I read it. It was Prof. Henry Drummond's "Natural Law in the Spiritual World." I was deeply impressed, not so much with his reasoning, which I disputed, but by one thought which fastened itself upon my mind: I felt myself standing upon the verge of earth and time looking away out into an eternity, and I had no hope. I felt intensely miserable: I felt I wanted to know God, for I was without hope, and I was without God, in the world. But I told no one my thoughts, not even my husband. I was ashamed to let anyone know that I felt that I was a sinner. We were about to start (my husband and I) for Europe, for Paris, where my only son is being educated, to spend the summer on the continent. But I felt I could not go in the condition I was. So I said to my husband, "Let me go West before we leave for Europe." He said, "Where to?" I said, "I don't know, I think I will go to San Francisco." He asked, "Why?" I would not tell him. But he agreed, and as we have friends, many friends, *society friends*," she added, "in this city, he thought it possible I might spend a good time here, and so I came a fortnight ago. A few days here with my friends only made me more miserable, for I could see that many of them were as heartily sick of the world as I was. So I left San Francisco and went down to the Hotel Del Monte at Monterey" (this hotel, one of the wonders of this continent, I visited when at Pacific Grove; it is a fashionable resort, at all seasons, of wealthy people), "there I found no relief; I wandered about the beautiful gardens, and walked along the seashore, but nature had no balm for my sickness. One day I lifted up quite casually, as I thought, a San Francisco newspaper;

I Was Startled with the Title

Of a paragraph on which my eyes fell, 'Healing by Faith.' I read it, and immediately the desire to see you became intense; I could not get rid of it, and after several days I determined to come up to the city and stop at this hotel and find an opportunity of seeing you. Two days have passed away, and until now I have not had the courage to make my request.

"That is all," she said, "except that I am so weary, not yet forty years old, and *worn out*. I have worked harder in society, in pleasure seeking and pleasure giving, than any

Washerwoman Ever Worked at Her Tub.

Oh! what must I do?"

Mrs. Dowie and I were both deeply moved. I told her how glad I was to see and hear her, and how thankful to God for the opportunity of telling her what she must do to be saved. I pointed out to her that the book she had read had been written by a true Christian man, that notwithstanding many differed from his way of putting some of his arguments, all who knew him admitted that his book was written in a reverent spirit, with a sincere desire to glorify God, and to bring blessing to man. I remarked that he had written the book praying that God, the Holy Ghost, would use it; and that it was most pleasant for me, as it would be for him, to know that God had used it, in convincing her of sin and of the emptiness and vanity of her life.

I then said, "But conviction is not conversion, and before you are converted you must also be convinced of the righteousness of Christ." I read to her the words contained in John 16 : 7-11. She saw she had an "Advocate with the Father, Jesus Christ the righteous." I then led her to see that

He Would Undertake Her Case,

and we united in prayer before our Father's throne, where she gave herself to him, and rose believing that she was justified, pardoned, blessed. She rejoiced, and very calmly, but very firmly, vowed that her whole life should be reversed; that her time, her talents, and her wealth, should be consecrated to God. She said, "In some matters it will be a hard fight, but I see and feel that I cannot return to the old life."

After further conversation I wrote a letter to the Rev. A. B. Simpson, of Madison Avenue Tabernacle, New York, introducing her to his kind notice and care; and she left us saying she would return the next day to her home in that city. We believe that she received not only pardon, but healing, for she left us saying that she had experienced both.

These two cases so widely different in character, will give our kind friends an idea of how the mission in this country opened.

[Extract from September number of "Leaves of Healing," pp. 82-99.]

San Francisco Mission and Its Closing Scenes.

It will be remembered that this Mission was conducted in the Young Men's Christian Association Hall, Sutter Street. The meetings in the afternoon grew steadily in numbers and in power, and a very large proportion of those attending were business men who left their offices and banks after three o'clock, to listen to the "Healing-room Addresses." Our closing afternoon meetings were large, and at last completely filled the hall, many sitting on the steps to the galleries.

The evening lectures were from the first attended by audiences which filled the building, and at last crowded it out. One of the morning papers of the city observed that "even standing room was at a premium." From the very first meeting we had after-meetings, attended on each occasion by many hundreds of persons, and it was our delight to see large numbers seeking openly at these meetings the Lord as their Saviour. More than one hundred and fifty persons thus professed to have found salvation in these meetings through faith in Jesus.

The work of Divine Healing went steadily on almost from the first, but during the last five days of the mission there were many striking miracles of healing, and numbers thronged us seeking the Lord for healing, swelling into hundreds.

It is our intense regret that in every mission we cannot see individually all those who desire to see us, but we feel it only makes us more earnest in making our message clear and plain, so that the people having received the teaching, may thus directly seek Jesus as their healer. We long for the day when multitudes will be healed without human touch. But when this work is in its infancy it seems to be with many an absolute necessity that they shall have the human helper, and we pray that God may send forth many qualified laborers into his great harvest-fields, for truly we see every day the fields are "white unto the harvest." The large numbers of Christians who professed to receive blessing during this mission greatly cheered us, and a very striking feature also was the numerous requests for prayer which came to us from every part of the city and State, and from all parts of America. These numbered many hundreds, and in not a few cases there were very direct answers.

But time would fail us to attempt any detailed account of our long series of over sixty meetings and after-meetings during that mission. It would be wrong, however, for us to omit to mention the special meetings for men, which at the request of the Young Men's Christian Association we conducted for four successive Lord's days. The crowded rows of earnest faces will never be forgotten by us, and the large numbers of men who found Christ as Saviour in these meetings make us deeply grateful to him who has thus condescended to use us so graciously.

The hearty co-operation of Mr. Henry McCoy, the Secretary, Mr. Johnson, the Assistant Secretary, the members of the Reception Committee, and large numbers of young men of the Association, was also most gratifying; and we owe it to them, and to God, to record our high appreciation of their constant kindness. Our janitor, "John," by his hearty good nature and unceasing devotion won the love of many hearts, and at our closing meeting a reference to his kindness elicited a burst of applause.

So it will be seen there were many things favorable to a successful mission. Yet there were not a few things unfavorable. The doctrine was little known and it was discredited by many who confounded it with Mind Healing, or Christian Science (modified forms of Spiritualism), which have invaded America and done much evil. We had also to contend with the apathy of many, and the antipathy of some, of the ministers of the gospel. We were very freely discussed (and the discussions were reported) at ministerial associations. On various public occasions reference was made to ourselves, and sermons preached in many churches on the subject of our mission.

But it may also be stated that a number of ministers openly avowed their adhesion to our teaching, and some of then openly assisted us on our platform and in the after-meetings; while others expressed their sympathies by their frequent presence and by kind letters.

I had also the privilege of preaching for my friend and brother, the Rev. M. Gibson, D. D., in the First United Presbyterian Church, and also in the beautiful Mariners' Church, the good pastor of which aided us throughout the mission. We were unable to avail ourselves of the invitation to preach for other brethren owing to the pressure of work in our mission.

Among the ministers who most effectually helped us, I would desire to mention gratefully the names of the Revs. N. W. Lane, M. D., and F. W. Clapp, Congregationalists; Rev. Mr. Arnold, Free Church; Rev. Mr. Sterrett, Methodist Episcopal, and others. The first-mentioned brother, Dr. Lane, minister and medical doctor, who was unable to be present at our closing meeting, sent us a kind letter expressing himself as follows: "You have my hearty appreciation of your labors of love for the Master and precious souls since you came among us, and I assure you I am in full sympathy with your presentation of a complete and full gospel for spirit, soul and body, which you so faithfully and successfully preach.

"I pray for you both daily in family worship, making mention by name of yourself and dear wife, and shall continue to do so.

"When I return I wish to take part in the Pacific Coast Divine Healing Association, and go forward to see the wonderful works of God manifested in the salvation of precious souls, their consecration, and the healing of the diseased. God bless you both greatly."

The Association to which Dr. Lane refers will, we trust, be formed during our second mission in San Francisco, which will be held in a month or two, and it is a great joy to us that such men as he and our beloved Brother Arnold, and others, will take a leading part, with many devoted men and women, in the establishment of such an organization.

We ask our friends everywhere to pray that we may be divinely guided in this portion of the work; for good organization promotes progress and insures success.

It was also pleasing during this mission to have the open testimony of several Christian medical men, in good practice, who attended our meetings and asked us to pray for their own friends and relatives.

There were also representatives, in intelligent teachers and prominent members and office-bearers, of many, if not all, of the evangelical churches of the city in constant attendance, and the appreciative letters which we have received would fill a respectable little volume.

The Closing Praise and Testimony Meeting.

This was held on the evening of Monday, July 9. The building was crowded to its utmost capacity long before the meeting opened, and every inch of standing room was occupied; one of the morning papers says, "Many hundreds of persons could not obtain admission." A song service preceded our entrance upon the platform, conducted by our kind friend, Mr. Chamberlain. We were engaged during that time in meeting with those who desired to testify, in the parlors of the Association, and it was with difficulty that we could thread our way to the platform, with the twenty or thirty persons who desired to speak.

The audience sang in fine style, "We are marching to Zion," and we felt as we heard them sing, it was an inestimable joy to be permitted to help those who on their Zionward way were groaning in pain, groping in blindness, and oppressed by the devil with countless diseases. We felt it was a recompense for our continuous and exhausting labor to see this great multitude of faces lit up with enthusiasm and expectancy, and looking around upon the blind who had received their sight, the lame who now had received power to walk, and the many forms of sickness which had been healed; we felt that we had indeed been privileged to be the bearers of "Leaves of Healing" from the "Tree of Life." After giving the glory to God, I presented the petitions for prayer which had been received since the previous meeting. Amongst these was one which was so beautifully answered that we cannot forbear giving it in detail, ere we proceed with the account of the meeting. I quote from a verbatim report of the proceedings now in my hands, written by Mr. G. H. Hawes, of 320 Sansome Street, San Francisco, a highly efficient stenographer and type-writer, who assists me to overtake my very extensive correspondence, and to report in full these meetings and special lectures.

The petition to which I have referred reads thus: "Please pray earnestly for a dear Christian lady who is dying; not expected to live until to-morrow morning. She is suffering agony, great and intense pain; oh! pray that she may be delivered from pain now—this moment, and that she may find in Jesus her deliverer."

Our prayer in presenting this petition, as reported by Mr. Hawes, reads as follows: "Lord, we thank thee for genuine requests, and if this sister is herself a partaker in this petition, we have no doubt as to the answer. We lay it before thy throne now in the presence of all thy people. We plead that the disease may be removed. It is not thy will that thy children should die in agony and pain; it is thy will that when we have served thee and our generation 'according to the will of God,' that we should fall 'asleep in Jesus;' that we should meanwhile obtain pardon from our sin, and that we should be saved from the power of sin and disease and death and hell, and all the power of the enemy. If it be thy will to give our sister sleep, we murmur not, but we say

Remove the Pain, Remove the Disease,

And we know we are saying it in accordance with thy will, and if she is co-operating with us in faith, then the answer has come to that silent room, and now thou art saying, 'Peace, be still.'"

The following morning I received a beautiful letter from the lady who sent the petition, Miss Laura V. Stone, 807 Leavenworth St., S. F., from which we quote the following words:—

"I wish to thank God for the instantaneous answer to prayer last night for the dear Christian lady who seemed at death's door. You remember that you prayed that she might be relieved from pain, and find Jesus as her healer and deliverer. The first part of the prayer was fully answered last night, as she passed a comfortable night without pain, and is much better this afternoon, although very weak. I have just come from her bedside, from which she sends you a message of thanks, and asks your continued prayers. She has been sick many, many years, a great sufferer, was unable to move hand or foot, not even her head from the pillow, and when moved by others the pain was most severe.

"Please thank God for what he did last night, and continue to pray that she may be kept free from all pain, and that her healing shall be perfected. Oh, how I long for this, that Jesus Christ may be glorified in that household, which is one of faith and prayer. Pray for me also. God bless you and keep you and your dear family, is the prayer of your sister in Christ."

Still quoting from Mr. Hawes' report, we find that in opening the meeting we said in prayer: "And now, Lord, we commend this meeting to thee. Bless this great company; bless those who are here as thy witnesses to thy saving, healing and cleansing power; some were great sinners; they feel themselves very unworthy; they are saved, they are healed; we give thee glory. Some, O Lord, are not as perfectly healed as we would desire to see; perfect their consecration and perfect their healing. And now we GIVE THEE ALL THE PRAISE. WE HAVE DONE NOTHING, thou hast done it all. Thine is the kingdom and the power and the glory. Let good go forth from this meeting through this beautiful city and State; yea, wilt thou bless all throughout this broad and beautiful land, and may multitudes hearing that thou art healing know

'That the healing of thy seamless dress
Is by *their* beds of pain,'

That they may know also, who are walking this world bowed down with suffering, that *they*

'May touch thee in life's throng and press,
And be made whole again,'

Even midst the streets of the cities. We ask it for Jesus' sake. Amen."

We then sang, "She only touched the hem of thy garment," and after the reading of Scripture by Mrs. Dowie, we made the announcements concerning our future missions, and recorded our thanks publicly to Mr. McCoy, the Secretary, and the members of the Association. The testimony meeting was then proceeded with. We first of all again gave God the glory and repeated our declaration that "we never healed anybody, that we never expected to heal anyone, that we never attempted to heal anyone, and that our Lord Jesus Christ, our Saviour and Healer and Sanctifier, had by the Holy Spirit wrought the work." We again defined our position with reference to Mind Cure, Mental Healing, Christian Science, and Spiritualism, declaring that with these things "we had not one thought in common, or one single desire to co-operate."

The first testimony was one that created intense interest and made a profound impression; it was that of

The Restoration to Sight of a Little Boy who had been Born Blind.

Quoting again from the verbatim report, we find that we said the following words: "Here is the little boy" (presenting him to the audience, a bright, intelligent little fellow, whose opened eyes were looking around in every direction with keen interest upon the meeting). He is a fatherless little boy. Is it not written of our God, 'He is the father of the fatherless?" This little fellow attended the meetings; he was blind. Dr. Barcon said he was blind from birth. I did not know he was here; he sat and listened to the word and received it. The good doctor had operated upon his eyes three years ago; he had done the best he could; he is a kind man and had taken a great deal of interest in the lad. The little fellow listened earnestly to the teaching, and heard me say to the people,

You Must be Saved First.

Then he told us that he heard us say in the after meeting, "Those who want to find salvation, stand up!" He said, "What does it mean, mother?" And she said, "As near as I can tell you, Georgie, it means that you are to give yourself wholly to Christ." He said, "That is just what I will do." And he did it.

So the next day he came into the meeting rejoicing in Christ. It was July the 4th, your great fire-work's day; my attention had been drawn to him, and I promised to see him that afternoon. When he came into the healing room with his mother (who is now present) we said after prayer, "Now, Georgie, are you sure that you are saved?"

"Yes, sir," he replied, "I am."

"When were you saved?"

"Yesterday," he said.

"How were you saved?"

"Well," he said, "I had been *trying to trust Jesus* all my life, and yesterday *I did it*, sir."

"Well, that is all right. Now do you expect Jesus to give you sight?"

He said, "I am sure he will, sir."

I laid my hands upon him and we prayed. When he opened his eyes, the little boy who had been blind from birth could see. Here is the result: the boy is now looking upon you with the power to see. Let me read the written testimony that his mother has placed in my hands to be read to this meeting, and she will afterwards herself rise and confirm the words:—

"My little boy Georgie was afflicted from birth with blindness. Three years ago an operation was performed by Dr. Barcon of this city. The boy was able to distinguish day from night, and sometimes bright colors, red and blue. For ten years he has been unable to walk, until now, without being led by the hand, when outside the house. He never saw an object, so far as we know, durduring these ten years, not a single object to know what it was. Jesus has now, through Mr. Dowie's agency, restored his sight almost entirely; he can now walk alone, see houses, chimneys, and small objects very readily. He can also see print of large size, and it can be read by him; something I never expected to see him do. My little boy is bright and happy now, and gives God all the glory. Praise his name forever."

"I was also," adds the writer, Mrs. Lula Ritchville, of 1241 Mission Street, San Francisco, "instantly cured of internal hemorrhage of some weeks' standing without any laying on of hands, at the first meeting I attended."

This letter having been read, we turned to the boy and said:—

"Now, Georgie, let us see you." (The boy was sitting on the platform behind us, and rose and came forward.) "What have you got to tell the people, dear?"

"I don't know, sir."

"Were you blind?"

"Yes, sir, I was blind."

"Can you see?"

"I can see very good."

"Who gave you sight?"

"Jesus."

"Well, now I do not know how to talk to the boy," continued Mr. Dowie, "he is only beginning to understand objects. Come now, when do you say it was you got your sight?"

"July the 4th, sir."

(This is Independence Day in America, and fireworks in the public streets and everywhere are continually going off.) "Did you see the fireworks?"

"Yes, sir."

"Were they very beautiful?"

"*Yes, sir.*" (Spoken very emphatically.)

Mr. Dowie said: "His mother told me that evening that he said to her, 'Don't you think, mother, God will forgive me if I don't go down to the meeting tonight; I do want to see these fireworks; they do look *beautiful.*'"

We showed him in the presence of the audience our watch, which he was able to distinguish at a distance, telling the people which side was turned to him, the open face or the back. We took a bouquet of flowers from the hands of one in the audience and asked him to point out the various colors; he described their colors without hesitation, distinguishing each color, and even shades of color. We showed him a little pair of peculiarly constructed folding nail scissors, which we use, which he at once recognized, and other objects, amongst which were coins, which he told us the value of. The last one that we held up was a silver dollar, and we said, "If you guess right you shall have it." He did so, and got it. We told the people also of how on the afternoon of that day in our rooms at the Palace Hotel we sent him upon a voyage of discovery, and how he went to every part of the rooms, and looked at unfamiliar objects, and made very remarkable observations concerning them. Amongst these was a certain round cylindrical black object, and he said, "Oh, ain't that a funny box." I told him to lift the box and put it on his head. He did so and found it was my silk hat, which completely covered his face.

Mrs. Ritchville, the mother of the boy, then gave personal testimony. She said: "He was about a year old when I discovered he was totally blind, although the doctors all said he was born blind. He has been very busy learning the names of things, and is learning by feeling and sight together; he feels and sees and then distinguishes objects, and after he has seen an article he knows what it is. He has to learn to see.

"When I was coming here to-night on the horse-cars, it was the first time he ever saw a horse. He amused the ladies and gentlemen in the car talking about it. He said, 'Mamma, the horse's tail is made of hair, I thought it was like a dog's tail. And look, mamma, he has a moustache on his head.'"

At this point the people laughed almost until they cried, and we closed that testimony, saying that it had often amused us to note the peculiar observations of those who had just received their sight. For instance, I had asked Georgie to say what the color of my hair was on top of my head, and he said, "You have none, you are bald." We believe Elisha was bald-headed, and so we are, at least in that particular, like one of the prophets. We have sometimes been mocked for this baldness; but we have never found it to be an infirmity. Those who reproved the ancient prophet at Bethel (2 Kings 2:23, 24) found that mocking a man of God was a serious matter; and there are still "she-bears" about, and "he-bears" also, for that matter.

A Little Girl 12 Years of Age Healed of Ulcerated Legs.

This was the next case presented, and from this difficulty she had suffered for six years. She walked up and down perfectly free, and her mother added her testimony.

Instantly Healed after Twenty-six Years on Crutches.

The third case which testified was one of great interest; it was that of Mrs. Coffin, of 54 Shipley Street, S. F., who had been healed after twenty-six years on crutches, during which time she had suffered great and almost constant pain. We will quote an account of this case from Mr. Hawes' verbatim report:—

"Mr. Dowie introduced to the meeting Mr. Charles D. Coffin, saying: 'This brother is present to testify on behalf of his wife who has been healed by the Lord during this mission. She came into my room on her crutches with Mrs. Dowie. I found her an earnest, consistent Christian, a member of the First United Presbyterian Church of this city, and she received from the Lord an instantaneous and perfect healing. Her written testimony is in my hands, but I will ask her husband to speak and tell the story more fully.' Turning to Mr. Coffin, Mr. Dowie said, 'How many years was she on crutches?' He replied, 'All her life.' Mr. Dowie continued: 'I may say the moment she was healed I was going to let her out at the side door; I do not believe in creating much excitement when people are healed. I said, 'Go home and thank God, and come to the testimony meeting.' She said, 'My husband is in the meeting, let me go and see him,' and she burst out into this hall; running on both legs. She made a rush for him, and they had a good kiss in public. But 'he is of age,' let him speak for himself."

Mr. Coffin said: "I cannot express to you how sorry I feel that my wife is not here to-night; we waited till close on to 8 o'clock to see if the baby would not be well enough so we could make the venture, and then I thought of her coming alone, but she had not been around much in the city. She was very anxious to come and tell how she had been healed. I know she will be waiting for me to come home and tell all about the meeting.

"She came here and listened to the Rev. Mr. Dowie teaching this beautiful doctrine, and day by day she grew in faith and believed his teaching fully, as being that of the word of God. She had seven open wounds on her limbs, and moving about on crutches kept up such an irritation, that at all times there was a suppuration. We had to attend to her morning and evening, if not oftener. We fixed her up 4th of July morning and came here to the afternoon meeting, and she went into the room with Mr. and Mrs. Dowie. She received a perfect healing, after Mr. Dowie prayed and laid hands on her in the name of the Lord. The first I knew of it was when she came running up to me, to my astonishment, with both arms extended, and she said, 'O Charley! Charley!' and kissed me. She came as quickly towards me as I could go myself towards her with my two sound limbs. And when we left this hall she walked readily downstairs to the cars, and walked from the cars to our house; she goes up and downstairs and does everything, and we have been *very happy*. She told me to-day she had been up on Market St. (one of the principal streets for shops in the city), and she took the baby with her. She had to carry it some way, and the baby probably weighs twenty-five pounds or more. She said she got along finely.

"We give God all the glory. We are so glad Brother Dowie came here; glad we heard him, and that through the teaching she has received faith to be healed, and I think she is permanently healed. When she was three years old she went to school with her oldest sister, and when leaving school she kind of hesitated on the top of the stairs, and the teacher gave her a slight push, and she fell headlong to the foot of the stairs, and she has suffered ever since and has had to use crutches. That was twenty-six years ago; she is now 29."

Mr. Dowie said: "Twenty-six *years on crutches*, and the Lord healed her in less than twenty-six *seconds* of time. [Hearty applause by the audience.] We will praise God for that." ("Amen," was heard from all parts of the hall.)

A Sufferer for Twenty-eight Years.

The fourth case was that of Miss Amy F. Wilcox, of 211 Oak Street, San Francisco. She had been saved and healed in the same hour. She had lost faith in God, and had passed through many dreadful experiences. We quote again from the verbatim report:—

Mr. Dowie said: "At one of our meetings when the call was made for sinners to seek salvation, this young woman (who then came forward) rose up on her crutches and came right up here to the platform. She sought salvation. There are many persons who saw her that afternoon—all who saw this girl sit here seeking salvation (for she could not kneel) and who saw her afterwards rise and walk without her crutches, will you please stand up?" (A number of persons stood up.) Mr. Dowie continued: "I see about twenty witnesses. She came up and she sought salvation; she found it. She sought healing; she found it through faith in Jesus. I never touched her; she laid down her crutches and she walked back to her seat without them, and she has been walking ever since. For twenty-eight years her limbs were diseased; for three years she had not been off her crutches once to go on the street, and but a little time in the house, but she could not walk for ten months past. This is in many respects a most peculiar case, and there are many things concerning it of which we cannot speak publicly."

Miss Wilcox then came forward and corroborated Mr. Dowie's testimony, and said, "I have never been on crutches since I laid them down here; I carried them home in my hand and left them standing behind the door, and I will give them to anyone who has not found faith in Jesus, that sweet faith in Jesus which enabled me to rest in him as my healer. Thank God, I have found him. I have suffered much; he has delivered me from great perils; it was a terrible battle, but God has won it for me and the victory is glorious." ("Amen" from all parts of the audience.)

"How long have you been walking," asked Mr. Dowie.

"Eight days, and I feel perfectly well; healed of all my diseases."

Instantaneous Healing without Human Touch.

The fifth case was that of Mrs. E. Barnes, of 303 Octavia St., S. F. It was a case of healing without human touch, instantaneous, perfect, and, so far as man can see, permanent. Mrs. Barnes said:—

"I would like to say to the people that I came in here simply out of curiosity. I was deeply interested in this little once-blind boy, and although I had never seen him, I heard of him, and I being a mother, and when young was blind myself for many months, I always feel interested in anyone who is blind. I had heard of this child's faith in Jesus, and felt sure he was going to get his sight when he came here. He was the burden of my prayer as I bowed down here in the meeting. I did not think of myself, but I was praying to Jesus, believing that he was the healer. After the meeting was over (it was very late) I had to go from here to Market St. to catch a car, and I found myself running; I stopped with surprise and found that I had been healed. I had an ulcerated leg for six months and had not been able to walk three blocks. I did not know where to put my foot for pain, and when I found myself running to catch that car I was astonished and said, 'Where is the pain?' I put my foot down again and I found no pain whatever. The next day I walked about all day long and felt no difficulty.

"I felt it was my duty to return thanks to God, and to encourage this gentleman in his work, and also that others may have faith in Christ. I claim that Christ healed me, and he has healed me perfectly. He will heal anybody else who put their trust in him. I feel that I am a new woman, for I am healed all through."

Mr. Dowie said: "This is a case of healing without human touch; I did not know she was healed, and you cannot attribute that to Magnetism, Mind Healing, Christian Science or Mesmerism. Is her husband here?"

"Yes," replied a voice from the gallery.

Mr. Dowie: "Is that all right? What have you got to say about your wife's healing?"

"Only that she is quite cured, sir. And I would like also to state that while in East Boston we employed four of the best doctors and they attended my wife for six months, and were perfectly useless. We had the homeopathists, the allopathists and all the pathists, but your doctoring has done the business."

Mr. Dowie: "Hallelujah! I believe in my Doctor. He is your Doctor; he is my Doctor; he is the Doctor of all his people."

"Now at this point," said Mr. Dowie, "I will ask a question. How many here believe that Jesus Christ is the healer? How many have received the doctrine which we have been teaching, and believe it to-night? Stand up." Nearly the whole audience seemed to stand to their feet, and they sang the Doxology, "Praise God from whom all blessings flow," with great earnestness. Mr. Dowie said, "Thank God for that. Now there is another question: How many of you who have been through this mission are not yet convinced? Please hold up your hands." After looking all around the audience Mr. Dowie said: "I reckon I will have to get a magnifying glass to see you." Some person cried out, "One."

"Well, the Lord bless him," responded Mr. Dowie, "it takes a good deal to convince that brother; he has the courage, though, of his opinion."

Healing of Mental Derangement.

The sixth case was that of Mrs. Laura M. Foster, of 1331 Union Street, San Francisco. Her name was at first withheld, but since then she has agreed it should be given; she rose up and confirmed the written testimony which she placed in our hands. It is in its details a very interesting case of healing, because it is the cure of a mental derangement. In her letter she says:—

"I write to tell you that through your instrumentality in these beautiful mission meetings I have received Christ; that he dwells in my heart by faith; I am saved. I have also to thank the Lord for the healing of a mental ailment. An eminent physician of this city, Dr. De Vecchi, said it was due to purely mechanical action; that which should have been thrown off from the system by natural channels was suppressed, which overcharged the blood-vessels of the brain, and caused irritation; my nature seemed to be changed; I doubted my friends and thought they were persecuting me, especially my nearest and dearest one, a most devoted and self-sacrificing sister. Life became a burden to her. My health was broken down, and I think she could not have endured much longer. A kind friend called our attention to these meetings, and after the very first my sister said she noticed in me signs of mental healing; the second day she tells me it was placed beyond a doubt. Our home from being a most unhappy one became the abode of joy and peace. My heart is unutterably full of thanksgiving, and my love and gratitude to God and to you cannot be expressed in words."

Mr. Dowie said: "Will the sister just rise for a moment wherever she is and confirm her letter?"

A very sweet-faced lady of about 40 years of age rose up and added a few words in a gentle tone of voice, saying, "That is all true, and I thank God for his great goodness."

Healing of Rupture without Human Touch.

The next case was that of a young man by the name of Mr. Jackson, who was healed of a serious rupture without human touch. He said: "I am very glad to testify on this occasion that I received healing through Mr. Dowie's ministry. I met him down at Monterey and told him of my case; he invited me to go to the meetings. I came two weeks ago and listened to him. I immediately believed the Doctor's teaching, and went to my room in prayer, and pretty soon I had so much confidence that I threw off my truss. I went along until the next Monday, when I had great pain for a short time; but I left it with the Great Physician; I had full confidence in his power, and willingness, and since that time I have felt no trouble at all, and I have not had on my truss for two weeks.

"I wish to return my thanks to Dr. Dowie and his lovely wife [Mr. Dowie exclaimed, "That is true!"], that I have found in Jesus Christ not only my Saviour, but my Physician and Healer, and to him I shall give all the glory. In the future it will be my highest endeavor to serve him faithfully, and to fulfill his will."

Salvation and Healing of a Well-Known Notary.

The next case was that of a very interesting one of a gentleman who professed to be healed only that afternoon. Quoting once more from the verbatim report, we find these words :—

Mr. Dowie said : "Now, friends, there is a case here to-night which I would not have asked to testify, but the gentleman came up himself to the private room where we were holding a little meeting before this, and wished to do so. The case is not as perfect as some of the others, but is deeply interesting. Mr. J. E. Brown is a Notary Public in this city, and he has been attending the mission continuously, walking in and out of this hall upon his crutches, which he had used for six years. He was not saved; he listened earnestly, and not a meeting has passed but what we have seen him in that corner listening eagerly to the word of the living God. I did not lay hands upon him until to-day, and now you will all see he is walking about without his crutches, although very feeble in his legs. I do not say he is altogether just as perfect as I should like to see him, but I rejoice greatly for many reasons in his blessing."

Mr. Brown then came forward, walking, and in answer to a call from some of his friends walked to and fro on the platform. The audience was much excited, and applauded earnestly, for Mr. Brown is well known in San Francisco. He said: "Well, dear friends, Christian ladies and gentlemen, through the interposition of a warm and dear friend of mine I was induced just a fortnight ago to enter the portals of this hall. Shame upon me, I have to confess that I have grown up from childhood in this State and have not attended a meeting of the Young Men's Christian Association. I had not been a stranger to the divine teaching, for my father and mother (now in Heaven) and all the rest of my family, are of the household of faith. But thank God my mother's prayers are answered. I was the wayward one ; in fact, my father's fortune was my misfortune, and there are numbers within the sound of my voice who know I was a pretty hard case. There was a general invitation extended here for persons to come up and be saved and seek the salvation of their souls. I ventured up here ["Thank God," from the audience], and I went down there and prayed earnestly to God for salvation and to escape from the thraldom of sin, and I arose convinced that I had been forgiven. ["Hallelujah!" from Mr. Dowie.] I consecrated myself to God, and I pledged myself on my knees that my subsequent life should be devoted to him and to doing good. I had said nothing about healing; I was following the program of the reverend gentleman's teaching. I think it is teaching, preaching and then healing. ["That is it," from Mr. Dowie.] I kept still; I asked God to give me strength, strength in my limbs, strength in my knees, and when I felt myself prepared for it I asked the Doctor—excuse me, sir, for calling you Doctor. [Mr. Dowie replied, "Never mind ! they all do it."] I asked him if he would lay hands on me and bless me,

"Now a few words in reference to my affliction. I was attacked with paralysis in 1882. Within the last three years I have been unable to walk without the aid of crutches, and consequently was totally unfit for the active duties of life. I gathered strength here with the spiritual comfort and consolation. A leading physician of this city long since pronounced my case hopeless. One very eminent physician told me, after making a diagnosis, that to take off the left leg would save the right; that was the only hope I had. It did finally affect the right leg. Since that time I have consulted physicians without help. Then I investigated Christian science, and went through that. I got the whole twelve lectures for $20, but I did not get cured. You get the whole business in twelve lectures, and you look wise and say nothing; that is about the program. That is a little digression, however. I asked the Doctor, I mean the Rev. Mr. Dowie, to lay hands upon me and bless me. I first waited upon God to ask him to prepare me for so great a favor. I made an effort to-day, and I went into his little room; he laid hands upon me after prayer in the name of the Lord Jesus, and I immediately walked about without the aid of my crutches. I have walked up here to this platform and about this building without them, and not only have I more strength in my limbs, but I have received in all my body and in all my spirit great comfort. May God bless the reverend gentleman and his dear wife. ["Amen," from the audience.] May God crown their efforts with fullness and success."

Healing of Spinal Complaint of Ten Years.

We again quote from the verbatim report: Mr. Dowie said: "I have one little case here, a very sweet case, a dear young lassie named May Jackson, from Sausalito. She had a spinal complaint for ten years. She had been treated by the doctors in a first-class surgical institute in San Francisco. She writes:—

"'For ten years I have suffered from curvature of the spine, caused by lifting. On Lord's day, June 26, I heard Mr. Dowie for the first time. I had never thought before of Jesus as my healer. The first time I heard him I felt sure that Jesus was the healer, and that he would strengthen my spine. I am convinced that if I had perfect faith I would have been perfectly healed, but now as it is I feel constrained to say that I am almost so, and that my spine is very strong, and that there is very little of the deformity left, and each day that little is passing away. I thank God with all my heart for his wonderful healing through Mr. Dowie. I shall go forth on my mission to China, not only with the blessed gospel that Jesus is the Saviour, but that he is also the Healer of China's millions. Thank you, dear Mr. Dowie, for your great help to me.'"

This young lady stood up and confirmed her written testimony, saying: "I thank God with all my heart for his great goodness, and Mr. Dowie for helping me to believe in him as my healer."

Mr. Dowie said: "If you would just study that sweet brevity, you would be a better preacher than I am."

Many Healings of Diseases of Women.

A number of ladies who had been healed of internal troubles which could not be detailed, then rose upon the platform, and in various parts of the building, who testified to their healing. One lady came forward and said: "I would like to say a word or two."

Healed of Hemorrhage of the Stomach.

"I came here from Michigan a year ago to seek my health in California; I was in very poor health. I saw in one of the San Francisco papers a notice of this meeting here, and I cut it out, and although it was my intention to come to this city during the summer, I hastened my visit so as to get here to these meetings; I came from the mountains a week sooner than I expected to come; I did not get here until three days after it commenced. I thank God I heard the Doctor, I had suffered fourteen years off and on, and I thought it was God's hand afflicting me to draw me nearer to Christ, but I have given that up in these meetings, and consecrated my body entirely to him. I think I shall never take medicine again. I thank God for it; that he brought me from Michigan to this State. Last Friday I entered the healing room. I got the evidence before that, that I would be healed. I said I did not want more than seven minutes. Dr. Dowie laid his hands on my head and the glory came, not only to my body, but to my soul and spirit. I feel to rejoice and I give God all the glory. The hemorrhage has entirely ceased."

A Mind-Healer Restored to God.

We then read a letter from a lady who had been led astray through investigating metaphysical science. She had left her church and Sabbath-school, and all the rest, seeking that as a better way. She sent in a petition early in the meeting, and she found restoration to God, spirit, soul, and body, and wants to warn others of the misery of going into this ridiculous, stupid Christian science, falsely so called. We then asked her if this was so, and Mrs. Willett, of 1521 Pine Street, San Francisco, rose up and confirmed what we had stated, adding earnest words concerning it, thanking God for her restoration from her backslidden condition.

Fifty Witnesses to Divine Healing.

Before calling upon the last brother to testify, we rapidly glanced through a number of written testimonials to healing which had reached us that day, more than thirty in number, but said as the hour was very late we would read no more, and we would only ask all present who had been healed through faith in Jesus during this mission to rise. In response over fifty persons rose. In answer to another request many more rose who had been healed through faith at other times.

Many Witnesses to Salvation and Blessing.

A large number of those who had been saved during the mission, then stood up, in response to our invitation. Many of them were very interesting and striking cases. In answer to another invitation to all Christians who had received spiritual blessing and help in the mission, more than six hundred persons stood to their feet.

We read a letter from Rev. Dr. Lane, which we have referred to, and thanked a number of the ministerial brethren present, especially the Rev. Mr. Arnold, for their help in connection with the after meetings. A brother minister then rose and testified to his healing, and after this Mrs. Dowie delivered the closing address. Again we quote from the verbatim report.

Mrs. Dowie's Closing Remarks.

"Mrs. Dowie said: 'I am sure we are all very much gratified to hear the testimonies. The Lord always sends somebody to testify of His healing power at the close of a mission. We have never seen a mission yet, even though that mission had been held only for a few days, but we have seen the healing. We always see the Lord's work as healer everywhere and at all times.

"I remember when we began this mission and we told you about these wonderful things, such as those about people rising up in the meetings and telling us they were healed while they were sitting there, that some of you looked incredulous, some of you almost doubted what we were saying. But you have come here night after night, and you have seen the things we talked about; you have seen the blind receive their sight and the lame walk, and the deaf hear, and those who have been healed of dreadful diseases of every description.

"We might have seen more blessing than we have seen if the people had been more faithful; but it has been a new teaching to many of you. Still I think as far as we can see, the results have been very gratifying. I am very thankful to God indeed for what he has done. We look upon this as just the beginning, and not as the end; that this teaching will go throughout this wide lands upon this great continent. Wherever we go we will carry it with us; we will teach the Lord Jesus is the same yesterday, to-day and forever; that He is with us at the present time, and that He heals all those who come to him in simple faith and love. Oh! it is a beautiful thought to see how Jesus teaches us, that as a sparrow cannot fall to the ground without his care, we know that our bodies are cared for by him, and that by his Holy Spirit he will heal and keep us and fill us with his power. I do long for the time when his people will teach it in all the lands; when little children will not be taken to the doctors and given drugs; and when they will be brought to the great Healer for all their sicknesses and diseases. Our Lord Jesus when in the flesh went about healing the sick and casting out devils, and all who believe in him received healing from him. As that dear brother said this evening, it is the teaching that is wanted; Mr. Dowie lays great stress upon this; we spend the greater portion of our time in all these missions in teaching. Jesus went about teaching and preaching, and *then* came the healing to those who believed in him.

In this mission the people have listened to the teaching and have received it. "Faith cometh by hearing, and hearing by the word of God," and then they have been healed and blessed.

We have not heard of all the blessing that has been received here; many who were healed have returned to their homes in various parts of this State. We could not expect to hear all in one night. Mr. Dowie has been unable to read one-half of the testimonies. But God has greatly blessed his people, and he will carry the glorious tidings forward that Jesus is our Saviour from diseases as well as from sin. Oh, rejoice in his goodness and power! We do not take any credit or glory to ourselves; if we did that we would not have received the blessing; of ourselves we feel empty and powerless, but when we consecrate ourselves to him the power comes, and his Holy Spirit manifests itself upon the hearts of the people, and wherever this teaching goes his Spirit instructs the people, and he answers confirming our words by signs and wonders and mighty works.

We then rose and said, "Now do not go away without giving God the glory in the beautiful Doxology. It is not 'Praise God from whom all *sickness* flows,' but let us stand and sing 'Praise God from whom all *blessings* flow.'"

The benediction was then pronounced, and the mission closed.

[Extract from "Leaves of Healing" for October, 1888, pp. 105–118.]

Record of the Mission in Oakland.

On the evening of Friday, 13th July, we met in the parlors of the Young Men's Christian Association on Broadway nearly two hundred and fifty representatives of evangelical churches in and around Oakland. The meeting overflowed the parlors of the Association into the larger hall, and there we spent a very enjoyable evening. Twenty thousand programs and tracts announcing the mission were placed in the hands of friends for distribution, and there was a very general expression of confidence that, notwithstanding many difficulties in our way, the mission would be abundantly successful; and it was. It was also proved that the difficulties had been by no means exaggerated, for in no place and at no time have we ever been assailed with more desperate falsehoods, misrepresentations and pure (or rather, impure) inventions of the press. There was also very considerable opposition on the part of the pulpit, and many sermons were preached at us by brethren who, it is very generally believed, now regret their utterances, for the most part. Still the opposition was steadily beaten down and the mission grew daily in power, until when it closed there was but one opinion even upon the part of our fiercest opponents, namely, that we had conquered. But we know well who conquered; it was Him to whom we have ever given the glory, and who has promised us the victory. To Him be all the praise, from whom is all power. We are more determined than ever to press forward wherever He directs us.

"Where my Captain bids me go,
'Tis not mine to murmur 'No;'
He that gives the sword and shield
Chooseth too the battle-field.

"Every battle I shall win,
Triumph over every sin.
'What,' you say, 'a victor be?'
Nay! not I, but Christ in me."

On the afternoon and evening of Monday, July 16, we

Opened the Mission in the First Presbyterian Church,

Where we continued it until Monday, July 30. The church is one of the largest and handsomest in the city, and with its spacious galleries and broad ground floor, it seats comfortably one thousand three hundred persons. The afternoon audiences grew steadily until the ground floor was fairly filled, and on the evening of our closing meeting every part of the building was seated.

It would be impossible to give in detail the many incidents which render this mission memorable. From the very first it was apparent that one portion of the Oakland press was determined to pervert our words and bring us into contempt with its readers. The Oakland *Evening Tribune* smuggled one of its representatives without invitation into our private preliminary gathering of friends on the Friday evening previous to the beginning of the mission. On the following evening, we were astonished to see what purported to be a report of the proceedings-which we had especially asked of all present should be considered *as purely private*, the meeting having been convened by private circulars only. In the report of my speech I was made to say numbers of most absurd statements concerning my private life, and amongst other things I was said to have made an open confesion that for "twenty-six years I had been a victim to the filthy vice of tobacco smoking;" and also that I had once opposed Roman Catholicism, but I had learned better and didn't do it now. I complained of these misrepresentations to the reporter representing that journal, and he assured me then and on two subsequent occasions, that his report had been garbled and altered in the office. At last I saw that this paper was making no mistakes concerning me, but that it was deliberately lying on purpose, and I said so publicly, at the same time declaring my intention of taking no further notice either of it or of any other newspaper attacks upon me, from whatever source proceeding. This policy we have pursued undeviatingly until this present moment so far as our public writing is concerned, and so far as my public speaking, also. As in all our Missions, we first of all presented Christ as Saviour, and we had the joy of seeing numbers saved almost daily, and on one occasion no less than seventy persons under deep conviction rose from their seats, and came up to the platform at the after meeting seeking for blessing. There are many touching stories connected with these saved and restored ones in our missions already, which if told would fill a fair sized volume, but we cannot enter into details, for which neither our time nor these pages are sufficient; and, therefore, we shall hasten now, as in our previous letter, to

The Closing Praise and Testimony Meeting,

Which, as will be remembered, was held on the evening of Monday, July 30, when the spacious church was filled with an eager, earnest throng, who listened with intense feeling and deepening earnestness to the testimonies which came from the loving hearts of those who had "touched the hem of Christ's garment" and been healed. The same gentleman who reported *verbatim* the San Franciscan closing meeting, Mr. G. H. Hawes, again reported this meeting.

Before the public testimonies were given we had a most interesting meeting with those who were about to witness to Christ's power to heal, and when they entered the building with us we met a sea of upturned faces, and we felt indeed that grace was needed to those who were about to speak for the first time before such an audience. After the preliminaries and an address from ourselves, we first of all read a number of testimonies from those who had been healed without human touch.

Thirty Years' Infirmity Healed without Human Touch.

Mrs. Parthena Balkam, of West Berkeley, wrote, saying, "I was blessed on last Thursday; my hip is altogether healed. Please pray for me that I be kept. The swelling of my limbs and ankles has almost gone; my hip is altogether healed. My troubles have lasted for many years; my feet and ankles for thirty years have pained me all the time, and my hip trouble is of many years' standing. My husband, whom you prayed for, is better, and is holding on by faith alone for his restoration. I am seventy-five, and my husband is about the same age. I was made well without any human touch."

Mrs. Heath rose and said that she knew this lady, and knew her condition, and was able to testify that she had been most miraculously healed. She was also able to testify that she was in the meeting with her when she received the healing.

Instantaneous Healing of Long-Standing Lameness without Human Touch.

We then read a letter from Mrs. J. J. Cook, wife of the proprietor of the Stoneman House, in the world-famous Yo Semite Valley, in which she thanked God for the blessings which she had received through our teachings in San Francisco, and wanted also to thank God on behalf of her sister. She said: "I went into my room and in earnest prayer to God I asked him to take the trouble from her. She had been a long time lame and in much pain. Before I could go downstairs word came for me to go to her, telling me that suddenly she had been enabled to walk without lameness, and could stand erect. She had been bowed down from suffering for a long time. I went with joy and told her to give the glory to God. She wept for joy; she now continues walking with no lameness. I hear from her often, and she is as well as when she left me."

We then pointed out in this case that the healing had been given without any intervention on our part, and we had never seen nor known this lady's sister, who had thus been so miraculously healed.

Healing of Many Years' Affliction without Human Touch.

Mr. A. T. Farish, 1380 Ninth Ave., E. Oakland, writes:—

"I want to thank you. When holding your meetings in San Francisco I was not able to attend, as I am now seventy-eight years of age. I have been a member of the Presbyterian Church for forty years. I attended your meeting in Oakland for teaching, and I praise the Lord, and I want now to give him all the glory that the prayers that were offered have been answered, and that now I am healed of all my diseases; and I now ask your prayers and those of other Christians that my healing may be kept perfect."

This dear old Christian gentleman then continued to tell us of his eight children, twenty-five grandchildren and two great grandchildren; all of whom he asked us to pray for. He mourns that one of his grandchildren smokes, and asks us to especially beseech the Lord that he may have power to give it up.

After these cases, we read the written testimonies of persons then present who were desirous of publicly witnessing for Christ, and, after such readings, they stood up and added certain words of confirmation. The first of these was that of one who had been

Instantaneously Healed of Severe Sprains of Both Ankles and of a Severely Injured Arm.

Mrs. H. P. Penniman, of Piedmont Ave., Oakland, wrote: "Nine months ago I fell and badly hurt my arm, making me nearly helpless. Five weeks ago I fell again and sprained both my ankles. I suffered the pain and inconvenience, known to those who have suffered likewise. Dr. Dowie prayed with me last Thursday morning. Having long been a believer in divine healing and a student of its principles as revealed in God's word, I only needed my faith, not my knowledge, to be increased. God gave me that, upon expression of which, after prayer, Dr. Dowie bade me in the name of the Lord Jesus, and in the power of the Spirit, to walk, which I did naturally and at once. It was in a moment, I may say. In a few minutes I put on my boots, and within one hour was on my way to this church. At the same moment my left arm was also healed. I give this testimony in obedience to the command, "Go and tell what great things the Lord has done for thee." ("Glory to God!" from the audience.)

We explained a little more fully the case of this sister, who is a highly cultivated and widely known Christian lady, and sister of Mrs. Capt. Gove, to whom reference has been already made. We had accepted an invitation to breakfast with Capt. Gove and his family on the previous Thursday morning, and found that Mrs. Penniman was in a very helpless and painful condition. She had been compelled for some time to creep about her room on her hands and knees, and was unable even to use crutches, as she could not bear to have her feet touch the ground, from the extreme pain. We said to her, "Jesus is speaking to you now, speaking through my lips as his servant, and he is asking you a question, ' Wilt thou be made whole?'" She said afterwards in this building, on the same afternoon as that on which she was healed, that when we put that question to her she lost sight of us, and took it as a direct question from the Lord himself. We noticed her lips move; her eyes were shut, and at last we heard her say, "Yes, Lord," as if she was speaking to the Lord himself. We said to her, "Give me your feet." She said, "Take them, Lord, take them!" We immediately took her feet in our hands, in Jesus' name. They were much swollen, and we laid hands upon them, beseeching the Lord that she might at once be healed. In less time than it takes us to tell you she was able to walk; she walked upstairs in a few minutes, dressed herself, put on her boots, presided at the lunch table, walked upstairs, came down again, dressed for the meeting, walked out with us to the carriage, into which she stepped without any assistance, and drove with us to the church, where she testified to her healing before several hundreds of persons at the afternoon meeting. As it had been well known by large numbers of persons that this lady had expressed a deep interest in our mission, and was quite unable to attend the meetings on account of her serious injuries, it created a very widespread interest, and even a sensation, and was an instantaneous and perfect healing of a very marked character.

Almost Instantaneous Healing of a Little Girl's Injured Eye.

Julia Mills, a sweet little child about ten years old, placed her written testimony in our hands as follows:—

"I was hit in the eye by a rock which a boy threw with a sling-shot. I had been totally blind, but the Lord made them some better, although I was not at all well, for I could not bear my glasses off in the light, and my sight was very bad. But last Saturday I came into the Children's Meeting and you invited me with other children that were seeking healing into the parlor, and laid hands upon me, and God has healed my eyes."

Some of her friends who were present testified that the eyes were very much injured and are perfectly restored. We have seen this little girl as late as October 20, and her eyes were perfectly well and her sight quite clear.

Restoration of One Who Suffered with Imperfect Eyesight for Many Years.

John Ashworth, 160 Broadway, Oakland, wrote: "Through your teaching I have found my Saviour for all eternity, and I have found my Saviour is also my Healer. For fourteen years I wore glasses; have had very weak eyes, and in fact so weak that I was almost blind; nobody was able to do anything, and my eyesight these last few years gradually grew worse. I came to the meeting and on the afternoon of July 18 I asked you to pray for me; I received a blessing that afternoon, for I rested in Jesus that very day for salvation, and day by day my eyes have been getting stronger. I can read my Testament without any glasses; I feel stronger and happier in my mind, and new life, in fact, has come to me. I give all the praise to God. In conclusion, I pray God that I may have more faith in Jesus. This is the only letter in my life that I have written with my natural eyes. The Lord increase my faith, and he shall have all the parise."

The letter referred to is an exceedingly good, well-written letter; every word in it is well formed and apparently easily written. Since then we received, at San Jose, another letter from this young man, telling us that his healing had remained, and that he was doing everything without glasses. The young man himself stood up in the meeting and added to his written testimony these words: "It is the first time in my life that I have stood up in a church to speak, but what I have to say is that I glorify God."

Instantaneous Healing of Heart Disease without Human Touch.

Mrs. S. Ransome, No. 9 Fourteenth St., Oakland, wrote: "I desire to testify to you, and to the Lord, that without a touch from your hand I am healed of palpitation and of heart disease, which I have had a long time. On Tuesday after your prayers for the many petitions, I thought I must cry out for I had such a strange sensation at my heart, as if my heart was turning over in me, and all at once it seemed as if it had stopped. Then I knew that Jesus had healed me, for I came home better than I have done for a long time. I now give thanks to my blessed Jesus for his loving-kindness to me. I am willing to testify for him."

We said with reference to this case, "We did not know of this healing until she brought us this letter. We will ask the lady if she is present to rise and confirm her testimony." She at once rose and did so, saying: "I am the lady, and can truly say that I have been a long time suffering from heart disease; it was very troublesome; in walking up a flight of stairs or a block I was so fatigued I wouldn't know what to do. I got worse. I came in last week and sat in a seat over there. While the gentleman was praying I prayed to God that if my heart was not right, it might be put right, for I knew there was something wrong about it; it troubled me a great deal at times, and I could not sleep. All at once I felt a sensation as if my heart was moved and turned into its place, and I thought I must cry out for help, but all at once it stopped. I gave God the glory, for Mr. Dowie never put his hands on me. I walked home at 11 o'clock and never slept better. I praise the Lord for his goodness towards me. I have been healed ever since."

Restoration of Healing of One Who Had Been Totally Deaf in Right Ear for Eight Years.

Mr. A. F. Rudens, 11 Telegraph Place, San Francisco, said: "Christian friends, I desire to be a witness for Christ; I feel to glorify him; he has been my Saviour for three years. I have also known him to be my Healer for one year. But I have been deaf in my right ear for a little over eight years. I have tried doctors, different kinds of doctors; I tried four doctors to open my ear, but all in vain. On the 10th of July, by the mercy of God, I was led to Brother Dowie's rooms at the Palace Hotel, and there he prayed for me and laid his hands on me, and there I got hearing in the right ear for the first time that I can remember for eight years; I could close my left ear and hear quite good, and I can do so now. ("Thank God!" from many in the audience.)

Healing of Hip Disease of Ten Years' Standing.

Miss Josie Colienour, 1663 San Pablo Ave., Oakland, wrote: "I want to testify to the praise of our Lord Jesus for my healing. I have had hip disease ever since I was seven years old; at times the suffering was very great. On July 19 I went to Mr. Dowie; he laid hands upon me, and since then I have had no pain, and I can use my limb."

This young lady, who is seventeen years of age, rose and said: "I wish to say that every word of that is true, and I do realize that I am perfectly healed. I give God all the glory."

Confirmation of Previous Testimony.

Miss Wilcox, who testified in the San Francisco Mission, desired to witness for Christ again in this mission. She said: "I suffered for twenty-eight years with my ankle, and thirteen years with internal trouble; I am testifying for Christ that he is not only my healer, but my Saviour also. I have been four years disabled, for one year most of the time in bed, three years the 30th of this month on crutches. On the 2d of July I received healing. I have been for thirteen years afflicted with internal diseases which were very painful, very great, disabling me for work or household duties of any kind. I give God all the glory, I am healed, and I feel better to-day than ever I felt in my life; I can't remember when I ever felt as I do to-day."

We remarked that this girl had been seen by many in San Francisco at the moment of her healing. She came right up to the platform on her two crutches, and in pain and grief she sought mercy from God. She could not kneel; she put down her crutches on the platform and wept and cried before God. But presently the power of God came upon her; she not only found salvation, but to her astonishment she was put on her feet, and walked back to her seat, leaving her crutches upon the platform. She says she has been well ever since.

Healing of Epilepsy of Many Years' Standing.

We said: "We feel it unwise for certain reasons to give the name and address of the lady a portion of whose testimony we shall now read. It is wrtten in an exceedingly beautiful hand, but, for sufficient reasons, we cannot read it in detail. Many here will remember that this lady one day went into an epileptic fit at one of our afternoon meetings; how many of you saw that?" (Many hands were raised.) "It was the case of the lady to whom we now refer. The Lord used us on that occasion, and the next moment, as you know, she was able to walk about; the Lord delivered her; her mind was failing, but is now perfectly restored; there is every evidence that she is fully healed, and she has returned to her home in the country. She says: "I pray continually for wisdom to conduct myself rightly and to have only a pure heart and influence. Last night I was specially blessed in prayer; the Holy Spirit was poured in fullness into my soul; I communed with God; God is very near; I feel his presence ever with me. I was moved to pray that all who were praying for me may be blessed in their own soul by seeing the answers to their prayers for me, and my heart thrills as I remember the promise spoken in Prov. 10 : 22. 'The blessing of the Lord it maketh rich and he addeth no sorrow with it.' If there is no sorrow, of course there is no sickness. This morning my pastor asked me if I was healed, and I replied in confidence inspired of God, 'Yes, I am healed.' Praise the Lord for his mighty work."

The mother of this young lady also wrote a beautiful letter thanking us for our part in her daughter's healing.

Confirmation of Previous Healing.

Mr. Jackson, of San Francisco, who was healed of rupture in that Mission, again witnessed to his continued healing, and a great impression was produced upon the audience by its thrilling recital, and many exclamations of "Glory to God!" and "Amen!" were heard on every side. The young man spoke with eloquence and force, and is likely to become a Christian minister.

Another Confirmation of Previous Healing.

Miss Laura M. Foster, who was healed of mental ailment in the San Francisco Mission, again confirmed her testimony, adding many touching details. Her friends who were present also confirmed her statements. She spoke with much beauty of expression, and is perfectly restored after long mental darkness.

Healing of a Minister from Dyspepsia of Eight Years', and of His Wife after Seven Years' Sickness.

The Rev. Mr. Green, a pastor in Oakland, spoke as follows: "I want to say to the glory of God that I have been healed through Jesus a week ago last Tuesday afternoon. I came here into the meeting and I heard Brother Dowie say that Christ was not only able but willing to heal. I always knew he was able, but it always seemed as if he was not willing to heal me. I had been *a sufferer from dyspepsia for about eight years*, and I grew worse and worse. The last three years I could hardly fill my appointments. Five weeks ago I got very bad, so I could hardly preach. Three weeks ago I called to see a doctor in San Francisco, and after he examined me he said it was not so much dyspepsia as consumption, and my case was a very severe one. He prescribed some medicine; I used that for a week and grew worse; I went to see the doctor again and he thought I was very bad, and that I had better give up preaching. After I attended the meeting here

I went home, entered my room, and kneeled down before God, and said: "O Lord, I know that thou art able to heal me, thou art willing to heal me now." I put my whole trust at that moment in Jesus, and there and then I was healed and I stand here in perfect health to-night. I give all the glory to Jesus. ("Amen!" and "Thank God!" from the audience.)

Let me say also that Mrs. Green, my wife, has been sickly for seven years. We have been having a good many doctors, and it seemed as if they could not do very much good; the last physician we had told her she had not better take much more medicine. She attended the meeting here and last Saturday afternoon when she came home she exclaimed to me, 'Praise God, I am healed; Jesus has healed me.' She is in the meeting to-night and she wanted me to testify for her and to give all the glory to Jesus." ("Amen!" and "Thank God!" from many.)

Interruption by an Epileptic, Who Was Instantly Delivered.

At this point the meeting was suddenly interrupted by an epileptic who screamed out. We gave out the hymn, "Wonderful Words of Life," and hurried from the platform to the possessed one, who was struggling in a fearful fit, and was instantly delivered. In a letter which we received at San Jose from Rev. Mr. Coplin, we find that after her deliverance, and on that same evening, *she was converted*, and continues healed.

At this point the Rev. H. L. Harris stepped up with a petition for prayer on his own behalf, which was at once offered.

Healing of Internal Maladies of Fifteen Years' Standing.

Mrs. R. A. Scott, of Springfield, Massachusetts, rose and testified that she had been healed, through our instrumentality, of troubles of a very serious character which had afflicted her for more than fifteen years. This is a case which we cannot attempt to give in detail.

Healing of Eczema from Birth in a Little Boy.

Mrs. Stacy, 717 Eighteenth St., Oakland, said: "I give God the glory for what he has done through his Son, Jesus Christ, for our little boy, Charles D. Stacy, who had eczema from infancy. I have tried everything in the way of washes and ointment, but have never been able to remove it from his head. Brother Dowie prayed for him nearly two weeks ago and laid hands on him in the early part of the meeting. He also had a rash on his hands and all over his body, and that went away after laying on of hands. I feel to praise the Lord."

Healing of Five Years' Internal Troubles.

Mrs. Margarita Johnson, 1088 Twenty-fourth St., Oakland, next testified: "I thank God for having healed me. I have been sick for five years, and have seen ten doctors. For three months lately my back ached very bad and troubled me very much; I could hardly sleep; I grew worse and worse; the doctor gave me some medicine, I grew worse still and I went to see him again; he gave me another medicine and I grew worse, I was not able to raise my hand to my head. I came here to listen to the speaking of Divine Healing. Mr. Dowie said the Lord did not want us to be sick, but he would rather have us be well. He laid his hands upon me and I felt a great deal better. But after a few days I got wrong and worse again. So I went to the Lord again and I got right, and I asked Him to heal me, and he has healed me, and I feel better to-night than I ever did. I give God the glory."

Healing of Chronic Catarrh of Fifteen Years, and of Internal Disease.

Mrs. Smith, of Fruit Vale, near Oakland, rose and said; "I want to give glory to God for what he has done for me. I have had chronic catarrh in my head for over fifteen years. Mr. Dowie laid hands upon me and I felt a clearness in my head I had not felt for a long time. I expected the Saviour to heal me and he did so. I had also an internal disease; the doctor said he could not do anything for me; medicine would do me no good; could only give me something to relieve my sufferings. Now I praise Jesus I feel I am perfectly well. I give the glory to God; he has wonderfully blessed me; he is not only the Saviour of the soul, but the Healer of the body."

Instantaneous Healing of Lameness of Many Years' Standing.

Mrs. A. Billings, 734 Market St., Oakland, testified: "Glory to God I am healed. I have been sick for many years, and sick in bed lately for three or four months; then I was walking around a little with a cane. I believed that Jesus was able and willing to heal me, and he has. I was healed this afternoon when Mr. Dowie laid hands upon me among the 122 whom he laid hands upon to-day. I left my cane at home. Glory to God; I am quite well."

This lady testified in a clear, loud, ringing, triumphant voice, and was, as she says, one of a large number upon whom we had laid hands at one time that afternoon. When she had finished an aged gentleman walked up quickly to the front from the audience and said: "I came up here in company with my wife; I was sick for several years, and I, too, was healed at the same moment as my wife."

At This Point There Was Great Excitement

Throughout the vast audience. The old gentleman said there was a minister present who knew them, and he openly applied to him to confirm his testimony. The Rev. Mr. Corlander rose and confirmed the facts as they had stated them. These persons are well-known residents of Oakland, and their testimony, and appearance in confirmation of it, created most apparent excitement amongst the audience. After a verse of "All hail the power of Jesus' name" the meeting was calmed, and the testimonies proceeded.

Healing of Rheumatic Fever.

Mrs. A. J. Leveritz, Chase St., San Francisco, said: "I just want to say to the glory of God that during this mission I have received great blessing from God physically and spiritually. I heard Mr. Dowie one afternoon last week. I was aching from the top of my head to the soles of my feet; I went into his room; I had rheumatic fever. He laid his hands on me and immediately the fever left me. Glory to Jesus. I can recommend this blessed Healer; oh! how precious is his name."

Healing of a Little Boy from Eczema.

Oscar William Warner, of Mission St., San Francisco, was presented by his guardian, who testified, as the little boy did himself, that he was healed of eczema. We said to him, "But, dear, have you given your heart fully to Jesus?"

"Yes sir," he said.

"When?"

"The 8th day of July," said the little boy, and the remark was received with hallelujahs from the audience.

Healing of a Long-Continued Internal Trouble.

Mrs. Bradford, 23d St, Lynn, East Oakland, testified at some length of her healing, but we are unable to find time to report her testimony.

Mrs. S. C. Fisher gave similar testimony, but as the hour was late there was not time to read it.

Many Witnesses.

At this stage of the meeting we asked all who had received healing during the mission to stand to their feet. A large number did so, and thirty-one were counted close to the platform; but it was impossible to count all correctly. A number who were saved during the mission also stood up afterwards. About seven hundred persons who had received spiritual blessing also stood up and thanked God for it. Then the usual request was made that "all those who in this meeting have believed the doctrine which we have been teaching" in Oakland, that "Jesus is a present healer, please stand to your feet!" Almost the whole audience did so, and sang the Doxology with great fervor.

The meeting closed at a very late hour with a very eloquent and touching little address from Mrs. Dowie.

[Extracts from letter to "Leaves of Healing" for November, 1888.]

Record of the Mission in San Jose.

On the evening of Friday, the third of August, we met in the parlors of the First Methodist Episcopal Church several hundreds of Christians who had been privately convened by circular. The Rev. F. F. Jewell, D. D., presided and introduced us. The hearty reception we then received, convinced us that the Lord would abundantly bless our labors in that place, and so it proved.

On the following Lord's day evening, August 6, the mission was opened. The spacious and convenient church was crowded in every part, large numbers of persons standing throughout the whole service, and many were unable to obtain an entrance into the building. Our after meeting upon that occasion resulted in the open conversion of a number of persons, and we were delighted to hear the following day that the infidel husband of a lady, who had been instrumental largely in opening the way for us, had been converted in his own house, and that his conversion was followed immediately by that of every unconverted member of his family.

The afternoon meetings in the beautiful church parlors, nearly as extensive as the church itself, grew from day to day in power and in numbers until they overflowed the accommodation, and also the extra sittings and contiguous rooms, and the space around our feet on the platform. We never experienced a more blessed sense of the power and presence of the Spirit in any of our Missions than in these afternoon meetings.

The evening audiences steadily grew, filling the church from the beginning, and on many occasions crowding it to its utmost capacity, and occasionally beyond. Conversions were of daily occurrence, a number of backsliders were reclaimed, and we have the joy of knowing that many believers were greatly revived. The meetings were attended by many of the pastors and officers of churches in the city, and by quite a number of doctors. A number of the

Professors and Students of the University of the Pacific

Were almost constant attendants. Rev. J. N. Martin, Ph. D., professor of ancient languages in the University, was a specially earnest seeker, and we found in him a very valued friend, whose approval of our discourses (to nearly all of which he listened) was very precious.

The Work of Divine Healing

After the first few days proceeded steadily, and some of the cases created widespread interest. We laid hands upon more than 250 persons, and believe that a large proportion of these were blessed, a number were healed without any human touch. But beyond all healing, the deep spiritual blessing which the people received was the most marked feature of the mission, our teaching being greatly owned of God, and *for all the results we do heartily give Him all the glory.* It would be quite impossible to attempt to give details of all, but we shall now present, as in our former letters, an epitome of the verbatim report of the

Closing Praise and Testimony Meeting,

Held on Monday evening, August 20, when the building was crowded to its utmost capacity. This report was prepared by Mr. G. H. Hawes, as in former missions in California.

The opening prayer by the Rev. Dr. Jewell was very beautiful and touching, and as it is in type-writing now before us, we feel led to give it a place in this record. This prayer was especially realized by myself, for reasons which will afterwards appear.

"Father in Heaven, accept the gratitude, the thanksgiving of our hearts, of hundreds of hearts, before thee to-night, that in thy gracious providence thou didst direct our brother and sister to this place to conduct this Mission, to instruct this people, and to lead them gently on in the enjoyment and in the realization of the great privileges that open before thy people in the name and for the sake of our Lord Jesus Christ. And we ask thee to accept the gratitude of our hearts for the spiritual quickening that has come to so many, for the deep spiritual interest that has pervaded all these services, for the deepening and quickening of the kingdom of God within the hearts of thy children.

We thank thee, Father, for this dispensation of thy grace, for the visit of the Day-spring from on high; we bless thee that the Sun of Righteousness has arisen with healing in his wings, and we have realized the overshadowing presence of the Holy Ghost through these series of meetings. We bless thee, our heavenly Father, and pray that this spirit may continue, may this anointing abide, and may the spiritual tides grow deeper and stronger and increase in volume and in power until hundreds more shall realize the great salvation and rejoice in the fullness of thy love.

"We thank thee, our heavenly Father, that thou hast in answer to prayer and in response to the touch of faith on the part of so many, enabled thy church to realize not only that the Son of man hath power on earth to forgive sin, but even that the voice divine is heard, 'Rise, take up thy bed and walk.' And we bless thee that so many have exercised the faith through the encouraging voice of thy servant and hand-maiden and the quickening power of the Holy Spirit, and have been enabled to know that thou art the healer of their bodies. O blessed Lord, we thank thee for the pains that have been removed, for the pains that have been rebuked, and for the feeling that has been experienced and realized to thy people here. O Lord we thank thee for what has been accomplished; for the great increase of faith in the hearts of thy children; we bless thee for the skepticism that has been removed; we bless thee for the Spirit that has fallen upon those who were inclined to question and doubt and cavil, and so many that began with questionings, but have been enabled to see the hand of the Lord and rejoice that thou wast in the midst of thy people. Blessed be thy name.

"And now we come to the last night of this mission, the last interview of these gracious services, and we look up to thee and thank thee for thy presence through the days and the weeks of the past, and we realize thy presence now. Blessed be thy name, the Lord is in his holy temple to-night, thy presence does overshadow us. Father, Son, and Holy Ghost we adore and praise thee that thou art here to-night in the plenitude of thy mercy and grace. Oh! to-night in this room gathered here may there be many who shall reach forth and grasp the arm divine, realizing the healing grace of our Lord Jesus Christ.

"Now blessed Lord we pray that thou wilt be with our sister and brother as they shall go from us; O Lord direct all their steps, select for them their places of labor, attend them wherever they go, and oh! do thou grant to bring to thy great name glory by continuing to work through them for the release of those who are in bonds, and for the glory and good of the gospel. We ask it in the name of Jesus, our Redeemer. Amen."

We then delivered a brief address concerning the blessings which had attended the meetings, and the arrangements which were being made to continue the work.

We took the opportunity of recording our gratitude to our beloved friend and brother, the Rev. Dr. Jewell, who had aided us throughout the mission in an eminently wise and judicious manner, speaking of us and writing concerning us in the columns of the Christian press kind words, for which we can find no adequate expressions of thankfulness. We also recorded our appreciation of the kindness of many pastors and officers of churches who had sympathized with and helped us, eminent amongst those being the Rev. C. N. Aiflerbach, who presides over the German Methodist Episcopal Churches of this State.

At this stage we were about to refer to the numerous testimonies in writing which we held in our hands, and had just uttered the words, "Now the first testimony that we will take," when the Rev. Dr. Jewell rose before the sentence was finished, and said:—

"Beloved friends, I wish to say a word before Dr. Dowie begins to read; I want to observe the order that our brother has heretofore observed, and insisted upon observing, all the way through. I assume that these testimonies that he holds in his hand refer to cases of bodily healing; I assume that that is true; I want to put the spiritual before it, so as to observe the order that our brother has insisted we should observe.

"I want to bear testimony first of all to the great spiritual good that has come to me and to my people through this mission. I think we are all agreed in saying that the

Spiritual Life of the Church has been Quickened,

And that the spiritual tides have been deepened and broadened; that we are nearer the Lord, that we know the Lord better, we know him better than we did when our brother came to us.

"I am very grateful that my people have shared this precious privilege, these gracious opportunities; have been identified with this mission; we are one in these things, and we are thankful for these blessings, for it prepares us the better to do the divine will.

"I am glad we understand the Bible better than we did when Brother and Sister Dowie came; I am glad we understand the gospel better; I am glad it ministers more to us than it did when they came; I am glad that the great volume of truth has seemed to enlarge and broaden until really there has been

Grandeur, Beauty, and Glory Added to this Blessed Gospel

Of our Lord Jesus Christ; new departments of the gospel have opened themselves to us; you have opened new pastures upon which we are enabled to feed; you have introduced new visions of love and mercy that are really so refreshing and sweet to us, that we shall claim the privilege of feeding upon them when you are gone, to the glory of God, in Jesus Christ our Lord.

"We are thankful for all of this; for the great spiritual good that has come to our people. The gospel has been vindicated, and we are enabled to stand here to-day and say that the Bible as it has been expounded by our brother is more than ever, MORE THAN EVER, the representative of the full-orbed complete gospel, blessed be God, saving spirit, soul and body.

"We are trusting to-night that this good work begun here shall continue. We are trusting a little more than this; that God in his gracious providence will direct our brother and sister to our midst again after a little, that they may come back to us and see and realize by contact with us and communion with us, that their labor has not been in vain in the Lord."

This eloquent tribute from this eminent minister, who has labored long and well amongst the churches of his denomination in America (numerically the largest in this land) very deeply affected us, and made a deep impression upon the people.

We then referred to the fact that over eighty persons have professed to find peace in Christ during the mission, and a number of these stood up.

We then called for testimonies to healing through faith in Jesus.

Instantaneous Healing of Fifteen Years' Rheumatic Gout.

Miss Emma Hudson, of Peterboro, Canada, handed us the following written testimony, which we read:—

"I rejoice in having the privilege to testify for Jesus this evening; he is my Saviour, my Healer, my Sanctifier; I give him all the glory. Fifteen long, long, weary years, I have suffered with rheumatism; I was treated by the most skillful doctors; then going from place to place where we would hear of noted doctors. The same answer from all: 'No help—nervous, chronic rheumatism of the worst kind. Also, rheumatic gout; every drop of my blood poisoned; bones turning to chalk; may break at the least move; my joints twisted out one after another." That was my condition. I have been so sore, from head to foot, that it was agony to be touched—sometimes half an hour getting into bed. I dare not let anyone help me; and for several years I was too sore and weak to use crutches, even.

I had one earthly hope left; change of climate might restore me. I had to wait long for strength enough, even, to take the journey to California. My dear brother in Peterboro carried me into the bus, into the cars, tears stealing down his cheek, expecting that I would die on the road from Canada to California. This beautiful climate failed to restore me; my earthly hope was gone. I did not let my loved ones know (my dear brother is now with me) that day after day I was sinking; they had sorrow enough about me. If Jesus would only take me home, it would be better for them not to know of my suffering. All hope was gone But I was at rest, for I loved my Saviour, and I knew I should go to him. And when I thus got to the end of myself the dear Saviour sent Dr. Dowie and Mrs. Dowie to teach us these beautiful words, these wonderful words of life. I saw they were hiding behind Jesus; I saw they were presenting Jesus; I saw it it was Jesus' words they were speaking. Step by step their teaching led me on until I could say, 'I will be made whole.' They prayed for me; God answered that prayer. I felt, when Mr. Dowie laid hands upon me in Jesus' name, that I had touched Jesus; I was every whit made whole that very moment. Glory be to Jesus. ('Amen,' from the audience.) I feel I will want to sing through eternity, 'Praise God, from whom all blessings flow.' I thank God that dear Mr. and Mrs. Dowie ever came to San Jose, and I thank dear Dr. and Mrs. Dowie that they were willing to be used of God for my restoration. My heart is sad at the parting to-night; I look forward to the meeting up yonder.

"The Bible to me is a new book; Jesus is more precious to my soul. I long for everyone here to-night who has not touched Jesus as their Saviour and their Healer, to touch him now. He is waiting; he is willing; just trust him now, and he will save you; he will help you; he will cleanse you; he will keep you."

After we had read these touching words we asked the sister to stand up and show herself to the people, and add a few words. Holding her crutches in our hands, we said:—

"These are your crutches, are they not?" referring to a pair of crutches standing by the pulpit.

"Yes, sir."

"They belong to me, don't they?"

"I bequeathe them to you gladly."

I then asked her to tell the people how she came to the meeting that afternoon, and received the healing. She said:—

"I came to the meeting that afternoon feeling very helpless, and I felt there was no hope for me only in Christ; I felt Jesus did want to heal me, and the moment Mr. Dowie laid hands upon me prayer was answered; I was at once set free, and walked away without my crutches, which I have done ever since. That night I could not sleep, I did not care to sleep, I was so full of joy; and for two or three nights I could only praise. I feel the witness within that the Lord has done the work and I have been healed. I have had to commence like a child and learn to walk, but I am walking without any help, and I am going to trust him to the end."

The audience immediately upon the close of this testimony broke out singing "Praise God from whom all blessings flow."

A Spiritualist Converted and Blessed.

Mrs. E. Moran, of San Jose, wrote as follows: "I rejoice, dear sir, to tell you that God has through you removed the empty ark of Spiritualism from my deceived heart and brain. It is of the devil. And now, dear sir, Christ has spoken the word of power to me, and I am his altogether.

Healing of a Severe Cough of Twenty-five Years' Standing.

Mr. N. K. Potter said, "I wish to testify to the fact that I am through Christ healed of a severe cough of twenty-five years' standing during this mission and through your agency."

Healing of Two Aged Negroes.

Mr. Randolph Cooper and his wife, Mrs. Ann Cooper, two happy-looking aged Africans, testified to their healing of many complaints, and added to their written testimony some very touching words. These testimonies created great interest, and the audience at once broke forth with, "All hail the power of Jesus' name," which rang joyously out from every portion of the crowded building.

Healing and Blessing to a Family.

Mrs. John T. Bell, in a beautiful little written testimony, said: "I wish to testify to bodily healing and spiritual blessing for myself and children. We rest in confidence that the keeping power of Christ will preserve us from sickness from this time on." Mrs. Bell rose and confirmed her written testimony.

This was followed by another letter from Mrs. Jennie C. Panton, a lady who had been exceedingly helpful in arranging and carrying out the mission. She testified to the "inspiration and comfort received from the patient, loving teachings of the mission. Through them I am now able to say in confidence that I am quietly trusting God to do everything for me."

Mrs. H. V. Stever, sister of the foregoing, also a helper, testified to blessing received.

Mrs. M. E. H. Baird, one of the first and most efficient of our helpers, has also sent us a letter containing most beautiful testimony to the blessing received by herself, her husband, and family.

Healing of a Lady of Many Years' Troubles, Who Was Sent by Her Doctor from Her Sick-bed to the Mission.

Mrs. Mary J. Walker testified in great detail to her healing. She said: "Dr. Hunmer kept telling me about you and your work, and how he believed in Christ's healing. But I was in bed; I did not think of coming to you. Friday morning he came in and said that a neighbor of ours was coming; then after he left another neighbor came in and told me about the wonderful healings which were going on in this church. After she left I thought I would like to go, as I was suffering very much. I had only sat up a little at times and had not left my sickroom. I arose and came to the church, and that afternoon I was relieved at once, through your instrumentality in prayer by the laying on of hands, through faith in Christ, from all my complaints."

I Had Come out of My Bed to Get This Healing, and Went Home Well."

This lady's troubles were many and serious, but the details cannot be given.

Healing of Heart and Spinal Diseases of Thirty Years' Standing, and of a Tumor of Seven or Eight Years in the Stomach, Supposed to Be Cancerous.

Great interest attached to this case, for the poor sufferer had been so marvelously blessed. He was one of two patients concerning the healing of whom Dr. Bishop had already testified in one of our meetings. Mr. C. N. Lathwesen, who was then supposed to be dying, wrote to me under date of July 31 from Pacific Grove, saying, "Dear man of God, I implore your prayers in the name of Jesus for my healing. I have been sick for thirty years. I am now day by day looking for the Master to remove me to the mansions above; but if it can be his will I would like to be restored for God's glory, and to testify to his power to save to the uttermost. Nearly everyone in San Jose knows me in my afflictions."

This touching petition was handed to us at the opening of our mission by the poor sufferer's wife, who had come up for this purpose from Pacific Grove, some forty miles distant. She waited day by day upon the Lord with us in prayer, and at last returned to the Grove and told her husband that she did not believe he would be healed unless he came up to attend the meetings and received the teaching. Although he was in a dying condition, and enduring great agony, he was so impressed with his wife's earnestness that he made the effort, was brought up to San Jose and brought into the meeting in a most pitiable condition. Owing to the nature of the spinal disease from which he suffered, he had no control over the movements of his limbs, which jerked out in all directions, and added to the excruciating pain from which he suffered in his stomach and heart. But during the first meeting he attended, the power of the Holy Spirit came upon him. He received the teaching fully, and that afternoon was instantaneously and perfectly restored to health, and remains to this moment a healed man. He spoke from the platform, in broken English, the following words:—

"Dear friends, I wonder that I am here; but I praise God, the Almighty, that through his power and through faith in Jesus Christ now I am a well man. ["Bless the Lord," from Dr. Jewell.] I suffered for thirty years—thirty long years; I don't know if Job suffered more. ["Not so long, by any means," said Mr. Dowie.] I have many good physicians; many times I wring my hands in thirty years and say, 'Lord, take me away! oh, take me away!' but he didn't. But if I prayed, 'Lord help me with a little more faith, with a little more patience, with a little more grace and trust,' the Lord was so willing to hear.

"Last Friday, a week ago, the mercy came in such healing power, but I forget something I was going to say. For seven or eight years I suffered with a hard cancer in the stomach, and a long time, a heart disease trouble, and from the crown of mine head to my feet there was not an inch that did not pain me; not one inch except my poor hands, and I thank God, the almighty One, he left me them poor hands, because I have to make my living with them. [Mr. Lathweson is a tailor by trade.] Now I am a well man. Praise God in the highest! Through faith in our beloved, sweet Jesus, I am a well man. The cancer is dropped, the heart disease is gone, the pain is gone; where it has gone to I don't care; it has gone! it has gone! I lay in the hardest convulsions with the heart disease, and I struggle in every direction, and mine poor family sometimes sheds tears. I love my family from the bottom of my heart; they see me suffer, but I could not help it.

"I never see my wife so thankful in all my life as just this last ten days. I say for my own self, *Praise God!* I thank God in Heaven that he sent this dear brother and sister here, and through their meetings and loving-kindness they lead me. I am healed! and something more, my dear brother, I am a little more patient since I been well; I reach out my hand and say, Almighty Father, help me that I live in faith all my life, and live a devoted Christian all my life. That is what I ask." ("Bless God," from the audience).

We then said, "I think we will have that happy wife talk, for she went down to the borders of the grave and brought him up—was that it?"

She replied, "Pretty near it." She then came upon the stand, and said: "My dear sisters and brethren, we live a long time in this city and you all know us, and you know my husband; then you know me; I was with him. I thought I never could leave him alone on account of his sickness. Thirty-six years ago I married him, in November, and so long as I been married I never saw him well. Before I was converted, I pray sometimes every day and night—and often didn't sleep two hours—and pray God to open a way. And the Lord was gracious and sent this minister, Dr. Jewell, and he talk and preach, and I had a love for the Methodist Church since; and he was converted to the Methodist Church and have an opportunity to testify, go to the church and have the prayer-meeting; what we didn't have in our Lutheran Church. But this last year I see more in the Bible, and the Lord opened another way. I told my husband, 'Could you not take the faith to be healed?' 'Well,' he say, 'mother I have to suffer God's will.' And everybody tells me pretty near, that he will have a crown in Heaven if he suffers. I tell you its very easy to say, but anybody got a sick man in their family suffering day and night, its another thing. I know what I suffered with him; could not sleep the whole night, and the next morning sick, and the whole day sick, and he pray God to take him away and give him rest, or to send somebody that he would be healed. But the Lord waited till now—oh! my dear sister and brother, the Lord waited till just now.

"Eleven years ago he went East and wanted to die there, and said if he die there then I could come back to California, and if he die there I should fetch his corpse back. And I said, 'Father, I won't do that; if you can die here, you can die in California; I like beter you will die in California.' And I have to cheer him up all the time the best I know how; I believe he would be lying in the grave if I didn't cheer him all the time. I often tell him when we came to Minnesota, now go die, die if you can; but he couldn't do it; he have to wait, he have to come back to California, and he have to testify here that the Lord have power on this earth to heal. [Cries of 'Amen.'] I can testify here that he had got the cancer and the heart disease, and that he is healed. Praise the Lord for such a healing power."

(This lady was rather a stout woman, with a frank, hopeful, cheerful manner, witty in her manner of talking, and carried the feelings of the audience with her all the time of her speaking. All sitting upon the platform rose and shook her hand heartily as she was about to take her seat.)

Instantaneous Healing of Three Years' Rheumatic Gout.

Mrs. Vandegrift, of the Willows, near San Jose, desired us to testify on her behalf concerning her healing. She had been brought in by her husband in a carriage, and then he lifted her on to the crutches (which were showed to the audience), and after the address we saw her, laid hands upon her in prayer in Jesus' name, and every bone in her body was instantly set free. She testified publicly on two occasions, and had said to us on the previous Saturday, "I am perfectly free, from the crown of my head to the soles of my feet, from the rheumatic pain."

She stood and talked to Dr. Bishop and others for about twenty minutes after she was healed, and although she did not feel she could face the large audience in the church, she desired that glory to God should be given in her behalf.

Public Testimony of a Doctor to the Healing of Two of His Patients.

We then asked Dr. A. B. Bishop, who sat near to us, to speak as the Lord might lead him concerning the two previous cases, with both of which he was perfectly conversant, having been the physician in attendance upon them. We quote the following from the verbatim report:—

Dr. Bishop, a tall, intelligent, fine-looking gentleman, with a very benevolent countenance, rose in the gallery, and in a very impressive manner said: "Brother Dowie, it will be more to my credit to give testimony about some patients I have cured; but for the credit of the gospel and for the honor of Christ I will say that I knew these two patients, and these two persons have been healed, and they were great sufferers.

"I was called to see Sister Vandegrift about two years ago; I paid her a few visits, perhaps covering ten days or two weeks, and she improved under my treatment and went to the mountains; after that I had nothing more to do with her; I think she had no more medical services. She considered her case incurable, and silently suffered on. I have seen her since. I know, before her cure, her joints were swollen; her hands were almost unusable. I saw her after she was cured, and she said, 'See, doctor, how I can open and shut my hands as you can yourself?' As Dr. Dowie said, she stood in the vestibule of the church fifteen or twenty minutes without any support, without leaning against the wall, even.

"I met Brother Lathwesen first about five years ago, when I moved here. I was not called to treat him, because he considered his case beyond the reach of any human agency. I was not called until about two years ago, and when I was I found him suffering great pain; had trouble with the spine and spinal cord, and had convulsive movements in the arms and limbs. I treated him with electricity, to relieve the pain. I knew he was a great sufferer. I did not examine the cancer very closely, but I know he had heart disease of a very bad type. I have examined him since he says he was cured, and he acts like a well man.

"I like to give this testimony because it gives honor to Christ. I believe, as they state, they were healed instantly, and I think we all must admit that Christ has power on earth not only to forgive sins, but to heal the body."

We then, after thanking the Doctor for his testimony, asked Mr. Lathwesen to give us further particulars concerning the tumor, and who had diagnosed it as cancerous?

Mr. Lathwesen answered, "Dr. Nichols, of Rochester, and our neighbor, a druggist, both pronounced it cancer. I was in great misery and suffering. Dr. Nichols said it was cancer. Since that time I never asked any more doctors about it, because I knew it my own self. Now all that lump is entirely gone away and I feel empty there."

After Mr. Lathwesen finished, Dr. Bishop said he had noticed the tumor, but did not diagnose it, and that it was a very difficult thing indeed to diagnose correctly; but as far as human investigation was concerned there was every probability that it was a cancer.

Many Witnesses.

At this stage of the meeting we made the same request of the great audience present which we have made at the close of every mission, namely, that everyone in the meeting who was convinced that Jesus had power on earth to heal disease, and that he was the healer of his people, should stand to their feet. The response was immediate; it seemed as if the whole audience instantly stood up, and with great feeling sang the Doxology.

We asked all who had received spiritual blessing to stand up, and nearly all did so.

We then asked if there was any person who was not convinced that Christ was the healer, to hold up their hand. Only one hand was held up.

Healing of Internal Diseases of Women

We then took the opportunity of mentioning that there were a very large number of healings in this as in all other missions concerning which we could not enter into detail, a class which are more numerous in our missions than any others; diseases from which ladies suffer nameless tortures. I then asked all who had been healed to stand, and a very large number did so. The testimony meeting still continued.

Instantaneous Healing of an Abscess in the Side, of Many Months' Standing.

A young man named Mr. Hoffman, from Santa Barbara, who had been saved and healed in the mission, then briefly testified to his healing. He said: "I have been suffering for a long time with an abscess in the side. I came here a little over two months ago and have been doctoring ever since without any relief, until Dr. Dowie opened his mission. With difficulty I attended the meetings for a little while, but I was so sick that I was unable to continue to attend. I gave to my mother a petition for prayer, which she handed Mr. Dowie, but still I did not get the blessing. She then asked him, at my request, to come and see me, for I felt I was sinking. He did so, and after prayer he laid his hands upon me and immediately all pain departed; I was able to use my leg with perfect freedom, which I could not use before without great pain, and I attended the meetings at once, and have attended ever since without any pain. The abscess has all gone away and I feel perfectly healed." (Dr. Jewell exclaimed, "Bless the Lord.")

We then referred to the fact that he had been publicly baptized the previous Lord's day, and was a candidate for fellowship in one of the churches of the city. This young man's case created great interest, and he seemed in perfect health.

Healing of Paralysis.

The Rev. Mr. Hazen, a minister of the Methodist Episcopal Church, then testified to the blessing that he had received through the teaching in the mission without human touch. He said that ten years ago he had been stricken with paralysis; he had been healed for seven years. Then he gradually failed and had to give up work. He came home last Friday still feeling symptons of paralysis about him, "but hearing of these meetings and of the wonderful cures Jesus was doing here, I began to think whether it was God's will that I should suffer from this disease any longer. I came to hear Dr. Dowie, and I will simply say his words gave me great encouragement; and I will say in addition to that which Dr. Jewell has already better said, that *the Bible is a new book to me.*

"I believed in bodily healing before I came, but I never dared to teach, hardly to tell of it, to intimate friends, that God had healed me once or more. But glory be to his name, I have now been able to put my trust in Jesus for a perfect cure, and now I feel such a power and influence going all through my body as well as my soul, as I have not felt for years. So far as I can realize there are no symptons remaining of this paralysis. I am trusting Jesus for a perfect cure; I am resolved that all my powers of body, soul and spirit shall be given to him. I know he has healed me."

This minister's testimony created a deep impression upon the meeting. It was entirely unexpected by us, for we had never spoken to the brother, and had not known of the blessing he had received.

Healing of Rupture of Eight Years' Standing without Human Touch.

Mr. Herrick, of San Jose, said: "For over eight years I have been an invalid, brought on from overwork in the hot climate of Arizona; nervous prostration set in, a severe rupture took place, and I was unable to work; my mind was nearly dethroned, and I was disqualified from doing business. I came to this city of San Jose last October.

"During the meetings of last week I said to a friend, 'People are being healed down there to the church, and if they can be healed I know I can be if I trust the Lord.' On Wednesday afternoon I pressed my way forward amid the crowd at the close of the meeting to take Dr. Dowie by the hand. He was trying to get the people to sit down, but we all wanted to speak to him. I said to him, 'I came here to be healed.' '*Sit down!*' says he. I sat down." (We explained to the people that we did not mean to be rude to the brother, but that at the close of our addresses people thronged us in such numbers that we could not get to the work at all until they sat down.) Mr. Herrick continued: "It don't matter; you were quite right; thank the Lord I did as you told me, I sat down. In a few moments I felt that something ought to be done. I reasoned in this way: What is the doctor doing here? Does the doctor do the work, or is it the blessed Saviour? He had taught us it was the Saviour. I said, That is true, it is the Saviour, it is the work of Jesus, and I will take the Saviour at his word. The moment I said, 'It is the Saviour, and that I would take him at his word,' I felt an electric shock go all through my physical system, and where the most disease lay the shock seemed the greatest. I went into one of the side rooms where thirty or forty persons were waiting for the doctor. He came in presently and remained a few minutes, and his dear wife called him out. I sat there while person after person went into his room to see him, and I left without seeing him, but with the conviction that I was perfectly cured.

"I did not tell my wife that night, but I went to the Lord Jesus and thanked him. I pulled off the truss that had given me so much unhappiness, and laid it down, and I said in my mind, 'Lie there forever.' And the medicine I had been taking to help me along, I said to it, 'You remain there.' In the morning I got up happy in the Lord; said nothing to my wife that day, which was Thursday. I came on Thursday night, and a brother spoke to me, a very intelligent gentleman, and said, 'What do you think of all this?' 'I will tell you what I think: I believe in it,' I said. I then told him, what I have since told everyone, how I had been perfectly healed.

"The point I want to make is this: While Dr. Dowie is here instructing us how to get healed, let us remember it is not the doctor, but it is the Lord Jesus Christ who is the healer. When the doctor leaves us the healing may go on— perhaps not so well, but it can go on, and if we trust the Lord Jesus it will go on. Thank God, friends, I think this is the happiest day I ever spent in my life. Not only is my body healed, but my spirit is quickened, and I know more of the Bible to-night than ever I did before."

Healing of an Injury of Sixteen Years' Standing.

A gentleman who did not give his name told of his healing four years previously. He had been injured in his side by raking heavy grain off a reaper, and at a meeting conducted by Brother Newton he had received instantaneous healing.

Partial Healing of Many Years' Deafness.

Mrs. Martin, wife of Professor Martin, of the University of the Pacific, said that she thought she could not let the meeting close without testifying. She had attended the meetings, and followed our teaching closely, and fully received the doctrine. She had been a sufferer for forty-four years from deafness, and now, "through the ministry of Dr. Dowie," she said, "I have been very much relieved. I have hesitated," she added, "about testifying to-night, because I am not absolutely perfect in my hearing; but I am so much better, and believe so strongly that I will be healed, I feel my faith will reach up to it, that I felt that I ought to testify. I want you all to pray for me. [Dr. Jewell, "The Lord bless her."] The enemy," she continued, "in view of my not being perfectly healed, will try to make me weak in my faith, but I intend to believe in the grace of God for what has been done for me, and it is very much. I feel to give God the praise."

Healing of Six Years' Chronic Diarrhea.

Mrs. Baker said: "Last winter, through the ministry of Rev. Mr. Irvine, at Pacific Grove, I was led to ask him in a cottage meeting to anoint me, which he did, and I have been healed ever since."

Testimony of a Minister.

The Rev. Mr. Lawson, minister of the Wesleyan Methodist Church, San Jose, very feelingly testified to the blessing he had received through our teaching. He said: "The Bible seems to me to be a new book. Since I heard these teachings in these meetings I understand it as I never understood it before, and Jesus Christ seems to me to-night more really a personal Saviour than ever he has done before. I thank God for the spiritual good I have received in this meeting. I feel more able now to go forth and preach than ever before."

Mrs. Dowie's Closing Address.

After this impressive little testimony Mrs. Dowie delivered a brief farewell address, which made a deep impression upon the assembly.

An Invitation to Return to San Jose.

Dr. Jewell then rose and said: "Permit me, Doctor, to say a few words. I just want to ask as many as would like to unite in inviting Brother and Sister Dowie, if the Lord in his providence should open the way for them to come to us again, to rise and stand upon their feet."

The entire congregation rose *en masse* and the choir immediately commenced to sing sweetly and beautifully, "God Be with You 'till We Meet Again." Dr. Jewell continued: "I wanted to say a word also suggested by my dear wife to-night, and it seemed so sweet to me; it was this: that she had never been able to appreciate before the wonderful scenes that are given in the New Testament when the sufferers tried to press up to Jesus; she never could fully appreciate and understand it as she had within these few days. And when they were gathering around and pressing up it seemed to her, and it seemed to me, just as though we saw the scenes of more than 1,800 years ago when sufferers came and sought to press up to Jesus; and as they pressed around our brother we have seen him try to hide behind the blessed Jesus and to make them see that Jesus was their healer, not himself. Blessed be God for these precious memories. And now, will Dr. Dowie come again?"

We then rose and thanked our friends and the meeting for their kindness. It made our heart very full to see the gratitude and love which gathered round us, and we promised, God willing, to return to San Jose at the close of the next San Francisco Mission, which will be, probably, about the middle of November.

After a very touching prayer by Dr. Jewell, we pronounced the benediction and the testimony meeting closed.

Two Days' Visitation of the Bedridden.

The two following days, Tuesday and Wednesday, twenty-first and twenty-second of August, were taken up in visiting many bedridden patients in and around San Jose, a number of whom think they received healing.

A Personal Experience.

And now speaking in my own proper person, and dropping for the time our missionary and editorial "we," I desire to record with profound gratitude to my Lord, an incident which, although it is known to a few, has not become public property. I may head it

Instantaneous Healing of My Dislocated Shoulder.

My readers will scarcely be prepared for my telling them that during the whole of the three hours of the foregoing testimony meeting, I conducted the exercises with my left arm torn from its shoulder socket, although the fact was unknown to a single person in the building. The accident, if such I may call it, for it was in consequence of the sin of another, occurred within three-quarters of an hour of our beginning the meeting. It was a quarter past seven before I left with Mrs. Dowie the parlors of the church to return to my hotel for slight refreshment and the arranging of certain papers. As I came quickly out of the door I slipped upon the hard asphalt pavement on the skin of a piece of fruit, and fell with a tremendous crash upon my left shoulder. I arose at once, but not without difficulty, and found my left arm was hanging powerless by my side. "It seems almost as if it were broken," I said. Dr. Holmes, who was standing by (who with Dr. Hervey and another, and the two doctors already mentioned, make a quintette of believing doctors in San Jose), came up to me and said, "O, doctor, have you broken your arm?" I at once replied, "No, it cannot be, for God's word has said, 'He keepeth all his bones, not one of them is broken.'" A little crowd had gathered around us, from which I hurried away, asking them to go back and pray that I might be able to conduct the meeting. Accompanied by Elder Cadman, of the Presbyterian Church, East Oakland, and Mrs. Dowie, I proceeded to the St. James' Hotel in great agony. I asked the Lord if it was a sprain to heal me; if by any possibility it could be a broken bone, to restore it. But the answer did not seem to come. Pastor Afflerbach and others visited me immediately and prayed for me very tenderly. I asked them all to go back to the church and pray for me there in a private room. I then appealed to God that I should not be put to shame, nor dishonor the name of the Lord, by my inability to conduct the meeting. I immediately got power to move my arm from the elbow to the finger tips, and returned to the church convinced that the injury was a dislocation at the shoulder. But there was no time to have that set right, for the church was crowded with eager, expectant people, and the rumor had got abroad that I was injured and would not be able to proceed.

I went into Dr. Jewell's study and told him I had been injured, but said nothing as to the nature of it. After prayer we at once entered the building and conducted the meeting. While it was proceeding I felt that the bone was not only out of its place, but that it had slipped back and was pressing hard against my side, with every slight movement of my arm or body. But I received in answer to my unspoken prayer such continuous streams of heavenly power that although I cannot say I was at all times without pain, yet I was so completely lifted above all sense of pain that I neither manifested it nor felt it, for the most part, during these long hours. But immediately the meeting had closed I turned to my friend, Dr. Bishop, and said, "Doctor, come in half an hour to my rooms, at the St. James', and pull my left arm into its socket." I think he thought I was joking, almost, at first, and I know from what he afterwards said that he was sure I was mistaken; for it was impossible, he thought, for anyone to be in such a condition and do what I had been enabled by the Lord to do. It was still half an hour after the meeting before I could get away from the kindly throng who gathered around us, and it was more than an hour later before Dr. Bishop got to my rooms, through no fault of his own, because he was waiting in another portion of the hotel, and was told I had not returned. Therefore it was a quarter to twelve when Dr. Bishop entered my room. My arm had then been out of the socket for four hours and a half. Dr. Jewell, Elder Cadman, Pastor Afflerbach, and Mr. G. H. Hawes, our stenographer, were all present, with Mrs. Dowie. I then for the first time had my coat removed, and Mrs. Dowie retired into the next room. When my clothing was all removed from the upper part of my body it was found, just as I had believed, that the arm was out of its socket, and of course the ligaments were ruptured, and extravasation of blood must have followed. The doctor looked very grave, but I asked him to proceed to business, and I lay upon the floor, asking the friends to pray. The doctor placed his stockinged foot against my side, and with one gentle, strong pull the arm slipped beautifully into its socket with a loud snap. I neither felt, nor by any sound expressed, any pain: for while that act was performed I felt as perfectly free as if no such thing was being done. With a hearty "Thank God," I sprang to my feet.

"But you must be suffering great pain still," said Dr. Bishop.

I said, "No. I thank you for the friendly act, but now the Lord will do all the rest; I am perfectly healed."

He said, "You must be suffering pain?"

I said, lifting my arm over my head, and putting it to the farthest extremity upon my back, "No, there is no pain," and then grasping my friend's hands with my left hand, I showed them that all the power was in my arm.

After a few minutes' prayer and happy talk, we separated. I ate a hearty supper, retired to rest and slept soundly, leaning my head for a good portion of the night upon the injured shoulder. The next morning I dressed myself freely and easily, and found there was no inflammation nor injury of any kind. Dr. Bishop called during the day with a patient of his whom he desired me to pray for, and found that I was free from pain. I visited many persons that day, and dined with a number of friends, and the following day continued my visits, and from that time till now have never been inconvenienced by the injury for a moment.

This little incident, though not publicly narrated, has become widely known, and I humbly hope has helped to strengthen the faith of many. I only narrate it here that I may give all the glory to God, who for Jesus' sake by his Holy Spirit so mightily upheld me, and so graciously restored me. Gladly can I add my testimony to the truth of his word, "I am the Lord that healeth thee;" and to the declaration concerning his servants, "He keepeth all their bones not one of them is broken."

After the Mission.

We have received since the close of the mission a number of testimonies to healing, for which we cannot now find space, and many letters concerning the healed which are deeply interesting. We will content ourselves by giving one of these testimonies, and referring to one or two of these letters.

Healing of Ten Years' Broken Muscle of the Right Knee.

Mrs. H. A. Pryce, of 58 Santa Clara St., San Jose, writes: "I wish to add my testimony to others for the divine healing received through the Rev. John Alexander Dowie. I believe it was on the 3rd day of the mission that I was healed.

About ten years ago I met with an accident which broke the muscles of my right knee, causing me much suffering ever since. In addition to this four years ago I was afflicted with sciatic rheumatism, for which I had no relief at all until I visited the meetings, and entered the healing room of the Rev. Dr. Dowie and wife. I went in trusting in Jesus to heal me, and in about ten minutes from the time I entered that room I was entirely relieved from all my pain. I could walk as well as I could before being hurt, ten years ago. For this I feel very thankful the Lord, and also to Dr. Dowie and his wife."

Confirmation of Healings.

Dr. Jewell in a recent letter speaks in very kind terms concerning the blessing which has followed our mission. He speaks of their testimony meetings being times of great refreshing, and says, "Many speak the most pleasant and appreciative words of your presence and work here. We shall expect a great blessing when you return to us. We found Mrs. Vandegrift out-of-doors when we called last Friday; she is free and gaining strength; her faith is strong and her heart is glad. Brother Lathwesen has gone to Pacific Grove, a well and happy man. My own heart is wonderfully drawn towards the blessed work in which you are engaged, and I feel at times that I must qualify by study and communion with God for a better knowledge and understanding of this department of the gospel."

The following words are also quoted from Dr. Jewell's report in the *Christian Advocate*, the organ of the Methodist Episcopal Church on this coast, in its issue of August 29.

San Jose.

"The mission for divine healing, held in the First Methodist Episcopal Church, by Rev. J. A. Dowie, assisted by his estimable wife, has been a great blessing to our people. The Holy Spirit has been wonderfully and sweetly present in all the services, and hundreds are rejoicing to have had this time of refreshing from the presence of the Lord. The afternoon meetings have continued from half past two until five and six o'clock, and the evening services from a quarter to eight until half past ten and eleven o'clock, and even then the people would seem reluctant to leave the place where Christ, the great "world-magnet," was so exalted. We realized as never before the attractiveness of a "whole and perfect Saviour," and came to understand how the people needed to be "sent away" from Jesus when in his public ministry in Galilee. There have been several clear conversions and a general and signal deepening of the channels of spiritual life and power. The word of God has become clearer and its teachings dearer to scores and hundreds of believers. Several pastors and preachers, together with very many of the most thoughtful and deeply pious of our church members, have been in regular attendance, and have seemed unwilling to miss a single service. Oh, with what holy delight have these waiting throngs lingered and drank of the fountains to which they have been directed by these servants of the Most High God! Besides the great spiritual benefits realized, there have been several instances of bodily healing by faith in Jesus in answer to prayer. Amid tears and glad testimonies, the great congregation last evening, as the mission closed, by a rising vote invited these Heaven-commissioned and sweet-spirited evangelists to return and hold another mission in our church." F. F. JEWELL.

[Extracts from letter to "Leaves of Healing" for January 1889, concerning Mission in Sacramento.]

This Mission was held from Monday, September 17, to Tuesday, October 2, in the Congregational Church.

It was the least successful of all our Missions, so far as outward results were concerned; but there were fruits even there. "This people's heart is waxed gross" is perhaps the best description which could be given to the spiritual condition of that city, where sloth and sin produce a moral stupor and indifference to eternal things.

Our closing Praise and Testimony Meeting was held on the evening of Tuesday, October 2. We did not have this meeting reported by our short-hand writer, as we did in other Missions, so that the testimonies we now quote are from our own notes, and from the letters of the healed.

Testimony of a Doctor.

SACRAMENTO, CAL., October 2, 1888.

DEAR BROTHER DOWIE: I esteem it a privilege to testify that I have received great benefit from your administration of the Word, viz.: Christ will not send the Comforter fully into our being until the temple is purified. He has been knocking at the door of my heart for many years, and for many years I have been trying to keep the commandments, and forgot that He said, "Without Me ye can do nothing."

I can testify to the peace and the joy in the HOLY GHOST, and also the great physical relief which I have received through your instrumentality, and I believe

if I continue in Him, He will heal all my diseases. I now wish to do His will, in His own way, and I earnestly desire the best gift. Remember me in your prayers.
Yours in Jesus, G. DART.

To these written lines Dr. Dart added some very earnest words, and thanked God for our visit to Sacramento.

Healing of Twenty-four Years' Infirmities.

Mrs. N. A. Little, 208 Tenth Street, SACRAMENTO, wrote as follows:

"REV. J. A. DOWIE: With profound gratitude to GOD and His Son JESUS CHRIST, I write to thank HIM and to rejoice that He has sent you as His agent to help us to understand more fully His own power and willingness to heal diseases of the body, at this day, as well as when He was in the flesh on earth. I praise His Holy Name. I want to tell how much good your prayers and your beloved wife's have done for my daughter, Mary E. Little. We had the best doctors for her. All was in vain. But when you came to this city, I saw God's way of healing, and when you came to my house and laid your hands upon my daughter, God heard your prayer, and I do bless His holy name she has been free from her infirmity ever since. Her mind is now clear and she is free from pain. It must be Jesus and Him only who has done this mighty work for her. Many have been blessed by your coming to this city. I am yours in Christ."

Testimony of a Lady Physician, Who Accepts Christ as Healer.

Dr. (Miss) L. J. Kellogg, Seventh and I Streets, a much-esteemed Christian practitioner, spoke with much gratitude of blessing received during the Mission, and that from thence she took Christ as her Doctor. This lady, with a few others, was specially helpful to us in the work, and is now devoting much of her time to evangelistic efforts.

The First of Our First-Fruits.

Mrs. Elizabeth Browne, 1117 Fourth Street, who had been healed in the Palace Hotel on June 16 last, testified to her continued healing, and her words were confirmed by her husband and daughter, Mrs. Chambers. But as her testimony will be given in detail with many others in the report of our Testimony Meeting of October 28, we do not quote it here. Mrs. Browne looked well and strong.

Healed Through the Agency of Dorothea Trudel.

Mrs. Maria Reaser, V Street, between Tenth and Eleventh Streets, gave a very interesting description of her healing at Mannedorf, Switzerland, through the holy and great woman whose fame has filled the world, Dorothea Trudel. Mrs. Reaser says she used to remember his praying: "Dear Heavenly Father, I desire and demand of Thee all the souls that are led into my house; for I know that thou art able to save them and bring them to thy glory."

Healed Through Pastor Blumhardt's Agency.

Mrs. M. A. Dutschke testified to having received healing through the good pastor Blumhardt, who was so largely used in Germany a few years ago; and said that she used to hear him say often, "Jesus is Conqueror."

Healing of Lupus (Cancer) and Heart Disease.

Mrs. N. Hudson, 1408 J Street, testified of her healing, through the laying on of our hands, of these diseases. She says in a written testimony that the lupus had troubled her for nine years, and that she was under four doctors; but none of them could do her any good. She says it is now well; and also her heart trouble is gone. "Thanks be to God." We have seen this lady recently in our meetings in the Grand Opera House, while on a visit to San Francisco, and she declares herself perfectly healed, and looks quite well.

Twenty Persons Healed Witness Thereto.

Upon our call for all who had been healed to rise, twenty persons did so and a number professed to have been saved.

All Present Believe the Doctrine That Christ is Healer.

After a number of persons had testified to their healing, I called upon all present to say if they had received the doctrine that we had been teaching, and all present did so. Then we closed the Mission, grateful for the blessing we had received, and surrounded by a crowd of sympathetic friends, giving God all the glory.

Extracts from a Report of a Praise and Testimony Meeting, Held by Rev. John Alex. Dowie and Wife at the Grand Opera House, San Francisco, Lord's Day Evening, October 28, 1888.

[This meeting was held at the beginning of the third week of a month's Mission, and will be followed by the usual closing Praise and Testimony Meeting on Lord's day, November 11, when many others who have been healed through faith in Jesus will witness for him. There were about one thousand two hundred persons present, and the meeting lasted from 7:45 to 11:15 P. M., and was followed by an after-meeting, which was attended by some hundreds. A number of persons sought and found salvation, amongst them a man of above forty years old, who knelt and prayed for the first time in his life. Up to the date of writing these lines (November 7) 147 persons have openly sought salvation in the Mission, and many have been healed.—J. A. D.]

Reported by G. H. Hawes, 320 Sansome Street, San Francisco.

The meeting was opened by the hearty singing of hymn 162 from "Gospel Hymns,"—

"My hope is built on nothing less
Than Jesus' blood and righteousness."

Mrs. Dowie then read the 67th Psalm. "God be merciful unto us, and bless us; and cause hisace to shine upon us."

Mr. Dowie then offered prayer, presenting requests from many that were sick.

Dr. Dowie said :—

BELOVED FRIENDS: I desire to say that to-night we have many testimonies, some of which have only just reached me since I came upon the platform some of them in writing and some are present here to speak for themselves, and as the number is so very great, it would not be wise in me to take up much time.

My Secretary has handed me a list of those who have given in their names as being prepared to testify, and there are thirty on this platform, besides others in the audience. With the single exception of one person who is now present, I have not personally invited a single person to testify; their testimony is perfectly voluntary, and they have come forward of their own accord, and they are fully responsible before God and man for their own testimonies.

I would like to say a very few words in introducing the Testimony Meeting. I cannot to-night speak as I would fain do concerning the work generally, but I want to say this first of all: This Mission is a mission of healing through faith in Jesus Christ alone. There is not one person either here in this audience or anywhere else in this country, or in the wide world, *whom I have healed*. I have never healed anybody; I never have attempted to heal anybody, and there isnot one here to-night to testify to my healing power. There is some misunderstanding concerning this matter. It does not exist in the hearts of those who have attended our ministry, but in the minds of those who have not been present at all. I want to say most distinctly and clearly at the very beginning, that those who are healed are here to confess Christ as their Healer. I have been used instrumentally in teaching, in preaching, and as the instrument of the healing; but the teaching is not mine; it is the teaching of the Teacher of teachers. The preaching is not mine, but it is the gospel of our Lord Jesus Christ. The healing is not mine any more than the salvation which has attended this ministry; the healing is the healing of the Lord Jesus Christ. Make no mistake about it; whatever you may have read, or thought, or imagined, or seen written, there is no living being in the world who has ever heard me say I have healed; there is not a line from my pen—and I have written many thousands of lines in my time, many of which have been widely printed—which would warrant anyone in making such an accusation. CHRIST IS THE HEALER AND HE ALONE.

I am here upon a Mission. I am just on my way—although I am tarrying long at the Golden Gate—through your great continent, and I hope to pass through Canada and England, and by and by to return to my old home in Australia. Then I hope again, after a short tarrying, to go farther away to the East, if the Lord permits, and back again around through the West. If the Lord will, I give Him gladly the next ten years of my life to carry His Gospel of Healing to every place I can reach.

Now you understand I am not here to establish a sect or a church organization, but to minister to the whole "Household of Faith" without reference to denomination. I don't know Baptists, I do not know Presbyterians, I do not know Episcopalians—I do not know you by these names; I know you by one name, by the Name that is above every name, the name of Christ, our Lord. I thank God that I am enabled to minister without any fear, without any doubt, in this beautiful work. I thank God, too, it is without money and without price. I am trusting God for everything connected with this work, and what we have received we freely give, as we have freely received.

I think perhaps it would be well first of all before asking anyone to speak regarding healing through human touch, to give you some illustrations from the testimonies I hold in my hand of—

Healing without Any Human Touch,

In direct answer to prayer during this present Mission. If we were to attempt to give you anything like a full account of such cases of direct answer to prayer offered upon our platform for those whom we never saw, and some of whom we have never seen to this day, it would take all the night. I will give you some of those I have in my hand.

Healing of a Ten-Year-Old Boy from Blood Poisoning, etc.

On October 17, I received and presented to the Lord in prayer the following petition:—

"DEAR SIR: Having been myself cured most wonderfully at one of your meetings last July through faith in Jesus, without any human touch; and being sure that God does hear and does answer prayer, will you ask the Christians to-day to pray for a dear boy aged ten years, who has blood poisoning and a very bad eye. The little fellow is a great sufferer. His parents are believers, but I fear not as fully resting in Christ as I could wish. I believe Christ can do with him as he did with the Centurion's sick servant—heal him without bringing him here to the meeting, which it is difficult to do. Please pray for him, for earthly physicians can do him no good. I am yours,
"A BELIEVER IN THE GREAT HEALER."

This was an anonymous petition. Exactly a week later I received another letter, thanking God for the answer, in which she said that she had waited, so that there might be plenty of time to test the healing before writing me. She is here to-night. Her name is Mrs. Barnes, 513 Hayes Street, City. Her note reads as follows:—

"DEAR SIR: You will remember that prayer was asked last Wednesday, October 17, for a boy aged ten years who had blood poisoning, and such trouble with his eyes that he had to be kept in a dark room and was so sick that he was unable to walk about. To-day the little boy is perfectly well; he can see without even a shade over his eyes. His face is all well and clean, and he is able to run around better than he has done for a long time. I feel sure Christ has fully answered prayer. Three other doctors did him no good; I never saw such a wonderful change in any child in a week in my life. He is my own grandchild. Yours very respectfully." It is signed by Mrs. Barnes. I will just ask the sister to verify that testimony.

Mrs. Barnes, who was sitting upon the platform, immediately arose and said, "That is perfectly true, every word."

Instantaneous Healing of a Baby in Answer to Prayer.

The next case of direct answer to prayer which I select, is one written from 1123 Greenwich Street, City, dated the 27th of October—that is, yesterday.

"DEAR MR. AND MRS. DOWIE: Will you praise the Lord with me for the complete restoration of a dear child for whom you prayed in the meeting of the 17th of this month? The child was very sick; she seemed to us to be dying. She could not support any food whatever. At the same hour, the same moment, almost, that you were praying in the Opera House she was healed in my own home; and, without changing any food, she supports everything she could not support before. Every day she grows brighter. I have not written my thanks before, because I wanted to prove to some of your unbelieving hearers that the child is healed and completely and thoroughly restored. As for myself, I do not need the proof, for I know what the Lord doeth, he doeth perfectly. He did it in answer to your prayer. Praise ye the Lord, the Lord who is Jehovah, the Healer of His people. Yours in the Lord, J. L. BOILLOT-STECK."

If the sister is here, will she stand up. The lady arose from the platform and said, "That is perfectly so."

Immediate Restoration of a Dying Lady in Answer to Prayer Only.

Mr. Dowie continued: I have another testimony from Oakland. A lady was supposed to be dying during this Mission, and the Lord healed her thoroughly in answer to prayer. This is her own writing. She lives on Twenty-fourth Street, between Adeline and Market Streets, Oakland. This testimony was handed me to-night, and is dated yesterday, October 27.

"To the glory of our Lord Jesus will I give my testimony that by faith in Jesus and prayer, I have been restored to health. About three weeks ago I took very, very sick, and my friends did not believe that I would recover. I thought I was dying. We prayed, and we asked you to pray, and the Lord heard our prayers. On the very night you were praying for me in the Opera House I was healed of my sickness, and I am now well, and I wish to thank God and give Him all the glory now and forever. Your sister in Christ,
"ANNIE SODERSTRAND."

All those who know this lady, and know of her healing, will kindly stand up. (Seven rose to their feet. Mr. Dowie thanked them, and said he was informed that the lady was a member of the Swedish Baptist Church, Oakland.)

Mr. Dowie said: I do not know that it would be well for me to continue this line of testimony. I have a number of others in my hands, but while there are so many living witnesses, I think I will put aside the letters, and just ask some of the living witnesses to speak. I scarcely know where to begin. I am surrounded by those whom the Lord has blest, and I feel so thankful. I think I shall begin by asking a stranger in your city to speak first. There are some in your city now who have come from quite a distance to this meeting and been blessed, and there is one brother whose testimony I am intensely interested in. Not that I count one healing more wonderful in some respects than another, because we are very poor judges of that; but this case has caused a great deal of interest in San Jose.

It Is the Case of Brother C. H. Lathweson.

I hold now in my hand a report of the praise and testimony meeting held at San Jose on August 20, after our two weeks' Mission. The meeting was held in the First Methodist Episcopal Church, of which the Rev. Dr. Jewell is pastor, Dr. Jewell being present, and nearly as large an audience as there is here. Among those who spoke that evening I called upon my friend and brother, Dr. Bishop, an eminent doctor in San Jose He testified to the healing of two of his patients. One of these is with us to-night. He said that this brother who is here was beyond all question healed; that his case was known to a large number of persons present, and I am quoting what Dr. Bishop said from the short-hand writer's report, taken by my friend G. H. Hawes, 320 Sansome Street, who is reporting this meeting. This document which I hold in my hand is a very beautiful type-written report of that meeting. He gives me here Dr. Bishop's words, and the doctor says he is delighted to be able to testify for the honor of Christ; that he knows these two patients, and that they were great sufferers, and that they have been healed. After mentioning another case, which is not present to-night, and which I shall not refer to, he says he met Brother Lathweson first about five years ago, when he moved to San Jose. Dr. Bishop was not at first called in to treat him, because his case was considered to be beyond the reach of any human agency; but about two years ago he was called in and found him suffering the most agonizing pain He had trouble of the spine and spinal cord, and had convulsive movements continuously in all his limbs; he was a great sufferer; he did not examine the cancer very closely, but he knew he had heart disease of a very bad type. He says that Lathweson acts like a perfectly well man. He says he likes to give this testimony because it is to the honor of Christ. He further says: "I believe these persons were healed instantly, as they state, and I think we must all admit Christ has power on earth not only to forgive sins, but to heal the body."

Our Brother Lathweson has been a member of the Church of God for many years He was a sufferer for thirty years from spinal injury, from heart disease, and from a cancer that was diagnosed by Dr Nichols, of Rochester, a number of years ago, as cancer of the stomach. He suffered continuous agony. He will tell you himself how the Lord instantly healed him. 1 will just call upon him to tell you the story in his own way. You will kindly remember he is a German, and not accustomed to addressing a large audience. You will get the testimony from him and all here in a simple way, showing just how they felt about it, and what the Lord did for them, and how they were previously. I will ask him to put it in his own words. Dear Mr. Lathweson, will you now step forward and tell us what the Lord did for you, and how He had mercy upon you. Come, my brother.

Mr. Lathweson's Story

Mr. Lathweson then stepped forward and spoke as follows. The reporter noticed a marked improvement in his appearance since he saw him testify in the closing meeting of the San Jose Mission.

"MY DEAR BRETHREN AND SISTERS: If you are very quiet I try to speak so loud as possible, so as to make everybody understand what I mean and what I say. First of all I got to say, 'What a friend we got in Jesus; what a friend we got in Jesus.' Oh, my friends, this good Friend in Heaven, my Father in Heaven, through Jesus Christ, he was the best Friend I ever know in mine suffering in mine last thirty years. I suffered as I never saw anybody in the world suffer, and I never like to see anybody suffer that way. God forbid that mine eyes ever see such a thing. In mine suffering I beg God many, many times— hundred times, 'O Lord, take me away, if possible; I can't stand it 1 don't see any good work of me. I don't know what I am doing in this world. I don't see any good work of mine hands. Lord, take me away.' God shake his head, and don't answer me. He don't take me away; but that was not all. I see that He was not pleased to take me away out of this world; I has to pray another story: 'Lord, if possible, give me patience, patience, patience, and peace and a quiet life.' Then my Father was so quick to drop down all the patience I need, and all I want.

"And now them thirty years is gone. Thank God in Heaven, them thirty years is finished. Thank God in Heaven he give me so much grace and patience, and that it is now finished. Thank God through Jesus Christ that this my dear brother [the speaker here turned to Mr. Dowie, who had fervently exclaimed,

"'Praise the Lord;'" and with tears streaming from his eyes, lovingly embraced him The audience was deeply moved as they looked upon the pathetic scene] God fetch him to San Jose, to lead me on—with his dear wife—lead me on, and tell me the good story that Jesus Christ just now is able to forgive sins and to heal all diseases. That is the story satisfy me, and I came just as I was, and I go and throw myself in the arms of Jesus, and say, 'Lord take me.' And my Jesus was waiting—oh, how anxious he was waiting ! and mine heart was ready to receive it; and so he came down so low to his little one that he healed the body. And that was not all; he healed mine soul wonderfully, as it was never, never healed before—mine poor soul. I never enjoyed such a rest, such a peace, such a religion. What shall I say ? [The speaker turned inquiringly to Mr. Dowie. Mr. Dowie said, "Tell about being at Pacific Grove."]

"My wife came down to San Jose from Pacific Grove. I went there to get a little rest in Pacific Grove, but I didn't get any rest; I get worser and worser. So my wife had a little business, and came back to San Jose, and in that time I grown so worse and so bad and so low that my neighbors was afraid I would drop away any minute; and they was going to watch me. My wife was away two or three nights, and they was going to watch me in the night. I say, 'No, no, just go home; I got a good watchman in heaven; he take care of me.' My trust was always fully in God in mine greatest agony.

"My dear wife came the next day, and she was so sad. She say, 'Aint you going to be healed ?" I don't know what to say. Then I broke down and say, 'Oh, mother stop, stop now; I can't hear any more. I go to San Jose to-morrow, and if I got only one leg I got to go.' I went the next morning and my wife was afraid I would drop on the cars; she watches me every minute; every minute she watch me so particular; she thought I drop down in the car We came to San Jose, and the same evening—oh, my dear brother [grasping Mr. Dowie affectionately by the hand] that evening between five and six o'clock, as I said a little while ago, the dear Saviour came down and met me—met this poor feller, and healed body and soul."

Mr. Dowie asked, "How long did it take to heal you ?"

"I was ready and Jesus was waiting, and it take only, I suppose, that much," (striking his hands together).

Mr. Dowie said, " Did you feel it ?"

"In that time it seems to me as if it comes in here and roll down; (illustrated by placing his hands upon the upper part of his body and slowly moving them downward.) There was a hard cancer, liver disease, heart disease, and spine disease— God knows how much more—I don't like to tell the others. I pray always in my greatest agony, 'Lord, keep these poor hands,' because I have to work for mine living; 'Keep mine common sense, that I do my work right.' The Lord was so willing, he keep these poor hands and keep common sense, and so I keep working. That is all of this old body that was well—those poor hands and the brain.

"Now I am here. Now I am here. I know I am healed, and God knows it, and the angels know it; the angels is glad in Heaven; they had a great struggle with me, for when I walk I sink down."

Mr. Dowie said, "Show us how you can walk now."

"I walk like a young man. [He walked easily up and down the stage, and a tremendous applause burst forth from the large audience.] I feel like walking, and I am pleased to walk and my legs don't ache."

"Where is the cancer?" asked Mr. Dowie.

"I have not asked the dear Lord in Heaven where He left it, but it's gone—I don't know where it's gone to."

Mr. Dowie then said: "That healing occurred over two months ago, on Friday, August 10. I should like his dear wife to testify, she had a great hand in his healing. She brought him up to San Jose from Pacific Grove. Dr. Jewell said to me, 'One of my people is dying at Pacific Grove.' I received a petition to pray for him. It was for this brother. I got it through his wife, and then I said, and others said, ' You had better bring him here;' but some said, ' He will die on the way.' I replied, 'Never fear, the Lord will keep him.' As he says, he thought he was going to die on the way; but the Lord kept him. I should like his dear wife to speak for herself; but she can speak well for both. The Lord bless her. Come, dear Mrs. Lathweson, you tell us what the Lord did; I know you can, and we would like to have you do it. These friends have been members of the Methodist Episcopal Church for about fifteen years."

Mrs. Lathweson's Story.

She then stepped forward and said: "I can testify that I know that God has power to heal, and that he heals mine ears; that I was deaf—pretty near deaf. I have to set on the front seat to hear what the preacher preaches, and what I would not understand, I have to ask my husband what Dr. Jewell was speaking about. So I thank the Lord for what I received mine own self through the preaching, through Brother Dowie. I thought if that is true as he explains it, that we can just grasp it, I thought I want my share. So I received my share. Praise the Lord for that.

"So I talk of my husband's case. I know he was a sufferer for thirty years. When he first began to suffer he was not converted, and he was such a sufferer that I was praying hard for him. I was afraid if he goes on, the pain and suffering would overcome him, because if one has no religion in their heart they have no power to overcome such a sickness. I lay the whole thing before the Lord and say, 'If thou wilt.' I always say, '*If* thou wilt.' Brother Dowie says not to say '*if* the Lord wilt,' so I leave the 'if' out of my prayer now. He got converted, and then he could ask God to help him to bear the burden. But I have to see him suffering year after year. He lay on his bed and groan all night long, and I don't sleep. It is not so easy to have a husband, or a wife, that is sick all the time. I keep up the spirit; I never let him know I was sad. I say, 'Father, you see better times; don't be discouraged.' He could hardly stand the pain, and he have to work. I say, 'Father, Job, he was a man like we are, and he was once poor, and God know he was suffering. Everythings was taken away from him, and that was the case mit us. We was twice stripped of everytings, and that was making it so much harder for mine husband, we was so poor. I say, 'Father, the Lord knows best, and we see better times.'

"We came from Minnesota to San Jose, and the people say he was so ill, so sickly, he would die on the road. But I trust the Lord would keep him, and I thought he might be restored, and that he might help me to raise the children. I pray the Lord to heal my husband; but he don't; there was a lack. And when we come to California I thought the Lord will restore him now. I thought he would get well; but he never did. He got worse and worse, until this summer, as he said, when we went to Pacific Grove. I said, 'Father, there is a better time coming.' He say, 'Yes, a better time to my poor suffering body.' I says, 'You don't need to work; you have a better time.' 'Mother,' he says, 'let me be, let me die, and don't tell me it is going to be better.'

"I came from Pacific Grove to San Jose for that little business, and I hear that Brother Dowie was there; and they ask me if I would not go and have my husband healed. I sat a few minutes and said, 'I never heard of Brother Dowie that he heals anybody.' They say, 'No, he don't, but Jesus Christ heals them.' I says, 'I go and see if he is a messenger sent from God.' And I go to the church, and hear Brother Dowie preach; and sometimes I cry and sometimes I rejoice in the meeting, and I thought if my husband was sitting there he would just take it in, and he would be healed. So I sent him a letter; but he not come. People tell him that is not so; that it is all bosh; that we got no man any more preaches a gospel that the body could be healed through Jesus Christ. I say, 'I know better.' I send for my husband again, and then he don't come. They tell him he shall stay there, and don't spend the money and have the trouble. Then I thought I go mine own self and get him; and so I went. [A hearty applause from the audience.] I thought I would tease him a little. I say, 'Father, why didn't you come?' 'O mother,' he says, 'I couldn't, I couldn't.' 'Yes you could; the Lord would help you.' I said, 'Do you enjoy to suffer? The Lord would heal you if you go.' He say, 'Mother, don't say that; you know better.' But I thought I would have a little tease; but then I see he was so ill, that I was right away still. At five o'clock the next morning he got out of bed, and he say, 'Mother, we going to San Jose.' I says, 'I know you are going to be healed.' He says, 'I know it, too.' I tell him we have to sacrifice; we have to do somethings. If I would not go back, or went home, then we wouldn't be here. I tell you, sisters and brothers, had me and my husband not believed, we never would be healed; and I believe he would have been in his grave. Everybody tell me he couldn't live that way any more, he jerking and twisting and turning so, and shaking and suffering so much. I praise the Lord we got such a Saviour that comes down on this earth and heal the body. What a blessing I receive in my soul, you don't know. I feel sometimes I should go out and tell all the sick people, 'Go to the Lord and be healed.' Oh, I feel so happy in my heart. Pray the Lord that we be faithful to Him."

As this good old soul, the quiet martyr and hero of over a quarter of a century of pain, took her seat, the audience, which had been listening with the keenest sympathy and attention, made the building ring with a tremendous applause, as though each one present were eager to give expression to their feelings.

Are the Healings Permanent? The First Case in America After More Than Four Months.

Mr. Dowie said: "The first case of healing in which I was used in this country is a very interesting one. I arrived on the Pacific mail steamship, *Mariposa*, with my beloved wife and children on the 9th of June. On the 16th of June, seven days after I arrived here—I had a great many visitors at my rooms at the Palace Hotel—this lady came in. I am sorry I have not got my American collection of crutches here to-night; I intended to have them; they are in the cellar of my friend, Mr. Craig; but we shall have them here this day fortnight, when we will have another Testimony Meeting. This dear sister, Mrs. Brown, came in upon a crutch with a daughter, who is now by her side on this platform. She had been waiting a long time in the corridor. I was about to go away, thinking I should like to get some lunch, for it was very far on in the day. I did not need to ask why she came; I could see she was suffering, in every line of her face. We said a few words to her. I have an account of the case in my little magazine, "Leaves of Healing," published in August last. I asked her if she was a child of God. She said she was not sure. We went into the matter, and she gave her heart wholly to the Lord. I asked her to give her foot to the Lord. Drs. Lane, Parkinson, and Ewing, of Sacramento, had all said that her left foot must be operated upon, and there was danger that it would have to be taken off; that a part of the ankle bone must be taken out. It was what they call a 'bone felon,' and the disease was in the ankle. She had suffered for two years, and at the advanced age of sixty-eight years, she felt she would rather die than have the operation. She heard of our coming; she read the account of the *Chronicle's* interview with me, and she said, "That man is either a great fraud or a man of God." Her husband said, "I believe the latter." She came down from Sacramento; she told me her case; she found the Lord in my room as her Saviour. Then I laid hands upon her foot, and she was just instantly and perfectly healed. That was June 16, and it is now October 28. That was the first case in which I was used in this country, and she is here from Sacramento to-night, to tell the story for herself. Come, dear sister, tell us all about it. It is something to face so many hundreds of people, I know, but the Lord will help and bless you."

Mrs. Brown, who looked in splendid health, said:—

"I was sick with rheumatism about seven years, and then about a year and one-half ago I was taken with a dreadful pain in that hip; at first it run down to the foot, to the heel. I suffered that way for some three or four months—I could not say positively how long it was; the suffering was great. I sent for Dr. Lane, and he came. In the first place, he made inquiries about my foot,—what was the matter with it, and looked at it, and pronounced it a bone felon. Then he wanted to know if I had money to pay him—that was the next thing—to attend to it. I told him I had not. Now, this is Dr. Lane of Sacramento. 'Well,' ne says, 'that is a year's job, and you have no money to pay me; now go to the hospital; that is the place for you.' I naturally thanked him, and said, 'Well, I will see about it; maybe I will go.' He said, 'I will send the city doctor around to see you." I thanked him, and he did so. When he came he looked at my foot and said, 'I think that is a bone felon on your heel. The best you can do is to go to the hospital; that is the place for you.' I thanked him and said, 'All right; I will see; maybe I will go there.' Then I sent for Dr. Ewing, and he came and examined my foot, and he says, 'Well, it is a bone felon; your foot is all ulcerated; the heel bone is decaying. The best thing you can do is to have an operation performed.' I said, I am not able, in the first place, to have an operation performed.' He said, 'Never mind that; I will perform the operation.' Well, I did not say I would not have it done. He went away and he came back in a few days without my sending for him. He offered to perform the operation again. That was Monday; and he said on the Wednesday following he would come around and bring some physicians along with him, and would perform the operation for nothing; 'for,' he said, 'I like to see the blood flow.' Well, that disgusted me. I said, 'We will see on Wednesday how it will be.' So, on Wednesday he came, without my sending for him. I told him that I had finally concluded that I could not stand the operation, and did not think I was able to go through with it; that I would rather die with my foot in that fix than to die and have it operated upon; that I knew it would kill me—knew I could not stand it. He insisted, but I told him that I did not want it done.

"A few days after that, I think it was, we read in the *Chronicle* that Brother Dowie was here. I said to my husband, 'Well, I am going down to-morrow morning.' He said at first, 'I don't see what you are going for.' I said, 'Well, I am going to see the doctor; if there is anything in it, I would like to have the benefit from him, or, from the Lord Jesus Christ through him.' He says, 'You have no faith; you don't belong to no church; so I don't see hardly any sense in your going.'

"'Well,' I said 'I am going to-morrow morning.'

"He says, 'How can you go? You can't walk only with a crutch, and how are you going to get into the hack or on to the train?'

"I said, 'You will help me, and the hackman will help me, and I think I can find somebody down there, and with your help I can get on the train.'

"So the next morning I got up at 4 o'clock, and it took me till half past five to stand well enough to dress myself, and I had to have help to dress. I got into a hack, and I came down here, and I went to see Brother Dowie at the Palace Hotel; but I didn't think I was any Christian; don't think I am much of one yet—that is honest; I think I lack a great deal of being a thorough Christian at any rate. He prayed for me. Thank the great God that I was sent to him. I feel grateful to my God and to Jesus Christ our Lord that I was sent to him; and I was healed in—I could not say how quick—after he prayed for me. Him and his dear wife prayed for me, sinner as I was, and I was healed—well, in an instant. He told me to get up and walk, and I walked right off, and I can walk now, and I am pretty old—not so very pretty, but old. (She walked easily across the stage, and the audience cheered with great enthusiasm.) From that day to this I have never felt any pain like that I had before, nor any pain in that foot, and it is QUITE WELL; it is very well. On Christmas day at 3 o'clock in the morning I will be sixty-nine years of age."

Mr. Dowie said: "Didn't you give your heart to Jesus? Didn't you tell me you had given your heart to Jesus before I prayed for your healing?"

She replied "Yes, I did it."

"Then it is done," said Mr. Dowie.

The lady then added to her previous testimony, as follows:—

"I have a word more to say. Since that I have cooked for nine persons steady; got up at five o'clock every morning, done the washing for nine beds and all the cooking and the work of the house. I am well and healthy so far as I know." (A hearty applause all over the house.)

Mr. Dowie said: "That is the first case of healing in this country, and it remains perfect to this day. We have heard talk about Divine healings not standing; there is the first. If they do not stand, it is not because there is any failure in God's work of healing: the failure is in the person healed. Let our aged sister's story be a lesson to some who 'think themselves to be something, when they are nothing.' She had no opinion of herself, and, therefore, the Lord healed, and the Lord keeps her."

The Little Boy Who Was Blind from Birth.

"I have a little boy here who had been blind from birth, and he got his sight on July 4. There is a very widespread and false rumor that he is as blind as he was before, and I am going to show him to you here to-night. I would like to say a word about the case.

"I want the boy that was blind to be seen, and to give you a few words about himself. Now, there are numbers of cases of healing which do not seem to be just as perfect as one would like to see; and let me say here, there is a general impression that divine healing of necessity must be immediately perfect and permanent. That is not the case. Even our Lord Jesus Christ himself had some healings that were gradual. A man at Bethsaida was blind; the Lord laid his hands upon him, and he saw men as trees walking. His vision was imperfect. The word says that 'after that' the Lord met him again 'and He put His hands again upon his eyes, and made him look up; and he was restored and saw every man clearly.' Now, 'after that' in Scripture may mean not only an hour or a day or a month, but it may cover years. Now, it does not say how long it was 'after that' first laying on of hands that our Lord met the man again; but it does not matter if it was a day or an hour or a week. It established the principle that even through our Lord's own hands there may be an imperfect healing, not because He heals imperfectly, but because the faith of the recipient is imperfect. The word of our Lord is, 'As thou hast believed, so be it done unto thee.' Take, for instance, the two testimonies which we have just listened to. Mr. Lathweson believes in an instantaneous and permanent healing; Mrs. Brown does the same, and they both receive according to their faith. This little boy, a fatherless little boy, without previous tuition, and his dear mother having a hard fight to get a living, comes and receives an immediate but an imperfect healing. I did not understand why he did not receive perfect restoration of sight, but his mother told me the reason afterwards. She said when she took the boy to me she prayed that the restoration of his sight might be gradual. She got what she asked for. I have not seen the little fellow for some months until yesterday, having been away from San Francisco on Mission. It was publicly stated that this little boy had lost what he had received from the Lord, and, therefore, I asked his mother to bring him here to-night.

"Our sister and the boy testified on the evening of July 9, at our first Testimony Meeting, in the Y. M. C. A. hall of this city, that this little boy had been blind from birth. These are her words: (Mr. Dowie reads from the short-hand report of that meeting.) 'My little boy, Georgie, has been afflicted from birth with blindness. Three years ago an operation was performed by Dr. Barcon, of this city, and he was able to relieve his sight to that extent that he could distinguish day from night, and bright colors—I think red and black. For ten years he was unable to walk without being led. He never saw an object, so far as we know, during these ten years—not a single object—to know what it was.'

"'Since attending this Mission, Jesus has restored his sight almost entirely. He can now walk alone, see houses, chimneys, and small objects very readily. He can also see print of large size, and it can be read by him—something I never expected to see him do. My little boy is bright and happy now, and gives God all the glory. Praise his name forever.'

"'I was,' also adds the writer, Mrs. Lula Ritchville, 1241 Mission Street, 'instantly cured of internal hemorrhage of some weeks' standing without any laying on of hands, at the first meeting I attended.'

Mr. Dowie said: "Now, Georgie, come along; I want to show you to the people again. Now, stand by the light. Now, here is the little boy who was blind from birth. This bunch of flowers I hold in my hand he has never seen before, and I will ask him to pick out the colors. Georgie, did Jesus give you your sight?

"Yes sir," replied the boy.

When?

"July 4th."

You had never seen an object in your life, had you, to know what it was?

"No."

He could just see darkness and light; tell if somebody passed in front of him;

he had to be led about by the hand. Did you ever see the color of a flower previous to July 4, Georgie?

"No."

I want you to tell all these colors, every one of them; put your hand upon them, so that the people can see that you touch the colors.

(Pointing to the colors, the boy said, and correctly) "There is a sort of reddish white; there is white; another white."

Find me a very bright red.

"There is blue, and there is bright red."

Find me some green.

"There is green."

Yes.

"There is another white."

He has named and touched all the colors. The Lord has given the boy sight. (Applause.) Now, wicked persons have said this boy is blind. He does not know what I am going to show him. What is that? (holding up a knife in front of the boy).

"Oh, it is a knife."

What is that? (holding up a watch).

"A watch."

Which side?

"The back." (Clapping of hands all over the audience.)

You can read big letters, can't you?

"Yes, sir; some."

Did Jesus save you?

"Yes, sir."

And did you give your heart to him?

"Yes, sir."

And can you see just as well as you did July 4th?

"Yes sir."

He picks out all the big letters. It is a peculiar fact that this boy's sight is not better than when he first received it; but he is in an asylum amongst the blind, and I do not wonder. It is not right that those who can see should be amongst the blind; and I hope God will open up the way for this dear mother, and provide some other way.

Turning to the mother, Mr. Dowie said: "This boy was born blind?"

"Yes, sir."

Does he see the same as he did when he first got his sight?

"Yes, sir."

Do you, yourself, retain your healing?

"I certainly do. I never have lost my healing, nor has my son. I do not believe that God is such a God as to go back on His word. May God be glorified."

"There are quite a number of persons who have said that boy is just as blind as he was. I do not know his antecedents; his mother says he was blind from his birth. His neighbors say so, and everybody who knows him says so. All of those present who saw this boy when he was blind, please rise. [Mr. Dowie counted twelve, and some one on the platform said there were persons in the gallery who were overlooked.] Supposing that this boy had not been blind, I would not be to blame because people said he was blind. But he was blind; he could not distinguish anyone or anything; the Lord gave him his sight, and I want you to pray that the Lord will perfect it speedily. [Amens from the audience.] We shall now take

Another Case That Was Healed in the First San Franciscan Mission.

Because it is important that we should give some testimony from those who have been standing a little while. Among those who testified in the first Testimony Meeting was Miss Wilcox. She was ill for many years. She came to the Y. M. C. A. Hall on her crutches; she received the word; she laid down her crutches and prayed, and she walked away healed and saved."

Miss Wilcox Confirms Her Testimony.

Miss Wilcox said: "I give God all the glory. I am healed through and by the precious blood of our Lord Jesus Christ, and he has cleansed me from all sin. I was sick with this last trouble that was in my ankles four years and four months; two years, eleven months and four days I was on crutches. And a little over a year, part of the time, I was not able to be on crutches; I was in bed. On the second day of July last, I instantly received strength to walk, at the Y. M. C. A. Hall. I had not worn a shoe, to amount to anything, for three years last January; and I walked nine blocks without a shoe on my foot, and carried my crutches in my hand immediately after I was healed. Praise the Lord! There was so much swelling in my foot on the morning of the 2d of July that I could not even put a slipper on; the next morning, the 3d of July, I put on my shoes, and have been wearing them ever since; and I have been praising God day by day."

"How long had you been ill, altogether?" inquired Mr. Dowie.

"Twenty-eight years."

"How long on crutches?"

"Two years, eleven months and four days."

"Where are the crutches?"

"At 312 California Street: Mr. Craig's office. Twenty-four years ago I was given up by the doctors in Iowa, Illinois, Missouri, and Kansas, and here in San Francisco. The first doctor I went to hear was Dr. Douglass; he said nothing but amputation would do, and he would not take my case, because I would not have it amputated. I was under the treatment of Doctor Morse for four and one-half months. He said at first it could be healed, and then he said it would have to be amputated. But when he was ready I was not ready, and I said I would be healed."

Mr. Dowie said: "Show us how you can walk now." (Miss Wilcox ran lightly across the front of the large stage, and the audience vigorously applauded.)

A Business Man's Testimony to the Healing of His Family.

"I will now ask a gentleman who is manager of a leading Insurance Company, a personal friend, standing high in this city among commercial men, and who will carry the weight that belongs to his sterling character and social station. I will ask our brother, Mr. Hugh Craig, of 312 California Street, San Francisco, to step forward and give us his testimony." Mr. Craig rose in the audience, and spoke as follows:—

"Before I speak about healing in my own family, I will say that Mr. Dowie brought to me from New Zealand letters from my father and mother. My father is seventy years of age, and my mother sixty-eight, and they are Christians of many years' standing in the city of Auckland. The letters told me of the good work he had done in New Zealand and Australia. On his arrival my family were away; when they returned he was carrying on his Mission in Oakland. On the first afternoon that we were able to attend, Mrs. Craig was so unwell from an affection of the spine, and from which she had suffered for twenty-six years, she could only sit for half an hour, and then I had to take her home. On the next Sunday afternoon, we had Mr. Dowie at our house. On the previous Tuesday one of my little girls, when climbing a tree, slipped and caught her arm in a crotch of the tree and hung there a sufficient time to make considerable noise, and until we could run out to her assistance. It injured her shoulder, and it kept getting worse from this Tuesday until this Sunday afternoon. After the usual exercises before the children go to bed (we had been reading the eighth chapter of John), Mr. Dowie thought it was a little hard for the little folks, and said we would have another little lesson for them especially. He read, 'Suffer little children to come unto me, and forbid them not, for of such is the kingdom of heaven,' and explained the story, saying he thought these little children were sick, and had been brought to Jesus for healing, as well as for other blessing. Then he asked Jessie if she thought Jesus could heal her little sister's shoulder. She had been going around with her left arm hanging down, and not able to go out with the other children."

"'Yes,' she replied; she thought He was.

"He said to another child, "'What do you think?'"

"She said she thought Jesus would heal her shoulder.

"Mr. Dowie then prayed, saying about half a dozen words, asking the Lord Jesus to manifest his power; and he just touched her with his finger, and told her to hold out her hand. She held her hand out; the pain was gone instantly, and from that moment she was perfectly healed. This was my first opportunity for seeing anything of Divine Healing. I was astounded. Mrs. Craig and I talked this thing over after we went to bed, and we had occasion afterward to see a good deal of Mr. Dowie. Mr. Dowie prayed for, and laid hands upon, my wife, and the spinal trouble that Mrs. Craig had for twenty-six years at once departed, and is now entirely gone. She had also an affection of the vocal cords, for which she was treated by Dr. O'Toole. She suffered so much that sometimes she had to sit up all night; she lost her voice entirely, and was not able to sing for something like ten years. Now she sings morning, noon, and night, and that trouble has gone. It was removed by the Lord at the same time as the spinal injury. All this occurred nearly three months ago. The healing of the spine and vocal cords has remained, and Mrs. Craig is here and able to speak for herself." (Tremendous applause all through the building.)

Mrs. Craig then rose in her seat and said (being in the audience and speaking low, the reporter heard only a few words):—

"I am very thankful indeed for what the Lord has done for me. I have suffered a great deal of pain. I was afflicted with the troubles my husband has mentioned. Now they are entirely gone, and I am very well and comfortable. It used to trouble me to lie on my left side, but now I can do so as well as upon my right." (Another hearty applause.)

A Doctor's Testimony to His Healing.

Now I will have a medical doctor testify, our dear Brother C. F. Lane, of Tulare City, who sought the Lord for healing.

Dr. Lane said: "Friends, I have not words this evening to express the gratitude I have to my heavenly Father for what I enjoy this moment. I give Him all the glory for what he has done for me. I have been a Christian man for a great many years, and I have suffered a very severe affliction of my head, and general breaking down of my constitution for the last three or four years. I have been so afflicted with my head that I have not been able to exercise my brain. If I entered into a conversation my thoughts would go away so that at times I could not connect the subject. I had been praying the Lord to use me in the ministry as well as in the practice of medicine. But I have hardly been able to practice medicine or to preach, only occasionally, for three or four years.

"I say it to my shame that I have been skeptical in regard to healing by faith, as it is called. I have tried Christian science, and I have tried all the remedies for the restoration of my health. I came here to the city last winter, and went to Dr. McLane, and other physicians, to help me in this matter. All failed. This spring I thought I would go to the mountains. I laid in a stock of medicines and started for the mountains with my daughter. I grew worse all the time. We came back to Woodbridge and stopped over there at a friend's house, on our way back to the city. My daughter was taken down with a very severe affliction, and we thought she was going to die, and I scarcely got through myself. I stayed there. A dear brother came in one day, and he told me about Brother Dowie at Sacramento, and he gave me a pamphlet which he got from there, to read. Well, I thought to myself, I have heard so much about faith healing and Christian science that I don't believe there is much in it. I did not seem to have any faith; but when I heard Brother Dowie was from Australia, out of curiosity I thought I would go and hear him. I did not believe any 'good could come out of Nazareth,' because I left Australia to educate my family in America on account of the wickedness of the people. So I went to hear him, and it was the hearing that enabled me to lay hold of faith in Jesus Christ for the healing of my body. I have heard a great deal about divine healing, heard a great deal of teaching about divine healing, but I have been taught, 'Lord, thy will be done.' So I went along suffering and suffering, and saying, 'Lord, if it is thy will, heal my body.' I tell you, dear Christians, it came to the point with me that I almost rebelled against God, I suffered so much burning pain in my head. I almost came to the point that God had caused me to suffer.

But I heard Brother Dowie, and I have not words to express the joy of my soul. I heard the beautiful teaching. It was just like living in a new world. Brother Dowie showed me it was not my Father's will that I should suffer; that it was His will that I should be whole; that I should have strength and health of body. And just from the teaching and listening to Brother Dowie I saw a new light in the Scriptures that I never saw before. And I went home and told my dear daughter and wife that it was not the Lord's will that we should suffer; it is the work of the devil. Well, I just commenced right then and quit the medicine, and I trusted the Lord, and to some extent I was better, but I did not get right. But I realized that the healing process was going on in my system. I then came here and listened to Brother Dowie in these meetings. Last Sabbath evening I was at Lodi, and I had to sit way back in the far end of the church and listen to the preacher, and I could not bear to hear the sound of the preacher's voice, much as I wished it otherwise. But, Brother Dowie, now I can pray and sing, and my head seems as light and beautiful and comfortable, and I am filled with joy and peace; I never felt so in my life. Oh, it is faith in our Heavenly Father, it is faith in the efficacy of the blood of Jesus Christ who hath atoned for our sins and sicknesses, and it is His will which has wrought the work. I believe that God's children shall be well and have healthy bodies. I am resting in Jesus from moment to moment; I am getting better acquainted with Jesus every moment; when I lie down to-night I shall realize He is present with me. I say, 'Lord, I trust in thee to heal me perfectly.' I was not healed immediately—not perfectly when Brother Dowie prayed with me in the Palace Hotel, but I am getting better all the time; I am better this evening than I was yesterday. I have confidence in my Heavenly Father that I am going to have perfect health, and a sounder body than I have ever had, because I am going to trust and glorify him every moment. The Lord bless you all."

Mr. Dowie remarked, "The brother looks all right; he does not look as he did at Sacramento. Perhaps Miss Lane, his daughter, would like to testify."

Testimony of a Doctor's Daughter.

Miss Lane immediately responded, and in a very pleasant manner spoke as follows:—

"It gives me great pleasure to speak a word for Jesus to-night. One month ago I never thought I could stand before a congregation again; I thought I should never be able to speak again in this world. For a number of years I have been an invalid; I have been very delicate. For the last three years I have suffered very much from nervous exhaustion, which means that the whole body is sick from head to foot. Of late I have suffered very much from heart disease, and at times it has seemed as if death was very near.

"A few months ago we started for Oakland to attend a camp-meeting, and to also go to a cooler climate, as I seemed to be failing very rapidly. We came as far as Woodbridge, and the excitement of just meeting with my friends was too great for me, and I was taken down with severe heart trouble, and it seemed as if I must die; it seemed as if I could not live until morning; indeed, from one moment to the next it was thought I could not live; and I believe that it was only by the power of God through the prayers of my dear ones (*they wouldn't give me up*), that I was raised from that bed of suffering and from going down to the grave just in the bloom of youth, when I might work for Jesus. I am so thankful that the Lord has raised me up.

"Papa has told you that he went to Sacramento to hear Bro. Dowie and to learn something more particularly of the Divine Healing. They prayed for me there and I felt very much better, very much indeed. I laid aside medicines, and I just told the Lord if he did not heal me I would die; I did not want any more medicine.

"I might say that Brother Dowie has been charged with being a magnetic healer, and heals by the laying on of hands and magnetism. I wish to say that my case is a direct disproof of that false charge. In this city last winter I took treatment of one or two magnetic physicians, I think as good as ever have been on this coast, and I am very thankful to them; the last one I had worked for me very hard indeed, and he spent much time over me, and much thought; he did all he could to raise me up. I shall never forget that physician, and never cease to pray for him. There was another physician, of the Eclectic school, who tried with all his power to help me, *but all failed.* And I just asked the Lord to give me strength to come up to these meetings. So Jesus gave me strength to come and receive the teaching, and last Sunday I made up my mind that it was the will of God to heal me. Brother Dowie prayed with me on Monday, and I at once received great blessing. I don't feel as well as Bro. Dowie, perhaps, not so strong, but I am improving every hour. It is wonderful to feel the change wrought within me. It is wonderful to me to know what good has been done, what God has wrought for me; for He has raised me up from the very gates of death, and placed his life within me. God be praised!"

Mr. Dowie remarked: "That is a very good case. Of course she does not feel as strong as I do, for I have been looking to Jesus as my Healer for twenty-six years."

Healing of Twenty-five Years' Diseased Lungs.

I have a little testimony here, so beautifully written that I would like to read it:—

"312 EDDY STREET, SAN FRANCISCO, *October 28, 1888.*

"REV. JOHN ALEX. DOWIE—*Dear Sir:* I wish to express my gratitude to you and Mrs. Dowie for the benefit derived through your instrumentality, when you visited my sick chamber on the fourteenth of September last, and laid hands on me, praying for Divine Healing. I had been a great sufferer for over twenty-five years from a complication of troubles, chief of which was an affection of the lungs, and eminent physicians have considered my case hopeless. Although they had greatly improved during the past year, they had never been free from soreness and pain. Immediately after the laying on of hands the pain and soreness entirely disappeared, and has not returned. I believe them to be perfectly well."

Our dear sister tells us she has received further blessing. It is signed "Mrs. S. A. Kelley," and she is a sister of the reporter, who is reporting this meeting so perfectly.

Healing of Twelve Years' Stomach Disease.

Now I will have a commercial man of this city testify, whom many of you may know better than I do. He will tell you what the Lord did for him. I was asked by him to pray with him, and I was not used as I would like; but I believe through the teaching he found a point that had to be considered and put right, which was done, and he was healed. I believe he is an elder in the church.

Mr. G. N. Wood, engraver, of Sutter Street, San Francisco, then came forward and said: "Bro. Dowie is mistaken about my being an elder. I hold several offices in the Hamilton Square Baptist Church, but I am not an elder."

Mr. Dowie said: "You will have to be made one then."

Mr. Wood continued: "I would like to say a few words. I believed in this Divine Healing for a long time. Ten years ago I had a trouble in my head which I never told Brother Dowie of; a disease of the brain; and a sister in Oakland (some of the people in Oakland knew her, not living there now); I simply asked her to pray for me, for the relief of my head, and she said she would. I was unable to write any business letters, or scarcely a friendly letter; I could not calculate or do any figuring which was at all close. It was in the afternoon I asked her to pray for me, and the next morning I got up and my head was perfectly clear, and has been so ever since.

"I was not aware that Brother Dowie was in the city until the meetings in the Y. M. C. A. Hall four months ago had been going on for some time. I went there and heard several discourses. From there I went over to Oakland and heard other discourses.

"I had a trouble with the stomach which lasted me about twelve years, and I had suffered intense pain. Dr. McNutt pronounced it inflammation of the stomach. I think it was something worse than that. I came near dying last winter. At the time I went over to Oakland I was suffering considerably, and Brother Dowie laid his hands upon me at the hotel. I did not receive immediate relief, but I did feel the presence of Christ, and I felt at that time I was going to be healed, and from that time on I realized that I was going to be healed, but I did not get the healing right away. At the time he laid hands on me I promised to give up all medicine; I felt I ought to do it. But I got discouraged, and my dear wife (who is here this evening) wanted me to take a remedy which always gave me temporary relief; and I consented. This I have not told Brother Dowie, as I have not seen him since the Oakland meetings until last week, when I met him here in the audience, and only had a word or two. The medicine I took did not have the usual effect: it acted right the contrary to what it usually did. I then saw at once that I did wrong; I had gone back on the Saviour. I made up my mind then and there never to use any more medicine, and from that day to this I have not used a particle, and I have trusted to Jesus for healing. I had been praying right along for several days that I might be healed, for I felt too sick to work for the Lord. In earlier times here I have been a worker in several of the churches which I have been a member of. I kept thinking that the Lord would heal me, and I would go to work for him. But I did not get well. Then I said I will go to work just as I am, and trust Jesus for strength, and almost immediately I began to improve, and in a few days I felt as well as I did twenty-five years ago, and now I am enjoying the best of health, and I am as well as I ever was. I am enjoying very good health; so that I am able to attend to my business, and I feel strong physically. I have not had any return of this intense pain in my stomach. I have had a little soreness in the stomach occasionally, but I asked the Saviour to take it away, and it disappeared.

"I believe that Christ is my healer. I got light through Brother Dowie, and considerable help also from a brother who sits there in the audience. I am trusting I shall enjoy good health the rest of my days.

"The best of all is, that I feel renewed spiritually, and feel more like working for my Saviour than I have for many years. Praise God."

Our "Little Queen's" First Testimony.

Mr. Dowie said, "My little daughter this afternoon stood up amongst the healed folks who desired to testify here this evening. When we were coming up to this meeting I said to her, "Now, my little queen, when I asked the people who were going to testify to stand up, you did so. Do you really wish to testify?" She said, "Yes, papa." I have noticed from her expressive looks toward me during this meeting, that she expects to be called upon: so I will do so. She is only seven years and five months old. She has been with us all through our work, and has never spoken in public before. Now, little queen, would you like to tell what Jesus has done for you?"

With the grace of maturer years, Miss Esther A. Dowie, the "Little Queen," said: "I want to tell you that Jesus heals me always; that he keeps me well all the time. Once I burned my hand on a red-hot iron, and he healed it right away. He keeps me well all the time."

Mr. Dowie continued: "I am glad my little daughter is a Witness for Jesus. She is usually in bed at half-past seven o'clock, but when a Praise and Testimony Meeting is on, she is permitted to come, and it is a treat she always looks forward to with very great interest."

Healing of an Eight Years' Decrepit African Sister.

"Now, I am going to have an African sister testify. Her name is Mrs. Williams, and she lives at 459 Sixth Street, Oakland. She was gloriously healed in the Oakland Mission. Come, Auntie, tell us all about it."

Mrs. Williams came forward with a nimble step, and spoke with great vivacity as follows:—

"My brothers and sisters, stand up for Jesus. Hallelujah to his holy name. [Amen, from Mr. Dowie.] I stand here as a spectacle and a monument of the goodness of Jesus Christ. I give God the praise and glory. Brothers and sisters, I have suffered for the last eight years from the crown of my head to the soles of my feet, with neuralagia and catarrh in the head, and rheumatism in the left foot, and I could not wear shoes. Brother Dowie can tell you that. He can tell you how I looked when I first came into his meeting, and look at me now. I am sixty years old." (The lady was very dark, rather slender in form, but erect, tripped gracefully across the front of the stage, and appeared to be a woman of not more than thirty-five years of age, and possessing a great deal of strength and vitality. The audience cheered.) "I am sixty," she continued, "and I feel like sixteen."

"You will please excuse my speaking so loud, but I wish all the audience to hear; not to be ashamed for Jesus. Stand up for Jesus; be steadfast in your faith; be strong to stand up for him. Speak for him like a man of war. Hallelujah to His holy name! I am healed through this faith I have in Jesus Christ, in the blood of Jesus. You don't know how happy I feel. I hav'nt tongue enough to express his goodness. For eight years I could hardly earn my living. I went to Brother Dowie's meeting in the First Presbyterian Church, Oakland, and he prayed for and laid his hands upon me. I attended every meeting there, and from the time of his last meeting there, I have been out of bed at 6 o'clock in the morning, and going to my work; and to-morrow morning, by the help of God, I expect to go to my work again.

"When Jesus heals you, don't be ashamed to stand up and confess him before men; for, recollect, if you are, he will be ashamed to confess you before his Father and the holy angels in Heaven. Stand up for Jesus. He is 'a man of war,' and never lost a battle. He has won every battle, and he will stamp Satan under his feet."

Mr. Dowie shouted, "Hallelujah!" and the people clapped their hands. Mr. Dowie remarked, as the good woman resumed her seat: "I think I shall have to go down South; I like the Africans. God bless the African race." (Amens from the audience.)

Restoration of Sight in One Eye After Fourteen Years' Nearly Total Blindness.

I am going to have a dear girl, who had almost lost the power to see with the left eye until the other day, testify. Now the eye is perfectly restored. Her testimony is here in writing, and she will also speak herself. Her name is Annie Burkman, and she lives at 1320 Filbert Street, Oakland. She is a Swede by birth. She writes as follows:—

"On last Thursday I was healed of sickness in my eyes since I was one and a half years old. Mr. Dowie prayed and laid hands on me, and I was instantly healed."

Mr. Dowie said that with the affected eye she could formerly only distinguish light from darkness. The young woman then came forward at Mr. Dowie's request, and spoke in a clear voice as follows:—

"Since I have been seeing, I praise God all the time. I came from Austin, Texas, a few months ago. Down there two or three doctors think they could cure my eyes, but they could not. Brother Dowie put his hands on my head and prayed, and now I can see clear everything, everything. I know before when I get up in the morning my eyes were sore and shut, and I have to wet my fingers and help take them up, and now both eyes are quite clear. I give glory to God forevermore. I bless Brother Dowie that he come to this country to heal my sight. Brother Dowie pray for me, and I pray for myself. I was converted to God two years ago, and then I pray Him to heal my eyes; but I don't think I had faith enough. I could not receive it, until now I have it, and my eye is just as good as any one of yours."

Mr. Dowie said: "This is the first time I have seen her since the healing." He then asked her to put her handkerchief in the eye that had not been blind, and held his watch some distance away, and asked her what it was. She said, "A watch." He then held it a little nearer, but still a foot or two away, and asked her to tell the time. "Five minutes to ten," she promptly replied. Mr. Dowie, turning to the congregation, said: "I did not mean you to know the time; you had better stay on." He then questioned, "You say you could only distinguish daylight from darkness with that eye, until I laid hands upon you in Jesus' name?" "Yes, sir." "How old are you?" "Sixteen."

"The change upon her eyes is marvelous, and the disease in both eyes is entirely gone. Will those who know this girl, and who know that what she says is true, please to stand up?" Mr. Dowie counted seven. He said she was a member of the Swedish Methodist Episcopal Church in Oakland, under the Rev. Mr. Corlander's pastorate, a brother minister who was in sympathy most thoroughly with Divine Healing.

Healing of Congestion of the Brain and Four Years' Nervous Exhaustion.

Now Brother Edwards will testify. He is a commercial man in your city— Mr. C. F. Edwards, of 1010 Washington Street, and No. 5 California Market.

Mr. Edwards said: "There are a great many here who know me, and know I have been sick for the last four years. I have been under the doctor's care. My sickness was congestion of the brain, from which a great many thought I never would recover; I thought so myself. I have been going down gradually all the time, although I had the best physicians in the city; money was no object. I took the best care of myself that was possible. About four months ago I left the city; I thought I could not get well here; and that I would go to Oakland. I went over and staid with my brother, feeling very much discouraged and disheartened.

"But I heard of this Divine-healing Mission, and I thought, surely if the Lord is doing so much for others, he is willing to do something for me. And so I went into the Mission and heard this teaching, and the first two or three times I attended I was not very much impressed with the doctrine; but as I went it seemed as though I began to get new light. All of us who are sick are apt to think it was the Lord's hand that was upon us, and that is what I thought; and I was trying to be submissive, and trying to bear my affliction as a Christian. But when Brother Dowie taught me different; that it was not the Lord's will that I should be sick—well, I considered the matter, and I thought perhaps it is so, and, if so, then why should not he make me well? At last I saw it was God's will to heal me, and I just took my case to the Lord; I did not go to see Mr. Dowie or his wife; I said nothing to anyone; I just said, 'Here, Lord, I want to be healed.' And, as I went home from the meeting that night, the Lord gave me evidence right there that I was going to get well.

"I had been out of business for four months; the Lord seemed to tell me to go back to the city. I came back and went into business, and I have been in business ever since, and have not lost a day. It has been about three months since I went into business, and I am getting stronger and better every day; and I am trusting him for healing. I gave up medicine entirely, and have taken none for about four months. I am stronger to-day than I ever was. I tell this to the honor of God."

Mr. Dowie exclaimed fervently, "Thank God," and proceeded to say, after Mr. Edwards resumed his seat:—

"Now, that is the case of an intelligent Christian brother, a member of the Methodist Episcopal Church, who simply sought the Lord directly, and without any human laying on of hands, and he is now strong and attending to business. Where is the magnetism in that? I did not know of our brother or his healing until the other day, when he made himself known to me, and told me what he has told you."

"Now we will have some brief, direct testimonies. Brother Rudens, perhaps you and your wife will testify." (The gentleman mentioned and his wife stood up, and he gave his testimony, followed by her.)

Restoration of Hearing in One Ear After Eight Years' Deafness.

Mr. A. F. Rudens, of 11 Telegraph Place, said: "Dear brothers and sisters, I am glad I have an opportunity to testify to the glory of my blessed Saviour. For about one and a half years I have known that Jesus is our healer. I had a difficulty in my head for about eight years. For about three years I tried several doct°·rs, and used a good deal of medicine, but it was all in vain. For about five years I have not used any doctors or medicine. I thought I would have to be deaf in my right ear for the rest of my life until about a year and a half ago, when I prayed the Lord to open this ear; but somehow my faith was not able to claim the healing.

"In the Mission at Y. M. C. A. Hall, that Brother Dowie held, four months ago, I heard his teaching and I was thoroughly enlightened to receive it. My wife had her right arm affected by rheumatism, and I took her to Brother Dowie's rooms at the Palace Hotel, and asked his prayers for healing. After Brother Dowie had prayed for her he asked me how my health was. I said it was all right, only my right ear was deaf. He said he would ask the Lord to open it for me. He prayed for me and laid his hand upon my head, and after praying for me he went to a distant part of the room and told me to close up my left ear. He then spoke to me. At first I could not hear a sound, but the second time he spoke I could hear his words plainly. I could feel something move in my ear, something give way in my head, and I could hear his words very plainly. He said 'God is good.' He spoke again, and his wife spoke also, and I could hear every word very plainly, and have continued to do so from that time. Glory be to God!" (Great applause).

Healing of a Stiff Rheumatic Arm.

Mrs. Rudens said: "I wish to praise the Lord for what He has done for me. Last July I got rheumatism and could not straighten my arm, and everybody saw it. [Illustrated by holding her right arm out, and doubling the fore-arm and hand in so as to make a right-angle at the elbow.] I did not know how my arm would get straight; I did not go to any doctor; but suffered a great deal. I went to Mr. Dowie's Mission, and believed, after hearing his teaching, that I would be healed. I went to his rooms and he prayed for me, and my arm came out all straight, and has been straight ever since; no pain in my arms since. I praise God for all he has done for me." (Applause.)

Restoration After Twelve Years' Deafness.

Mr. Dowie then called on S. Edmonds, of 11 Telegraph Place, city.

He said: "I can testify to the honor of God and of Jesus Christ. For twelve years I could not hear in my left ear. I sat in the audience in Mr. Dowie's first Mission, and I thought if that is Christianity I want to have it. I prayed for the restoration of my hearing in the meeting. I went home and when my wife spoke to me I found I could hear with my left ear. Then I gave God the glory."

Healing of Many Infirmities.

Mr. Dowie announced Mr. Wm. Donald, 220 Third Street, city, as one who had been healed of many troubles. Mr. Donald said:

"There are a great many here who have heard me testify of my healing a good many times. It was not through Mr. Dowie's teaching and preaching nor that of anybody else that I was healed. I was in my bed, not able to do my work, not able to move around, and one day I asked the Lord to give me strength to do my work, and before fifteen minutes He revealed Himself to me as my Healer, if I would trust in Him. I said, 'Yes,' I would. Previously I was very skeptical about Divine Healing; I did not believe in it. I did not get perfect healing right off, but about six months after I was perfectly well, and I have been well ever since. The Lord is my Healer, and I praise Him for it all.

"I am glad Mr. Dowie is here; we have often wished in our meetings we could see this great work done. I believe the Lord has heard our prayer and sent him in our midst, and he has taught us how we may be healed, and how we may be used to those round about us. I praise the Lord for what He has done in my case. and I am well to-night."

Healing of Life-Long Headache.

Mrs. Edward Leach, 1333 Union Street, city, testified: "I have suffered from severe headache all my life long; scarcely a week passed without having to stay in bed. I have trusted the Lord for healing, and since then I have been troubled no more. It was in the first Mission. Mr. Dowie knew nothing of it until his return from the Oakland Mission. My husband is here in the audience and can say the same."

Her husband immediately arose and said: "I thank God that I can corroborate my wife's statement. While it seems marvelous, it is not so; for 'Jesus Christ is the same yesterday, to-day, and forever.' I thank God for what I have seen and realized of His healing powers in my wife."

Healing of an Ulcerated Leg.

Mr. Dowie then said: "Mrs. Barnes, 513 Hayes Street, city, a member of Simpson Memorial Church, was healed during our first Mission instantly, and I will ask her to again testify to-night because wicked rumors are abroad, even in one of the city M. E. Churches, that she is as bad as ever. Her husband had occasion to rise the other night and contradict these statements. I will ask Mrs. Barnes to tell what the Lord did for her, again. It was a remarkable healing."

Mrs. Barnes came forward and said:—

"Dear Friends: For the first time in my life I heard of Mr. Dowie on the fir. of last July; I had never had faith in Divine Healing. I heard that little Georgie Richville was going on the 2d of July to have his eyes opened. Previous to that I had suffered from bad limbs, with ulcers, and had tried several doctors in the East and in this city; but they had made me worse, and I gave up doctoring. Well, I went to the meeting because I was interested in this little boy who was then quite blind. I had never seen him, but had heard of him. When prayers were offered for him, I did not pray specially for myself, but I prayed that Jesus would show his power on the dear little boy, and give him his sight. To my astonishment I found it was twenty minutes to six when our meeting was over, and I had to be home by six o'clock; so I hurried out and got into the car on Market Street. I went to Grant Avenue and then to Market Street. Before I went to the meeting my leg was in great pain, and above the calf of my leg it was raw, and a big wound nearly as large as a dollar in one place. When I went out it was so late, and I was in such a hurry, that, before I knew it, I was running down Grant Avenue as hard as I could to try and catch the car. When I got to Market Street I remembered my leg, and thought, 'Where is the pain in my leg gone?' I was so astonished I did not know what to do. Presently the car came along, and when I got home my supper was late, and I had to rush around. On the morning of the 4th of July I prepared to go out, and I walked about the whole day long. On the 5th of July I went around to tell Mr. Dowie what a healing I had received; a healing which I retain to this moment.

"I want distinctly to say Mr. Dowie never spoke to me, never knew I was in the hall, never knew a word about it until I gave him my testimony; and it is a wicked, false story to say that my leg is now as bad as it was. My leg is better than it has been for twenty-five years. My husband is in the hall and can confirm what I say."

Mr. Barnes arose in the audience and said: "I can simply say that my wife is perfectly correct in every detail. I will further state that while we were in East Boston, Mass., she had Doctor Hand, Doctor Campbell, and Doctor McMichael; they each did as much as they could, but all amounted to nothing. She went to the Allopathic Hospital and to the Homeopathic Hospital, and she got no relief; the leg remained very bad indeed. Although now it has been turned back to its natural size, there is evidence of what it has been. Some have said, 'You did not say who these doctors were;' so I have given their names, and they are some of the best physicians in East Boston, Mass. She remains perfectly well."

Mrs. Barnes added: "I am perfectly willing that any medical gentleman, that is, a real medical gentleman, should visit me at my house, and see my foot and leg."

Mr. Dowie remarked: "I hand you over to Doctor Lane! We are all satisfied, however, that the Lord's work was done, and that the Lord's work remains."

Healing Through Doctors Cullis' and Simpson's Agencies.

Mrs. Blanchard, 330 Sanchez Street, city, said:—

"Five years ago I was anointed in the East by Doctor Cullis and was restored from sickness, and have taken Christ as my healer and physician from that day to this. Last December I took cold in my neck and it became stiff. I did not take any medicine. When Doctor Simpson was here he anointed it, and it became limber. I went to see my pastor and showed him what the anointing was, and that I was restored. I have been so ever since. The pastor was Mr. Hall. He came in to see me in my sickness."

Healing of Many Years' Internal Disease.

Mr. Dowie said: "The next to testify is Mrs. Margaret Johnson, 723 Eighth Street, Oakland. I may just say in this case, that our dear sister cannot be expected to give details."

Mrs. Johnson, a Swedish lady, spoke as follows: "I would like to say that Jesus is my Saviour and he is my Healer. I have known him as my Saviour for fifteen years, but I have not known him as my Healer until Mr. Dowie's Oakland Mission, the 18th of last July. I heard the teaching, and I could feel and see where all the sickness came from. I thought before that the sickness came from God. But I felt I could not, when I knew better, stand it any longer, and I asked the Lord to help me get relief very quick, for I knew I could not stand it long. The next morning I was more sick than ever, and I was wondering what I should do; I felt I would not be able to sit up in the Mission, and I did not know whether to take medicine. I took medicine and I threw it up. I said, 'That is the last I will take.' I went down to Mr. Dowie's meeting in the afternoon, but I was filled with pain from head to foot. I had been sick for six years, and been taking medicine all the time. I have seen eleven doctors; the last one was Dr. McLane in this city, and he told me I could not be cured for many months.

"That afternoon I came into the healing room, and Mr. Dowie laid his hands upon me, and I felt every pain leave me; I moved and stepped, and I did not feel anything, the pain passed away so quick. But after that I did not feel so strong as I wanted to be, and I doubted and wondered if I was really healed. One night I heard a voice say, 'Satan hath desired to have you, that he may sift you as wheat; but I have prayed for thee, that thy faith fail not.' I wondered what was going to happen; if I was going to be sick again, and I wondered if I was healed or not. I moved and I felt I was all right; but when I stood up, I felt as if there was a chain around me just above my knees, and my feet and legs felt heavy. I said that is the work of the devil; I aint going to have it. But I had it until Saturday, and during the time I caught cold and felt very sick. On Saturday morning I was wondering if I was a Christian or not, and if I had done anything to keep the blessing away. And I went to God and asked him to forgive me my sins and heal me according to his own promise. And I seemed to hear, 'Peace be still; I have heard you.' I felt as if somebody was opening the chain and it dropped off. I stretched out my hands and said, 'Lord, can I touch you?' And I felt something overflow me, and I felt so happy and light. I felt that I was healed; I felt as if I was just swimming in the River of Life. I was so happy I could not sleep at all, and I laid there all the night rejoicing. I now feel well and strong; I have been perfectly well for two months."

Mr. Dowie said: "This was a serious case of long standing—internal troubles. I cannot say any more about it, but any lady who can read between the lines can understand. Our dear sister's body was just made anew."

Healing of Many Troubles.

Mr. Dowie said: "Now a word from Mr. J. A. Mansfield, of the Silver Star House. The brother is unknown to me, but he tells me the Lord has healed and blessed him elsewhere."

Mr. Mansfield said: "I praise God because of his blessings to my soul. It was through faith in Jesus alone that I have been kept in health, and through the sanctification of the Holy Spirit I have several times, when at the point of death, been brought back again. I knew at the time it was through the power of Jesus that death was overcome. Whenever pain would come I looked to Jesus, and instantly the pain would go away. It is as when a person commits sin. You know the word of God says, 'Sin not,' and that seems to be the command taught to me in reference to pain. When we sin we can come to Jesus as an advocate, and the sin is instantly taken away. So it is with pain. I look to Jesus as my healer, and it is instantly taken away; it disappears. I have faith in Jesus, and am trusting him for all things."

Healing of Kidney Disease.

Mr. Homer Dray, 707½ Stevenson Street, city, said: "In March, 1884, I had been suffering a long time with an affection of the kidneys, and had taken bottles and bottles of medicine; all for naught. One night in my sufferings the thought came to me something like this: 'Why not ask Jesus to heal you?' and I immediately turned my eyes towards Jesus in prayer, and I dropped to sleep praying. In the morning I awoke just as hearty and as well as any man I had in my camp. I give all the praise to Jesus."

Healing of Heart Disease.

Mr. Dowie then called on Mrs. Bills, 326 Larkin Street, city, saying that she had been cured of heart disease and other troubles. Mrs. Bills said:—
"I can say to the glory of God that since the first of last May I have been enabled to take Jesus as my healer. For some months previous to this I suffered from heart difficulty and other troubles. Being a child of God, I was trying to take Jesus as my healer. I felt my faith was weak. I asked some of the people, some of the faifhful ones, connected with an organization to which I belonged, to pray for me, and Jesus healed me. Since that time I have been perfectly well, and I give all the glory to Jesus. To-night, by the goodness of God, I am well in spirit, soul, and body."

Healing of Ten Years' Chronic Neuralgia and Spinal Injury.

Mrs. Pereau, of Bristol Street, West Berkeley, said: "I am so glad that I am able to glorify God and tell of his healing power. I was a great sufferer with neuralgia for ten years, which became chronic; also an affection of the spine, not able to lay on my back. I attended the meeting in Oakland, and listened to Dr. Dowie's teaching. I took Jesus for my Healer, and I have not suffered any since. The Lord be praised."

Mr. Dowie exclaimed, "Thank God! The sister has come a long way to witness for Christ."

Healing of Many Troubles.

Mrs. Mary C. Littell, 817 Nineteenth Street, San Francisco, said:—
"About ten years ago I read in the precious word of God that Jesus was my Saviour and my Healer, and I have lived with him ever since, until he has come to be a complete Saviour. Since taking him as my Healer, I have never had a physician. My husband can testify that Jesus keeps me and saves me. I do not see why every Christian who reads God's precious word does not see that Jesus is the Healer as well as Saviour. I praise his name that he has kept me by his power. Glory be to God!"

Healing of Chronic Neuralgia.

Mr. Littell said: "I can testify to the power of God to heal. I had suffered for several years with neuralgia in my head. Brother Brown, who is in the audience, and some others who used to belong to a Mission that I and my wife used to attend, know this to be true. I, like many others, was opposed to this doctrine of Divine Healing. Through their teaching I was led to call upon Jesus. One morning as I left my home I was so ill that I said to my wife, 'I may be back in a few moments, and if not, I may be dead." On the corner of Valencia and Nineteenth Streets I prayed, and my faith reached to the very throne of God. I called upon Jesus to heal me then and there. He did, and I have never felt the pain from that day to this. I give God the glory."

More Than Sixty Witnesses.

Mr. Dowie said: "All that have been healed in any of our meetings through faith in Jesus, just stand."

After counting them he announced there were sixteen in the meeting and about twenty-eight on the platform, and at least twenty had gone away, as the hour was very late. Mr. Dowie said: "Now, I may say I have a number of written testimonies; but at this late hour of the night [it was past eleven o'clock] I will not detain you longer. I think you are about the most patient people I have seen for a long time. Now, we are just going to close this meeting; but we are not going to send the people away without giving them an opportunity to give their hearts to Jesus, and we will have an after-meeting, as we always do."

At Least a Thousand Believers in Jesus as a Present Healer.

Mr. Dowie said: "Will all those in this meeting who believe that Jesus Christ is the Healer, and that the doctrine which we have been teaching is the doctrine of our Lord Jesus Christ, just stand to their feet." (The larger portion of the great audience were on their feet.)

Mr. Dowie exclaimed, "Thank God! May the Lord grant that we may have a mighty Association to promote this work in this city. ["Amen," from the audience.] My wife reminds me to tell you that these meetings are continued every day through the next fortnight, save Wednesday next. Will you bring the sick along?"

"All who have received spiritual blessings in this Mission, stand to your feet." (Another large body of people rose.)

"Hallelujah! hallelujah! I thank God for it. We cannot do any more now than sing the Doxology, but the moment this meeting closes we shall have our after-meeting."

After singing the Doxology, Mr. Dowie pronounced the following

Benediction:

"And now, beloved, abstain from all appearance of evil, and the very God of peace Himself sanctify you wholly; and I pray God your whole spirit, and soul, and body be preserved entire without blame unto the coming of our Lord Jesus Christ. Faithful is He that calleth you, who also will do it. The grace of our Lord Jesus Christ, the love of God, and the fellowship of the Holy Ghost be with you over. Amen."

POSTSCRIPT.

Twenty-Three Years' Deafness Removed During the Meeting.

At the conclusion of the above meeting, an after-meeting was held, to which several hundreds remained. Immediately the meeting was called to order a young man rose and requested permission to speak. He said he had been entirely deaf for twenty three years in the right ear until that evening, and that during the meeting he had asked in prayer for the restoration of his hearing and had received it. He spoke somewhat as follows:—

"I have been deaf in my right ear for twenty-three years. When two years old I had a terrible sickness and could not hear in that ear since then. I have been in this country four years; have been a Christian for four years; I have believed in this doctrine of Divine healing ever since I have been a Christian. I do know the reason why I was not free before: it was because I did not give up everything to Christ. I have been here in San Francisco for four months. I give up everything for Christ. I was smoking, and so I gave that up, and felt more pure from it. This very afternoon and this evening during your meeting I asked God to heal me. I had to listen before very much indeed; and now as I was sitting here I hear better and better, and then, all at once, I hear in that ear too."

Mr. Dowie then asked him to close his left ear and to repeat after him the words he would then say. "God is good."

He answered, "He is."

Mr. Dowie said, "But will you please repeat my words after me? Put your finger in your other ear. Now, 'God is my Healer.'"

The young man replied, "He is my Healer, too."

Then Mr. Dowie said, "You will please say the very same words which I say."

He said, "Yes."

Mr. Dowie then said: "Jesus Christ, the same yesterday, to-day, and forever." The young man exactly repeated these words, hearing only with the ear that had been totally deaf. Mr. Dowie then told him to go to the farthest back seat in the Opera House, over one hundred feet distant. He did as directed. Mr. Dowie again told him to put his finger in the left ear, and to listen to what he said with the right ear only, and to repeat the words, "God is love." "I am the Lord that healeth thee," "I am the good Shepherd; the good Shepherd giveth his life for the sheep;" all of which, with other expressions, were repeated perfectly back from his position at the end of the building. The young gentleman was a Norwegian, about twenty-five years of age, and gave his name as Thorvald Ber, 655 Howard Street, San Francisco.

[The following paragraph appears in *The Pacific Herald Holiness* of November 8, and is from the pen of an eminent minister of the Methodist Episcopal Church, who is at present laboring in and around San Francisco, as an Evangelist. His home is at Niagara Falls, and he has been much used of God, both in England and America. We may add to his kind words concerning our present Mission the fact that up to the moment of writing these lines (Thursday evening, November 8,) over one hundred and sixty persons have openly sought the Lord for salvation in our meetings; and that over five hundred persons profess to have been saved in our five months' ministry in this State. To God be all the glory!]

Rev. Mr. Dowie's Meeting.

It has been our privilege to attend a good many of the meetings conducted by the Rev. John A. Dowie in the Grand Opera House in this city during the month of services now coming to a close; and I praise God for the wonderful power and blessing of God which has been experienced in the meetings. I profess to be able to distinguish between truth and error. I believe no man can deceive me with unsound doctrine or hypocritical pretensions either. And I do say, to the glory of God, that I have never heard sounder gospel truth taught by any man than by Brother Dowie. His teaching on faith for salvation and healing seemed to us on last Sunday to excel anything I had ever heard. It carried me back in thought to the wonderful teaching of John Wesley, whose utterances on faith seemed to be, and no doubt were, inspirations from God. Mr. Dowie does not heal the wounds of the daughters of Zion slightly. His denunciations of sin of all kinds are convincing and powerful. God is evidently owning his labors in the conversion of hundreds of sinners, and many clear cases of divine healing are wrought through his ministry. The blind have received their sight, the lame walk, and no doubt diseases as incurable as leprosy are cleansed away.

It is much easier to persecute and misrepresent such a man than to imitate his example, but it is dangerous business. "Touch not mine anointed and do my prophets no harm." To have carried through such a series of meetings for a whole month successfully in San Francisco amid all the excitements of a Presidential election, has been a wonderful achievement for the glory of God and the good of suffering and perishing humanity. To God be all the glory.

J. E. IRVINE.

END OF FIRST EDITION.

Praise and Testimony Meeting Held in the Lyceum, San Francisco, on the Evening of Lord's Day, November 11th.

As in other cases this report is the work of Mr. G. H. Hawes, 320 Sansome Street. There was a very large audience present, and after introductory exercises and the presentation of many petitions for prayer, and announcements connected with the organization of the newly formed Divine Healing Association, we stated that over 170 persons had professed to be saved in the Mission within the last 28 days. The first person whom we asked to testify was Mr. M. C. Ryan, of 503 Commercial St., San Francisco.

For Twenty-five Years He Had Lived without Prayer,

And had been converted in the Grand Opera House, in consequence of the spiritual impressions made upon him at our testimony meeting of October 28th. His testimony was a very characteristic one, and he seemed to be a typical American workingman. In giving his experience, our reporter says, "He spoke in a frank and earnest tone." He told the assemblage that he had always claimed to be a moral man, never a drunkard, and never looked for anything in the shape of Christianity. He felt that the dictates of his own conscience were a sufficient guide, and said: "As long as I went through the world and did not cheat my fellow-men, and was contented with myself, I thought I was quite ready to lay down at any time and meet my Maker. I have told this to a great many Christians when they talked to me about my soul, and I considered myself as good a man as any Christian. But two weeks ago to-night I was standing on the street and I heard a man testify for Christ. I don't know who he was, but his words made an impression upon me. He said, 'If you don't want to go to our church, to which I invite you, you can go to the Salvation Army, or you can go and hear the Rev. Dr. Dowie; he will do you good and it won't cost you anything.'

"Well, I 'piked' out for the Opera House, and when I went in I got up pretty close to the stage. I see the faces here of some who testified that night. Their testimony seemed to me very strange, but they came with such force that I was under conviction right there. I tell you, my friends, if a man was ever close to hardened infidelity on this earth, it was me; but now I feel and know that I am a different man. I have often heard Christians say that they felt that they had been freed from sin and all desire of sinning, and that the Spirit of God had got into them. I always thought that was bosh; it was all talk. But, friends, I give it to you to-night that if I ever spoke the truth in the world, it is a reality in my case.

"And another strange coincidence happened here this very day. When I was sitting here in the audience I found myself right alongside of a Judge belonging to Denver, my own town. I don't know whether he is here or not. Is Judge Jeffries here?" There being no response, Mr. Ryan continued: "He is not here, I guess, else he would say so. I was so interested in what Dr. Dowie was saying that I did not notice who was sitting alongside of me; but something occurred that caused me to look around, and I saw the Judge. He said, 'Great God, Mr. Ryan, what are you doing here?'

"I said, 'Judge, I have been seeking the Lord, and I have found Him.'

"He said, 'Good for you.'

"I said, 'Ain't it better to be found here than in the saloon?'

"He said, 'You would never find me in a saloon.'

"I said, 'You know me long enough to know it is not my resting-place either; it is a place that has no pleasure for me, but this place has.'

"The judge went away rejoicing. He says he is going to tell all my friends in Denver that I am a Christian, and I tell you, friends, that I reckon they will be more surprised than when they heard Harrison and Morton [the newly elected President and Vice-President of the United States] were elected.

"But I want to tell you about my conversion. On the night of the last testimony meeting I staid until the after meeting, and for the first time for many years I knelt down and prayed. As I was going out I spoke to Mrs. Dowie, and she sent me home full of conviction. She told me the passage of the Bible to look for, told me to pray in faith to God, and that I would be all right. I went home, and I will say before my Maker that that night was the first time in my life since I left my mother that I had ever got on my knees; and I have continued it night and morning since. I feel at peace with God through faith in Jesus Christ; I know that he is my Savior." ("Praise the Lord," and "Hallelujah," from many.)

"For twenty-four years I have lived without prayer, and now I am praising and praying all the time." ("Praise the Lord," from Mr. Dowie.)

This testimony was received with great interest by the audience. Mr. Ryan spoke in a particularly impressive and simple-hearted, manly way. He continues to be an earnest worker in connection with the newly-formed Association, and is doing much good, as also are many of the other converts in the city.

Healing of Cancer in Switzerland without Human Touch.

Mr. Dowie said: "I want Mrs. Dowie to read a very beautiful testimony which has reached us, of divine healing, from a lady, whose case I mentioned. She would like to have been here herself, but cannot, as she has given birth to a beautiful baby; she has to stay at home to take care of it. Now Mrs. Dowie will read her testimony. She is a very excellent lady."

Mrs. Dowie before reading the letter said: "This lady spoke her testimony last Thursday in our meeting; she intended to have been here to-night and have spoken it again, but the circumstances mentioned by Mr. Dowie have prevented "

"1123 GREENWICH STREET, SAN FRANCISCO,
November 11th, 1888.

"Six years ago I was very ill over in Switzerland. The Doctor Monsieur de Montmolin, one of the first doctors in Neuchatel, declared I had the beginning of a cancer in the womb. He came every other day for several months, and as I got worse every day he told me that I had but one more chance of recovery, and that would be an operation. I was shrinking from suffering and had lost faith in his, as in all doctors', treatment, and would not consent. I had been a child of God for nearly ten years then; had worked for my Master as a deaconess in Mrs. Pennefather's Deaconess work, Mildmay Park, London, N., but had not known Christ as my healer.

"So I lay one morning, it was the 27th of April, 1882, helpless and suffering, in my bed. I could scarcely move, when suddenly there came the word that healed them of old to me: 'All they that touched Him were healed.' I had read these words many a time, but now they came to me with Holy Ghost power. 'Is that true? Does it really mean what it says?' I asked myself. 'Christ did not turn one away; all were healed?' Then came the devil's argument: 'Yes, all who touched Him were healed, but that was nineteen centuries ago; the time of miracles is past.' I got sad again, when God sent another word: 'Jesus Christ, the same yesterday, to-day, and forever.' Satan had to be silent now. I put the two Scripture passages together, and said again: 'Is that true? Does it mean just what it said, "'All they that touched Him were healed,'" and, "'Jesus Christ, the same yesterday, to-day, and forever'"? 'Well, then, I am going to take Thee at Thy word;' and I left my bed, dressed myself, and went out into the kitchen to ask one of the girls to give me some heavy work to do. They would not, and urged me to return to bed, as I was too ill. But I took a tub of clothes, went out to the lines and hung up two pieces. When I was about to hang up the third piece the pain was gone. I came into the house jumping for joy, telling the girls the Lord had healed me.

"The next day the doctor came. I underwent one more examination, after which the doctor shook his head. 'What is the matter now?' I said. 'Well,' he answered, 'your sickness is treacherous, as all this kind will be. I don't see anything of it, but you'll come to me in three days and see.' Then I told him Christ had healed me by faith, and henceforth he would be my healer. And so He is. Since that time he has been my healer, and my children's healer, and He has led me out in the highway of holiness and health, and taught me to lay hands on the sick, and they would recover *through* Jesus.

"But the other day my baby was very sick." (The healing of this child is given in our last letter.) "The voice came, 'Go to Bro. Dowie with that case.' When Mr. and Mrs. Dowie were teaching in the Y. M. C. A., I was engaged in Mission work every evening, and could not attend the beautiful meetings; and, sad to say, I was told by some Christian worker not to believe, and to enforce it they took the passage, 'A stranger will they [my sheep] not follow, for they know not the voice of a stranger.' But when dear Sister Dowie held her meeting for ladies only, I was disengaged, went, and then I saw it was not the voice of a stranger, it was Christ speaking through one of His children.

"And now how shall I praise the Lord for having allowed me to take part and listen to the beautiful, wonderful teaching of one who is not the voice of a stranger, but one who speaks the words that give life and health to all who believe, the words of the great Shepherd, 'I have come that they might have life, and that they might have it more abundantly.' T. L. BOILLOT."

Mrs. Dowie continues: "Mrs. Boillot sends me this: 'DEAR MRS. DOWIE: I promised in the meeting on Thursday night to give my testimony this evening, but I am unable to be there in the body, so I have written it down while sitting in bed; so please excuse my scribble. I am praying with you in spirit this afternoon. Your sister in the Lord.'"

Healing of an Episcopalian Minister at Saucelito.

"I have a letter which I will read:—

"'DEAR MR. DOWIE: The Rev. Mr. Reed, a minister of Saucelito, for whom you prayed at Sacramento, wishes to give thanks to God [I like this—'thanks to God'] for his recovery. He had been given up by physicians, and was supposed to be dying of consumption. May God bless you and dear Mrs. Dowie.
'Yours in Jesus, MAY JACKSON.'

"Is little Miss May Jackson here? [She made known her presence.] Is that so, dear Miss Jackson?"
"Yes, sir."
"You are authorized to send this letter?"
"Yes, sir."
"He is your minister, is he?"
"Yes, sir."
"The Lord bless you. Miss Jackson was healed in the first Mission."
"Now I am always glad to get somebody healed belonging to the ministry. The Lord bless Mr. Reed."

Instantaneous Healing of an Aged Scotch Lady Who Had Been Afflicted with Rheumatism for Twenty Years.

We then read the following letter, written by Mrs. Mary Castell, 530½ Olive Avenue, San Francisco:—

"MR. AND MRS. DOWIE—*Dear Servants of the Lord:* At your request I write you these few lines. I attended your meetings, and listened to your lessons on faith. After one of the meetings I went into the healing room, and after you had laid your hands on me, in the name of the Lord Jesus, through faith in Him, I was perfectly healed. My limbs and ankles were very weak at first. They have been strengthened very much since then. Glory to God. He hears and answers prayer for His Son's sake. My trouble is rheumatism.
"Your sister in Christ."

Mr. Dowie asked: "Is that all right?"
"Yes, all right," responded an old Scotch lady in the audience. She then got up and commenced to speak, when Mr. Dowie said: "Come up close to the reporters. You are worth looking at." She then stood beside the reporter's table, and said:—

"The first day that I went into the Mission I was so bad with my legs that when I got up to go out I didn't know how in the world I would get about. I have been afflicted for twenty years. I suffer particularly when there is a change of the weather. In the last year I have been very lame, and suffered more than tongue can tell. I would go to bed, and perhaps for two hours, and sometimes for half the night, I could not sleep for the aching. In this weather we have to-day I would have been just terrible bad if I had not been healed."

Mr. Dowie asked: "How long did it take to heal you?"

"A moment." ("Hallelujah!" from the audience.)

Glory to God; I am delighted to see you.

She added: "The grand baptism from the Holy Ghost was as good as the healing, and my soul is full. Glory to God." (This produced much feeling in the audience, and there were hallelujahs and clapping of hands.) Mr. Dowie remarked that she was from Edinburgh, Scotland, the place he himself came from.

Instantaneous Healing of Eight Years' Rheumatism.

Mrs. Agusta Anderson, residing on Third Street, below Mission, San Francisco, wrote as follows:—

"This is to certify that I have been laid up with rheumatism for the last eight years, so that I was helpless and could not even dress myself, and the pain was intolerable, until at last I found relief and instant healing through faith in the Lord Jesus, when you laid hands upon me yesterday in the Grand Opera House. I hope that others will do the same, giving themselves to the Lord. I wish to thank you and to thank God, who uses you in this work."

Turning to the lady, Mr. Dowie inquired, "Is that true?"

Mrs. Anderson, who was on the platform, came forward and said: "That is true, and I have been happier than I have been in all my life. From that moment I felt the pains go away. I have had such feelings and been so lifted up that it has relieved me from all unhappiness and all sorrow. I believe in Christ. Friday I felt I ought to give myself to Christ, and yesterday I promised Christ I should be His, and I was healed at once.

"I used to be so unhappy I could not sleep at night. I say, May God in Heaven help me. I don't get no help. I did not give my heart to Christ. I thank the Lord that I had to do it, and I never will go back. I have been eight years ill. I could not lift a spoon to my mouth. I could not handle a knife. For four years I could not do any work."

Can you do everything now?

"Yesterday noon I went over to a lady friend of mine, who is sitting right there, and she asked me to sit down and dine with her, and she asked me if I would take some coffee, and it was the first cup of coffee I have been able to lift to my mouth for the last eight months."

(Mr. Dowie asked the lady she referred to, if she would stand up and confirm that. The lady did so, and gave her name as Louisa Zeigler, residing in San Francisco, at 71 Natoma Street. Mr. Dowie asked: "Is that so?")

"Yes, sir."

How long have you known her?

"For three years."

Mrs. Anderson then continued: "She knows I have been unable to dress myself; I had to wait until someone come around the house and ask them to help me put my clothes on; I could not button my shoes; I could not reach my hands to my head. I can now put my hands to my head, and to my back—I can do everything. A week ago I met a gentleman on the street, Mr. Dan McCarthy. I lived in their house when they were first married; but I had not seen him since I had this trouble uptil then, and he and his wife shook hands with me, and I nearly fell on the sidewalk, and I screamed, and said, 'Don't double my hand so much as that.' He told his mother-in-law I was so bad with rheumatism he felt awful sorry for me. Now I can shake hands with everybody and anybody, thank God."

(The lady while speaking illustrated how she could use her arms by raising her hands to her head, placing them far behind her back, and reaching down to her feet, not only doing it with apparent ease, but gracefully.)

Restoration of Sight after Twelve Years' Blindness.

The following letter written by Mrs. Gleason, of 187 Turk Street, San Francisco, on behalf of Mrs. Castro, of San Pablo Ranch, West Berkeley, gives an interesting and detailed account of her healing, which has attracted much attention in the social circle to which Mrs. Castro belongs, and has also interested many specialists who have treated this lady in vain for many years. The case has made a profound impression, and has been followed by much blessing to many persons.

"DEAR DR. AND MRS. DOWIE: I feel it a great privilege that I have been permitted to witness and give testimony to the visitation of Christ in our midst with His healing power, bringing His word to us with living reality. This morning I was too late to bring to the Lord's table the dear sister who was so blessed in the restoration of her sight, but I was not too late to listen to the story of her healing, with the earnest request that I should give it to the meeting as a thank-offering in part for the unspeakable blessing. I dare not attempt to give it in the language of her inspired soul, inspired so thoroughly with the spirit and love of God.

"She said: 'When I went into the healing room the first week of the Mission I had never seen Dr. and Mrs. Dowie before. I explained to him that twelve years ago I was thrown from my carriage, receiving a spinal injury. From that time for about a year a star cataract formed over each of my eyes, slowly but surely shutting out all earthly objects, as well as the faces of my loved ones. All these years I have prayed for patience to bear my affliction, appealing in vain to the best surgeons we had, getting always the same sad sentence, "No human skill can reach your case; the knife would destroy all hope." So I rested until I was led to Dr. Dowie, believing, as I had heard he taught, that Christ was the same yesterday, to-day and forever. After the discourse I sought the healing room, and I felt a soft hand, as though it were the hand of an angel, and Mrs. Dowie's sweet voice rose in prayer. As she prayed I seemed to hear a voice saying, "Daughter, thy sins are forgiven thee," and when Dr. Dowie laid his hands on my eyes I felt distinctly the cataracts give way, like bursting asunder; I arose and instantly saw quite a number of objects and the figures of those around me. You can only faintly imagine the joy of such a ray of sunlight, such a certainty that my God still loved me. Over a week passed and I went about, as the Scriptures say, "Seeing men as trees walking," and in certain lights other things dimly. At another meeting Dr. Dowie said, "I would like to see you again, when I believe the Lord will perfect the healing." Wednesday, 10 o'clock, was fixed upon, at his rooms at the hotel. We had a little talk, as the Dr. calls it, although he had worked all night. He took a seat in front of me for a moment, then went behind me, telling me to try and realize that Jesus, my healer, was in his place, while he laid his hands again on my eyes and prayed. We all prayed earnestly. That sacred moment may I never forget, feeling the presence of the Holy Spirit filling the room. Dr. Dowie then led me to the light. There is no language to describe what followed; I had the joy of seeing my friend's face I had never seen before, other faces, the hands on the watch, books, colors, etc.'

"Now I must tell you how we went from there to the Opera House meeting, and taking in many sights on the street, enjoying even the shop windows, for, as she expressed it, it seemed as if she had just returned from a long journey. Two days after still more wonderful sights met her clearer vision, when she read a sign. Added to this blessing of sight she has been greatly strengthened in mind and body, enabling her to walk on the street as she has not done all these years. This morning I found her both cheerful and happy, her sight growing clearer every day, and I might say, every hour. When she says, 'Whereas I was blind, now I see,' we praise the Lord we are not like the Jews, for we believe and know who our Healer is."

Mr. Dowie said: "This lady the Lord has given sight to after twelve years, and may He be glorified." ("Amens," from the people.) "I take no glory; all glory be to Him who does it." (Cries of "Hallelujah.") Mrs. Castro was present in the meeting and confirmed the testimony. She is attending our present Mission and progressing daily.

Instantaneous Healing of a Lady Who Came on Crutches.

Mrs. Elizabeth Rodenbach, of Foley Street, Alameda, said: "I came on crutches to the Opera House two weeks ago, and now through faith in Jesus I have got healing. My leg, which was very much injured, is getting stronger and stronger. I did not have the use of my right limb, but now I can walk without crutch or cane. I was about two months on crutches. After Mr. Dowie laid his hands upon me I was able to leave his room and walk away from the Opera House and carry my crutches."

Salvation and Healing.

Mr. Edwin McDonald, lodging at the Empire Hotel, San Francisco, gave a very interesting testimony. He spoke of having first heard us at Sacramento during our mission there, and had been deeply impressed. He came to the city and found salvation and healing in the Opera House; he was healed of rheumatism. He said: "I am not so much amazed at the healing of my body as I am that our blessed Savior, who saves perfectly, saves and keeps a rebellious sinner such as I have been. I have been the chief of sinners, not a moral man at all. I have earned quite good wages and had an iron constitution; but I sought pleasure in all directions; I have been a pugilist in the ring; I have done everything that was sinful, except that I never murdered anyone, but I have done everything else; to think that God would pardon, save, and keep a man like me and put me where I am now, seems amazing. Healing seems very little in comparison, and it came very easily to me. I feel that I am thoroughly converted and that my name is written in Heaven, and by the grace of God I will never take one step back."

He then gave details as to how the word we had preached had been blessed to him, and how the testimony of Mr. M. C. Ryan in a meeting of the Salvation Army had impressed him. He had heard Mr. Ryan say, "I have been led to Christ through the wonderful words and the wonderful works of God which I have heard and seen in the Grand Opera House; the things that I have seen in Dr. Dowie's meetings at the Opera House would confound Bob Ingersoll; I believe it would convert him if he were there."

Mr. McDonald continued: "When I heard Mr. Ryan say that I enquired where this Opera House was, for it was there I wanted to be, as I had heard Mr. Dowie in Sacramento.

"The first night I came I sought the Lord and he took me in; he saved me; he healed me, and he keeps me all the time. Hallelujah." ("Amens" from the audience.)

This young man has been instrumental since his conversion in leading a considerable number of persons to Christ, and is working daily with us in our present Mission, bringing in many every day to seek salvation and healing. His energy is amazing, and he has entirely consecrated this month to this service of God in connection with our Mission, and has laid aside his work (that of a carpenter) for the time being.

Healing of a Russian Lady of Consumption.

Mr. Dowie then introduced a Russian lady by the name of Madame Faodoroff. He said: "I may say I had the very great pleasure a while ago to receive a request for prayer from St. Petersburg. May God bless the Russian nation; I hope to go there some day.

The lady stepped forward and said: "I can praise the Lord to-night that I am on the Lord's side, and the Lord is on my side. I am only a short time in this State, and I have given my testimony quite often in all the churches and meetings wherever I have been. 'It is said, 'We shall confess, or else the stones will speak.' It is three years ago since I found the Lord Jesus for my Savior and for my healer. My body has been broken down with consumption. I think everyone knows what a disease that is; there was no help for me. Two of my brothers were doctors; they died. We had three drug stores in all. What was in there they tried, but no help. It was ten of us in the family, but they all died of this disease. So I know it was coming on me; I know there was no help. Of course the doctors were trying to save me, but they could not. I never had a thought for a moment that I could live.

"I was brought up as a child of the Roman Catholic Church, and you know that is nothing but a dead religion. Afterward the Lord was with me in my young age; I wanted to find the Lord, and I went to the Lutheran Church, but I did not get what I wanted; I wanted more. Then I seen death come before me, and the Professor told me, 'You can live no more than three weeks.' Well, I knowed it, for the way I cough and pieces of my lung come up as big as a hazel nut; I thought I could not live. I didn't care; I only wanted to know that I could be saved.

"Then a lady taught me about Divine Healing; that was down in the East. I never would come in a Christian meeting like this here, for I thought I would lose all the religion that I ever had. I did not have faith to touch the Lord, but I pray that the Lord give me faith to believe and touch his garment; and I went on and pray all night, 'Lord, is it Thy will, give me faith that I may touch Thee, that only my soul may be saved.' I don't care for the body. As I was brought in the meeting I seen the happy faces of the Christians, and, 'oh,' I says, 'I have what the Lord give me in silver and gold, but I have not what my heart wants,' for I know that I didn't have everlasting life. But in a moment I believe that Jesus was able to overcome my sins, and when I cried out, 'Jesus of Nazareth is passing by; save me now,' (I know Jesus was near by), he took me up and called me his daughter. And I know in a moment when I gave my heart to Jesus I was healed. It was well with my soul, and I was just as well as I am now standing here before you. And He spoke to me and says, 'There is no death for you; there is everlasting life.'

"And since the three years ago I am rejoicing. A good many say that this is Mind Healing; but I know what the Lord has done unto me; He has given everlasting life. And a good many say of these meetings of Brother Dowie's, that is Mind Healing. O my Christian friends, come and try this Mind Healing; what you can't buy for money, but only by the blood of Christ." ("Amens" from the congregation.) "Come and give yourself entirely to the Lord. The Lord Jesus Christ is willing to save you and to heal you. Oh, what a joy is this having everlasting life.

"I was healed three years ago in Chicago. I was supposed to be dying at that time. It was by my faith in Jesus." (Applause.)

Healing of an Injured Hand of 27 Years; Injured Feet of 16 Years; Catarrh Since Infancy; Serious Injury to the Right Eye; and Dislocation of the Arm.

Mrs. H. Sparman of Sutter Street, near San Pablo Avenue, Oakland, said: "I want to thank God for sending His Son on earth to heal and to save the people. I praise Him for healing my hands which I have had chapped for over 27 years.

Nearly 16 years ago I used to wear too small shoes, and my feet got to be all spoiled; some of my toes were all cramped up." (Mr. Dowie interjected, "You deserved it.") "Last Thursday, after hearing your teaching, I went to the Lord and told Him all about it. He had healed me, through your agency, of my injured hands, and I asked Him to heal these without any human touch. When I was undressing I found to my great surprise that my toes were all straight and my feet in right shape. Before my feet used to pain me all the time, but I am now quite free. I give God all the glory."

Mr. Dowie turned to a large, heavy-set man on the platform and asked, "Is that lady your wife?"

He said, "Yes, sir."

"And you know her toes were crooked and are now straight?"

"Yes, sir," he said.

The lady continued: "I have had catarrh since I was an infant; now the Lord has healed me. Thanks be to his holy name.

"Over nineteen years ago I was in Stockholm, Sweden, and I had pimples all around my eyes. [Mr. Dowie, "Why, there is a whole catalogue."] I went to the greatest professor there, whose name was Busardo, to get my eyes cured, and he gave me some salve to put on, and, after using the medicine, I became blind in my right eye, and during the last few years I could see but little in that right eye. But the Lord has healed me now in that eye, so that I can see with it very well indeed. Glory be to God. And then there is another thing. [Mr. Dowie, "What a catalogue!"]

"I had my arm out of joint July 28, and I asked Mr. Dowie, when in Oakland, to pray for me. The Lord healed me, and I can now do my house-work, and I don't feel any pain in it at all, and give God all the glory."

Healed of Rheumatism and Dyspepsia.

Mr. Carl Sparman, who spoke in somewhat broken and indistinct English, gave his testimony. He is the husband of the lady last above mentioned. He said: "I was very much troubled with rheumatism and dyspepsia for many, many years. I drink medicine like a mule drink water. When others buy a pint I buy a gallon. I take no less than twenty-five bottles of one kind of medicine, and it do me no good. A week ago to-morrow I come over into the Opera House to hear Mr. Dowie, and he say how Jesus can heal. Then I think that is true, and that I will give up myself entirely to Jesus. I go to him, and the next morning I found something there; I found Jesus. Jesus has healed my wife from everythings, and so he has me. Just as he has saved me, so he has healed me. I give glory to God for what He did for me. That time when I prayed all the pain was taken away, and never came back.

"I thank God, also, for the healing of my family. My boy was sick last Wednesday, and my little girl four years old was sick. I say to my wife, there is only one way to do; pray to God to help us, for we cannot use any medicine now. I don't put my horse in the wagon and go for the doctor any more. All what I got belong to God. My wife and children belong to God; I give up all to God. And when we prayed God heard, and He healed, and I thank Dr. Dowie for the teaching."

Repetition of Former Testimony of Healing of Twenty-three Years' Deafness.

Mr. Thorbald Ber, 655 Howard Street, San Francisco, who was very remarkably healed during the previous testimony meeting, whose case was mentioned in a postscript to our last report, arose and said: "Friends, I got to tell you to-night what Christ did for me. He saved me four years ago, and two weeks ago, in the Grand Opera House, during such a meeting as this, he healed me. I had been deaf in one of my ears for twenty-three years, and when someone was testifying that they had been healed, I asked the Lord to heal me, and so He did, and I thank Him for it to-day."

I tested him in various ways, requesting him to close his right ear, and every test was instantly responded to. This case created a great deal of interest in the meeting, and has made a deep impression upon large numbers of young men in the city.

Testimony of Our Reporter, Mr. G. H. Hawes.

Mr. Dowie said: "Now I have got one most important testimony before we close. I want you all to hear this testimony. My dear friend, the reporter of all our testimony meetings, a gentleman well known in the stenographic world, and whom I want to thank publicly for the excellent manner in which he has reported our testimony meetings, said to me this afternoon, 'I feel like speaking to-night, Doctor.' Then I said: 'You shall, and I shall be very glad to hear you.' He said: 'I would like especially to mention what I witnessed of your own healing.' I said, 'Tell whatever you like.'

"Our friend wants to speak now as the official reporter of my meetings. He has reported all our testimony meetings, save the one at Sacramento. He has been with me all around the Missions, and he is reporting this meeting to-night. While he speaks his assistant will take down what he says. Now I just want Mr. Hawes to speak as he may be led. I again express my personal thanks to him for the excellent way in which he has done his work, and for his volunteer testimony."

The reporter mounted the high platform, stepping from the top of the table on which he had been writing, and was received by a welcoming hand from Mr. Dowie. Then, turning to the large audience before him, he said:—

"It has been my privilege, friends, to witness and experience a great many wonderful things during my life, but among the most remarkable, and which I can never forget, are those I have experienced the last four months in connection with Mr. Dowie in his testimony meetings and assisting him in his correspondence, where I have seen and known him as many of you have not; where I have seen him replying to this great mass of correspondence, which had already accumulated in great quantities when I first met him, in July last, while conducting the first Mission in San Francisco. I would like to say in a general way that I have been surprised at the numerous testimonies (which I have reported, and afterwards written out, and therefore had an opportunity of scanning and considering very closely), in regard to the great variety of cases that have been healed, and the severity of them; the organic troubles of long standing, among all classes and nationalities, male and female, young and old. I have talked with some of those who have been healed, who have gone into details, perhaps, more than at the public meetings, and they have described to me strange and wonderful sensations when undergoing the healing process, showing that a powerful and subtle force was operating upon them. You have heard these testimonies, and I will not dwell upon them.

"After I had been with Bro. Dowie for some time and saw that these cures were effected, and were permanent in character, I had a strong desire to have him visit one who is very near and dear to me, a sister with whom I have spent nearly twenty years in California. She has been an invalid for over twenty-five years, and has suffered more than tongue can tell. Early in life she became a victim of that dreadful disease, consumption. She was told by Dr. Fitch, a celebrated lung physician of Massachusetts, that she could not long survive. She has also been afflicted with serious heart difficulty, spinal disease, and other troubles. A year ago she returned from the East to California, after spending five years in the New England States. For some months after her return she improved considerably, but last May she was taken severely ill. She was troubled with great derangement of the heart, sleeplessness and nervous prostration; was only able to sleep two or three hours a night for weeks, and appetite very poor. You can imagine what a condition she was in under these circumstances. While her lungs were not seriously affected, she was never free from soreness in the right lung, which she felt very keenly whenever she moved, raised her hand or took a long breath.

"I asked Brother Dowie to visit her sick chamber, but waited a long time before he did; he was so constantly employed and the pressure upon him was so great from the sick and suffering and dying, that I almost despaired of ever getting him to the house. But after his return from the San Jose Mission, he and his dear wife went to her bedside, prayed and laid hands upon her. Although she had been suffering for several days before with pain, it all immediately ceased. The pain in her lung, and soreness, entirely disappeared, and not a vestige of it has since returned, and that was several weeks ago. The action of the heart greatly improved. In the latter part of May she had an attack of neuralgia of the heart, which physicians consider very dangerous. A prominent physician in this city who was attending her said he never saw a patient in such agony, and come so near death, and live.

"Two weeks ago to-day Brother Dowie and his wife again visited and laid hands upon her, with still more remarkable effects than the first visit. For a time she experienced a sinking, deathly sensation, and became speechless, but soon a marked change occurred, new life and strength poured in upon the system, and she exclaimed, with brightened countenance, 'Oh, I am better! yes, I am feeling better!' And she has kept on 'feeling better' and improving from that time to this, and she told me yesterday, if it were pleasant to-day and she had a carriage to take her, she felt she was able to come to the meeting. Now here is a remarkable result that transpired under my own eye.

"But I desire to particularly mention another event I witnessed which has not been mentioned in any of these meetings that I am aware of. It occurred in San Jose at the Closing Praise and Testimony Meeting. I arrived there a little while before the meeting commenced. Brother Dowie left Dr. Jewell's church at quarter past seven; he had laid hands on about one hundred and thirty persons, and was hurrying away from the throng that still pressed around him, to return to the hotel for supper and prepare for the evening exercises, when he suddenly fell heavily to the ground or pavement, striking upon his left side and arm, having stepped upon a piece of fruit. When he arose his arm hung powerless at his side, and he could not even move the fingers of his hand.

"He walked to the hotel in company with Mrs. Dowie and a few friends, where I met him at his rooms. He was suffering great agony, and large drops of perspiration were on his face. Refreshments were brought in, but he ate but little. He prayed earnestly to God for help, you may rest assured. Soon he began to feel a little relief, and began to move his hand and the arm below the elbow. We were in doubt as to just what the injury was, but were fearful it was of a serious nature. Eight o'clock drew near and he said it was time to go, and he boldly led the way back to the church, which was then packed with an eager, expectant congregation. Pausing a moment to pray with Dr. Jewell in an anteroom he ascended the pulpit, and he carried right through one of the grandest and most successful meetings I have reported. He was overflowing with cheerfulness, and the meeting was unusually long. At its close a large number shook hands with him. He then quietly told a doctor who was present (Dr. Bishop) to come around to his hotel, as he thought his shoulder was dislocated. The doctor looked in astonishment, and said it could not be possible, and he able to conduct that long service.

"Arriving at his rooms in the hotel, the doctor made an examination and discovered at once that the shoulder was out of joint. He asked Brother Dowie to lie upon the floor, and the doctor proceeded at once, with my own strength added to his, to draw the arm into its socket. Not a sound escaped his lips, nor expression of pain was seen in his face, and, as the joint entered the socket with a snap, Brother Dowie bounded to his feet, swinging the arm over his head, exclaiming, 'Thank God! Thank God! I am all right!' The doctor said he really felt he ought to put some arnica on it, but Mr. Dowie replied, 'The Lord will do the rest.'

"About three days after this I met Bro. Dowie at the Palace Hotel, in this city, and my first question was in regard to his arm. 'Just as good as ever,' he replied, and stooping down and picking up a chair by the lower front round he held it firmly in the air with his left hand, above his head. His words needed no further proof. I have never had my shoulder dislocated, but I am told that those who have, frequently carry their arm in a sling for four or five months afterwards. I think that is a very remarkable experience, and it came directly under my own observation.

"I wish to also add that when I have been privately with Bro. Dowie receiving dictations of his correspondence, I have been distinctly conscious of a stimulating power, and I seemed to be in the midst of a fountain of health, the very air permeated with energy. Anyone who looks upon the rich, glowing color in his face can see his physical condition is splendid.

"I regret very much, as a citizen of this community, in which I feel a just pride, and which claims and has had the reputation of being liberal in thought, generous and full of hospitality, that it should have the stain upon it of having called Bro. Dowie and his wife frauds and imposters. If the great work accomplished through our Australian friends had been of a directly opposite character, the criticism would exactly fit. When the great mass of testimony gathered here, which is going forward and will continue to do so throughout our land, is read, and then when they learn of these strange and unjust accusations, they surely must think that we are a people who delight in the propagation and cultivation of sickness and disease.

"What a terrible thing this sickness is; it turns a beautiful home into a dungeon of despair, and those within it are victims and prisoners chained and tortured by these nameless ills, and multitudes before the natural end of an earthly life is reached, pass into the common mystery of death. Through these beautiful and potent ministrations a great number in our midst have been released before our eyes, and fresh hope inspired in hundreds of sufferers who have not yet passed under the healing hand. As the gratitude and thanksgiving of hundreds who have been made to rejoice through this health-giving service goes forth and encircles our beloved Brother and Sister Dowie, I know it will lift them far above all the obstacles and difficulties placed in their way, and that they will feel themselves enriched a thousand fold." (A hearty applause.)

A Multitude of Witnesses.

Mr. Dowie then asked all who believed the Lord Jesus was the present healer to arise, and almost instantly it seemed as if the whole audience arose to their feet. The hour was very late, and the meeting, which was a joyful and enthusiastic one throughout, closed with the glorious doxology.

Extract from Letter Sent to "Leaves of Healing."

Our letter of December 15 contained the report of the closing praise and testimony meeting (at the end of a thirty-two days' Mission), held on November the 11th, in the Lyceum, San Francisco, and we therein referred to the month's Mission which we were at that time holding in the Central Presbyterian Church, San Francisco. That Mission closed on the evening of Lord's day, December 23, and we quote the following facts from the

Report of Closing Praise and Testimony Meeting Held at the Central Presbyterian Church, Golden Gate Avenue, San Francisco, Monday Evening, December 23, 1888.

(Reported by G. H. Hawes, 320 Sansome Street, S. F.)

A large audience was present, completely filling the building, which seats about 1,000 persons. The platform and the space around it was entirely filled with persons who had been healed through faith in Jesus, at least eighty in number. Our friend and brother, the Rev. L. M. Schofield, pastor of the church, happened to be absent from the city, to his great regret, as he subsequently stated in public.

We expressed our gratitude for the kindness shown by Mr. Schofield, and the officers and members of the church, during the month, and especially recorded our gratitude to God that our brother, the pastor, had accepted the doctrine and was preaching it.

We referred in our opening remarks to the gracious season of communion at the Lord's table which we had enjoyed that afternoon with many hundreds of believers in that place; and to the fact that a number of ministers had been in friendly and sympathetic attendance upon the meetings during the month. Amongst these we specially noted Rev. Dr. Hannon, pastor of the First Methodist Episcopal Church, South; Rev. Dr. Kimball, editor of the *Pacific*, the organ of the Congregationalists, who spoke and wrote to us and concerning us very kindly; and Rev. Kincaid, minister of the First Baptist Church of San Francisco, who heartily invited us to hold a Mission in his church, and from whom we had accepted an invitation to preach on the evening of Lord's day, December 30, which we subsequently did to a large audience, completely filling the building. The Rev. Dr. Tileen, president of the Swedish Lutheran Church on this coast, and other German and Swedish pastors, had also been present and expressed their sympathy with us and acceptance of the doctrine which we taught. These facts we feel it a privilege to be able to record.

We also had the pleasure of introducing to the great assembly the local Vice-President of the Association, the Rev. Dr. C. F. Lane, late of Tulare; the Secretary, Elder Cadman, of East Oakland; the Treasurer, Mr. G. Wood, and the Council of ten brethren and sisters.

We had a very large number of written testimonies in this Mission, and we introduced the stream of witnesses with a number of these.

Instantaneous Healing of a Dying Child without Human Touch.

On the afternoon of Saturday, December 15th, we received the following request for prayer: "Please pray for a baby now at the point of death with pneumonia only one block distant."

This petition came by the hands of Mrs. Carrie Strayer, 516 Van Ness Avenue. The following day (Lord's day) I received this answer: "God heard your prayer for that beautiful baby yesterday. At the time you were praying—from 3 to 4—a sudden change for the better was apparent, and it is now healed. Accept the gratitude of the happy parents."

At our request Mrs. Strayer rose and confirmed this testimony. In advance I read the following letter from the parents of the child: "Our baby was ill nigh unto death with pneumonia. She is three months old. She was suffering intense pain. Mrs. Strayer, a stranger to us, entered the room and asked if we would like to have the baby prayed for by you in the church. We had no knowledge or experience in healing through faith; but after her explanations we gladly assented to the kind service of her taking the request to you. We did not know at what hour prayer would be offered, but we all noticed a quick and decided change in the baby for the better at the very time that we subsequently found that you had prayed. The doctor calling at the same time pronounced her a different child."

Then they went on to tell us that the imminent danger was all passed; that within a few days her recovery was perfectly assured, to the great wonder of all who saw her at the worst. "We gladly and gratefully express our heart-felt thanks to God, who came to us in our great need, when our dear baby was sick; and also thank you and the lady who called and first opened to us the possibility of Divine Healing."

Another Baby Healed Instantly without Human Touch.

Mrs. Rawlinson, of 1217 Lombard St., San Francisco, testified that she had brought to us a petition for prayer on behalf of a baby of a neighbor. The following day she wrote: "The little three months old baby you prayed for last night passed a good night, and is improving." Mrs. Rawlinson then testified that the child was perfectly healed, and she expressed on behalf of the parents their gratitude.

Instantaneous Healing of a Fever-Stricken Child.

We spoke of a number of similar healings in the Mission, and said: "A dear grandmother brought to me a baby the other day. It was very ill, and supposed to be in great danger. It had a very severe fever and was instantly healed. Will the grandmother rise and tell us about the case."

Mrs. Charlick, 214½ Grove St., San Francisco, rose and said: "My daughter has sent you a letter of thanks concerning this case, but as I was used in bringing the dear child I would like to state what occurred.

"My grandchild was sick, and my daughter asked me if I would go and bring some medicine for the child. I said, No; but I proposed to her to bring the baby to see Dr. Dowie. She did not take very kindly at first to my taking it to Dr. Dowie; but I persuaded her, and I brought it. It was very sick, and burning up with a fever, and could not hold up his head until Dr. Dowie laid his hands upon him, and in about five minutes I took the baby away *perfectly free from fever.* He had not eaten scarcely anything; but when I got home he ate and went to sleep. That was two days ago, and he has been well ever since. The fever at once went right away. Before I left Dr. Dowie's room the fever was entirely gone, and the little fellow began eating on the way home, for he asked me to buy some crackers, and he ate heartily when he got home."

The letter to which Mrs. Charlick made reference was as follows: "A few days ago my darling baby was brought to you by my devoted mother, Mrs. Charlick, and she brought baby back to me free from fever and greatly changed for the better, through your prayer, and is perfectly healed. Neither myself nor my husband are such Christians as we wish to be, but, oh, do pray for us that we may become such." (Amens from the audience.)

We remarked that these three cases illustrated two distinct forms of Divine Healing: The first two without our seeing the children, by the direct power of the Lord; and in the last by the laying on of our hands, but the power of the Lord being identically the same.

Instantaneous Healing of Cataract on the Eyes.

On December the 7th we received the following petition for prayer: "I have a cataract forming on my eyes. Please offer prayer for me that by the power of the Lord Jesus Christ it may be removed." We did not know who sent this, as it did not bear any name. Fourteen days later another letter was handed to us, as follows:—

"DEAR SIR: I was told by three of the finest oculists in this city that I had cataracts on both eyes. Since attending your meetings I have been perfectly cured. I can see, and I read both fine and large print. I have been a Christian for many years, and now I have consecrated my life afresh to Christ. I felt a little hesitancy in testifying, as I wished to be quite sure that my statement would be correct. MRS. C. M. SMITH."

It appears from what we were told by this sister that she received the healing one afternoon amongst some thirty or forty others whom we prayed for and laid hands upon at the same time in a ladies' meeting. We then asked the lady to rise. She did so, and confirmed the testimony above recorded, saying that she lived in Springfield, Ill., and now lives in Berkeley, Cal. Her case was corroborated by several persons present who knew her, and the healing seemed to be a very perfect one.

Healing of Twenty Years' Internal Disease and Spinal Injury.

The following letter was then read:—

"206 KEARNY ST., SAN FRANCISCO, December 23, 1888.

"REV. MR. DOWIE—*Dear Brother in Christ:* I here testify that I have been healed by divine power of an internal complicated disease, of which I have been a great sufferer for twenty years. I was confined to my bed for three years. But my physician saw I would die if I longer remained in bed, and he procured for me a very complicated spinal brace and support, which he fitted to me. Through that instrumentality I was able to get up from my bed nine years ago, but I gained strength very slowly, and have never been able to do without it until about two weeks ago, when, after listening to the teaching of this beautiful healing doctrine, I was healed through faith in Jesus, the great Physician, instantly. I wish to express my gratitude to Dr. and Mrs. Dowie for their efforts to bring me the knowledge of this glorious light. May God bless you and your work. Sincerely yours, MRS. L. A. WILCOX."

We said: "This lady at a meeting of ladies told us her case in detail, and how she had taken off the spinal brace, without which she could not move a single step for nine years. She was in the meeting this afternoon at the Lord's table and could not be out at the meeting this evening, owing to family arrangements, and sent this written testimony. Will her friends who are present corroborate this testimony?" This was done by several persons present.

Healing of Catarrh of Twenty-six Years, and Imperfect Sight of Five Years.

We said: "It will be good now to take an illustration of how the Lord uses the testimony of those who hear the doctrine and go into other parts of the country telling their friends and neighbors of what they saw and what the Lord has done. From Borden, Fresno County, we have a very beautiful letter from Mrs. C. C. Easton. After referring to some other matters, she says, 'We want to tell you, dear sir, that since my return to Borden, after hearing you in Oakland in August, my faith has been strengthened in many ways; I have great blessings both spiritually and physically. I thank God that from what I saw and from your preaching I was enabled to accept this blessed truth that Jesus was a present healer.

"'I must tell you of my dear brother, who was healed by divine power after hearing me tell of the glorious work you were doing by the power of Jesus. He has been a Christian for twenty-three years. He has suffered from catarrh for twenty-six years. While talking with me after my return he said, "If such blessings are for others, why not for me?" There and then he prayed that God for Jesus' sake would deliver him from all his troubles. Now I wish to say that from that time he has been perfectly healed. He has had no trouble with his head. He had used spectacles to read with for five years. He discarded them at once, and now reads fine print by lamp-light for two or three hours at a time.'"

Healing of a Dying Man.

We said: "A few days ago we were asked to pray for a man named Delano, living at the Montgomery House, 613 Mission St., San Francisco. He had been given up to die by a number of doctors. Our friend, Dr. Lane, who is now on the platform, visited the case, with others. They tell me he was given up by six physicians. This afternoon we received the following note from this man: "'Praise God from whom all blessings flow,' your prayers have been answered. I want to say the tumor is going away very fast. I can raise my head quite straight. Pray earnestly that I may be perfected.' Two evenings ago, Thursday, February 7th, this man testified publicly at a meeting of the Divine Healing Association, San Francisco, over which we presided. He stated that he was entirely healed. The healing of this man was witnessed to by several persons in the audience."

Healing of Nervous Exhaustion, Dyspepsia and Other Troubles of Twelve Years' Standing.

Mrs. C. E. Shilabeer, of Solano County, spoke as follows: "I want to testify to the glory of God that I have been healed through faith in Jesus and your teaching, of nervous exhaustion. I had dyspepsia for about twelve years. About sixteen months ago I took dumb ague, which left me a perfect wreck in mind and body. I had four doctors. Then I went to the Springs and came home worse. My husband was advised to take me East; so he took me to Boston. I tried one of those Christian Scientists, and I do think with you, Bro. Dowie, it is the devil's own work. I know I would have been better off if I had never went near that woman. I came back no better. I heard of Dr. and Mrs. Dowie holding these healing meetings in the Grand Opera House, and I came down to the city nervous and aching in every limb. You were talking that afternoon, among other things, of the necessity of giving ourselves up entirely and trusting in Jesus. I said I shall trust Jesus and give up medicine, and I did so, and from that day I began to get better. I was just thinking yesterday how strong I was getting. I am quite well of all my nervous trouble. I thank God for sending Dr. and Mrs. Dowie among us. I feel they will be the means of bringing great blessings to many, and bring many to Christ. May God bless them both."

Healing of Rheumatism of Six Years' Standing.

Mrs. A. Darby, 214½ Sixth Street, San Francisco, said: "I wish to express my thanks to God, and I rejoice that it was His will to send Dr. Dowie out as His agent to enlighten us and to help us to understand more fully the power and willingness of Jesus to heal the diseases of the body now at this time as when here in the flesh. Bless His holy name. For six years I suffered from rheumatism from the crown of my head to the soles of my feet. I tried almost everything I could get, with only temporary relief. All the time I was asking God to bless the means I was using, but for the last two years some of our best physicians have told me that I could never be cured. But since coming to your meetings and hearing the teaching of Jesus through you so beautifully explained, I do thank my Heavenly Father for the blessings received both spiritually and bodily. My rheumatism has almost entirely disappeared, and I believe I am now healed. I have taken Christ as my only physician. I am resting in Him. Praise the Lord, I feel quite well."

Healing of Internal Complaints of Many Years' Standing.

Mrs. Meyer, 407 O'Farrell Street, San Francisco, wrote her testimony, which we cannot publish, giving glory to God for her perfect healing.

Healing of a Minister's Wife in Ontario, Canada.

The Rev. J. E. Irvin, Ontario, Canada, sent a telegram to us asking us to pray for his wife, who was in a very critical condition, on December the 1st. On that date he writes us from Niagara Falls, as follows:—

"MY VERY DEAR BROTHER: I believe I ought now to write you this morning, and say to the glory of God that answer to the prayer which you offered has been perfectly given. We have had a wonderful victory in prayer. It is now about an hour ago; we have expected you would be praying about that time."

We would add that the brother who writes this letter had been attending our Mission in the Grand Opera House and had been recalled to his home by telegraph, owing to the dangerous illness of his wife. Recently we received from him a long letter, telling us that he had been greatly encouraged by his visit here, and helped by all that he saw and heard. He sent us at the same time an excellent little tract which he had written, and a program of meetings held at his house attended by many ministers from the neighborhood, in which he taught the doctrine of Divine Healing, and gave accounts of the work in which we have been engaged.

Healing of Twenty Years' Suffering from a Bone Felon on the Right Hand.

Mrs. Rawlinson, 1217 Lombard Street, testified as follows:—

"I suffered for over twenty years from a bone felon on the thumb of my right hand. I applied to many doctors for relief, and got none. All told me I must have my thumb taken off. This I refused to have done. At last to my joy I heard Dr. Dowie's teaching in the Grand Opera House, and through faith in Jesus my thumb has been perfectly healed."

Mr. Rawlinson, husband of this lady, rose and confirmed her testimony.

Healing of a Young Lady Doctor.

Dr. Mary D. Fletcher, of Fresno, returned thanks for her restoration to health through faith in Jesus, after illness from what might have been a serious fall. We said, "She is Elder Cadman's sister, and he will perhaps speak for her."

Mr. Cadman said: "I will only say, dear friends, that my sister-in-law had been very sick, and she was obliged to leave Fresno and come home to the folks. When she came home my father told her about this teaching, and in her room alone he knelt by her bedside and asked God, in the name of Jesus, to make her strong. She is a Christian. She wanted to do all she could for Christ. She felt that she could not while she was weak. She got the blessing. She never saw Mr. Dowie. The blessing came alone in her own room."

The Restoration of Hearing to a Deaf Mute.

A few weeks ago we said we had a petition to this effect: "Please pray to Jesus to heal me. I am a deaf mute. KATE BRADLEY."

This young lady, at her own request, testified yesterday afternoon publicly, and showed all who were present that she could hear. Will all those who were present who heard Katie Bradley repeat the words after me that I spoke into her ear, stand. About fifty persons in the building rose. It was a very interesting sight to see this dear girl, who had been a deaf mute from her second year (now apparently about nineteen), repeat the words that were spoken to her. She sent in a little thanksgiving note, which we have mislaid. The case is not perfected, but we trust will be.

Healing of a Skin Disease.

Mrs. Desmond, of No. 3 Golden Gate Avenue, testified to the healing of her little son, who had a very bad rash over his whole body, and is now quite well.

Healing of Whooping-Cough.

Mr. and Mrs. Edmonds, 451 Jessie Street, S. F., returned thanks to God for having healed their child of whooping-cough in direct answers to our prayers.

Healing of Consumption, Catarrh, Diseased Eyes, and Sores on the Face.

Carl Sparman, of Sutter Street near San Pablo Avenue, Gaskill Tract, Oakland, a lad about fourteen years old, made the following statement:—

"I praise the Lord that He has healed me. First of all he healed my eyes, which were badly diseased, after you laid hands upon them. A little over a month ago I was getting pretty sick. I coughed and spit up something, and my mother came in in the morning and took out what I had spit up, and asked me how I felt. After I had told her she said, 'My boy, you have consumption, I fear;' and she told me I had spit up some of my lung. She said that Jesus was the only one that would heal me, and now it would be either life or death. My papa said the same. We went over to see you. I was very ill. You prayed for me, and I at once became stronger. The next day I came over again with my papa to see you. I saw you before the meeting. You again laid hands upon me in the name of the Lord, and I was healed entirely. I am well.

"I also had my nose all stopped up, and my head covered with big sores, and pimples on my face. I looked more like a dead person than one alive. I had the sores over three months. Inside of a week after you laid hands upon me they all disappeared. The pain in my side went away, and Jesus healed all that. I praise the Lord for all that He has done for me. He is my Saviour, and healed me spirit, soul, and body. He is my beloved Saviour." ("Praise the Lord," from the audience.)

The father of this lad stood up and confirmed the testimony, and said: "On the 4th of December I brought to Dr. Dowie my other little son, who had very bad catarrh, and trouble with his feet, but the Lord Jesus healed him."

Healing of a Severe Cold through Mrs. Dowie's Agency.

Mr. Richard Smith, 2515 Larkin Street, said: "For the glory of God I give thanks that he used Sister Dowie as an agent in his hands for the complete healing of a severe cold which I had for several weeks, and which had settled in my right lung, causing me to cough and spit some blood. On the day I was healed I was so sick that I kept my bed nearly half the day, and then I went to the meeting at the Opera House. But Dr. Dowie was so busy he could not see me, and I saw Mrs. Dowie and asked her to tell her husband to pray for me, not expecting she would administer to me. But to my surprise and joy she placed her finger on my breast on the right lung and said, 'Pray to Jesus that the pain may be taken away now.' We prayed, and that night I felt myself perfectly well, and have not been sick since."

This hearty looking old gentleman confirmed his testimony by striking several hard blows on his chest with his fist. We said: "That will do; you look healed. You thump yourself pretty well. If anybody else thumped you like that you might cry out."

Healing of Seven Years' Internal Trouble.

Mrs. Hassler, 2650 Folsom Street, San Francisco, said: "Dear friends, for the past seven years I have been afflicted with a severe chronic trouble, for the cure of which I have sought the best physicians in the State, but only obtained temporary relief. Until a few short weeks ago I felt I would never be healed. But thank the Lord I heard of Dr. Dowie and the work already accomplished through him in this State. I was anxious to see for myself and attended one of the meetings. I was fully convinced by his beautiful teaching that through faith in our Lord we could be healed through prayer. I had sought for relief in medicine, but in vain. No man could help me. I asked Dr. Dowie to lay hands on me and pray for me, and since he did I have felt myself better, and believe I am well."

We said: "The details of this case cannot be entered into. Like hundreds of other cases, it comes under the generic term of diseases of women.

"Another of those cases, and perhaps one of the most serious we have seen in the Mission, will now testify. We are not often staggered, but when Mrs. Dowie informed us of the details we felt just for a moment the exceeding gravity of the case, but we had faith given to us to pray for her healing, and thanks be to God she was perfectly healed."

Healing of Internal Troubles.

Mrs. Della B. Scarfe, 1320 Mission Street, said: "Myself and husband have attended all the Missions, and have received the teaching and accepted Jesus as our healer. On the 30th of November I went into the healing-room at the Central Presbyterian Church. Dr. Dowie prayed with me and laid hands upon me, and I felt the blessing come. I feel now I must give up all human doctors and trust to Christ for perfect keeping. I have not taken or used anything since whatever. I praise God I was perfectly healed of that terrible trouble, a healing which could not possibly be effected by any human remedies. I am getting stronger and stronger all the time."

Healing of Many Years' Catarrh.

Mrs. Anna B. Anderson, 547 Minna St., San Francisco, said: "I want to say to the glory of God that during this Mission I have received great blessing. I have had catarrh in my head for many years, and I suffered much pain. Dr. Dowie prayed for me and I felt like a new person, and I am going to trust the Lord for keeping. I am healed."

Healing of a Little Boy.

Adolph C. Jacobs, 507 Leavenworth St., San Francisco, said: "On December 7th I was attacked with a severe pain in both my temples and with dizziness in my head. My mother sent me on an errand, thinking the fresh air might do me good. I had to rest several times on the way on account of my increasing weakness, and I felt very, very ill. When I returned home I laid down, and my mother, who had been attending your meeting, told me to pray, and my sister went and asked Mrs. Dowie to pray for me also. Prayer was offered for me by Dr. Dowie in the evening at the evening meeting, and just about 8 o'clock, when prayer was offered, I suddenly felt myself as well as ever, and I am quite healed. I give God all the glory."

Healing of a Young Man Who Suffered from an Internal Complaint, and Was Injured by a Heavy Timber Falling on His Back; and Also Healing of His Sister in Scotland.

Kenneth McDonald, Golden Eagle Hotel, San Francisco, said, speaking in a broad Scotch accent: "About the third week of Dr. Dowie's Mission in the Grand Opera House, I was persuaded by Edwin McDonald (a young man who was saved and healed in the same Mission) to attend the meetings, which I did, with blessing to my spirit, soul and body. I received Jesus as my Saviour and my healer. I was healed of an internal complaint which troubled me.

"I asked prayers for my sister in Scotland, Parish of Gairloch, Ross-shire. She was perfectly helpless in her lower limbs, but the very day that prayer was offered for healing for her in this city by Dr. Dowie, my father wrote me, and said that, contrary to all expectation, she was able to get up and walk about. [Praise the Lord and amens from the audience.]

"The first week of this Mission I was hurt by a timber falling across my back. I went to one of the meetings, but, as Dr. Dowie was pressed by the people, I thought I would go home without relating my accident to him. But my friend, Edwin McDonald, would have me wait until he could lay hands upon me, which he did just as he was going out of the door. He laid hands on my back and the pain instantly ceased, and all the trouble of that accident passed away, and I was able to go to hard work the next morning, and I am quite well now. I give God all the glory."

Healing of Internal Troubles of Many Years' Standing.

Mrs. Carrie Strayer, of 516 Van Ness Ave., said: "I have been suffering from ill health for a number of years, which caused great nervous prostration, the principal trouble being in my head. Just here permit me to relate a dream. I pay no attention to dreams, as a rule, and I have had very few in my life. But the morning previous to my healing I had been attending your meeting and I was strongly impressed. I dreamed I saw a beautiful bird, white in color, flitting about me in the mazes of dream-land, and ever and anon it would return and alight on the left side of my head, close to my neck. This was repeated many times, the bird always returning to the exact place. The next day, December 19th, the Holy Ghost descended upon my poor weak head and body, quickening my spirit, soul and body, through faith in Jesus. Peace has come to me that I knew not of, and great spiritual revelation, and a restoration of strength in my head, which has not left me. I can testify to the positive healing power of the Holy Spirit in the meeting from the very first."

Healing of Cancer in the Tongue.

Mrs. King, of 1265 Center Street, Oakland, said: "I have had cancer in the tongue and throat for several years. Under Dr. Dowie's teaching I received Jesus as my healer. He has perfectly healed me, and keeps me whole to-night. Praise His name. I give Him all the glory. The cancer has entirely disappeared. Dr. Dowie laid hands upon me during his Mission in Oakland in the First Presbyterian Church, last August. The cancer was an active cancer. I could not bite a piece of bread, and was suffering constant pain. I have had many doctors. I will name three who recently treated me: Dr. Miller, Dr. Donnelly, and Dr. Darrin, on Powell Street, in this city. They gave me little hope. The cancer became very active, and was eating away my tongue. There were two holes in my tongue, but they are entirely gone, and I am perfectly healed.

Healing of Internal Cancer.

Mrs. Boillot, 1123 Greenwich Street, gave a very interesting account of healing of internal cancer seven years ago in Switzerland. We gave the details of this case in our report of the testimony meeting in the Lyceum on November 7.

Oakland Cases of Healing.

Some reflection having been cast upon the genuineness of the Oakland cases, we asked all those who happened to be present from that city to rise. Over ten did so.

Confirmation of Restoration of Sight in One Eye after Fourteen and One-half Years' Blindness.

Miss Annie Burkman, of 813 Peralta Street, who had been blind in the left eye for fourteen and one-half years, and disease in her other eye, again testified that both of her eyes were entirely healed of the disease, and that she could read quite clearly with the eye that had been blind from her infancy. We held up our watch at some distance from her, and she read the time with the eye which had been blind. It was then thirty-five minutes past nine o'clock. Our watch was held about three feet from Miss Burkman. We then remarked that this was the case concerning which an Oakland minister publicly said that she was just as bad as ever. This young lady testified shortly after her healing in the Grand Opera House.

Confirmation of Healing of Broken Instep of Thirteen Years' Standing.

Mrs. Elizabeth Rodenbeck, Foley Street, Alameda, also healed in the Grand Opera House, testified to her continued healing. She had come in on crutches, and walked away without them. When we asked her if she was perfectly healed, she said, "Yes; shall I show you?" Without waiting for an answer she walked quickly up one of the aisles of the church, and the audience broke out into an applause.

She also testified that she had been saved and spiritually healed in the Mission.

Healing of Heart Disease of 5 Years' Standing, and Confirmation of Oakland Cases Generally by One Who Knows Them All.

Mr. John Svenson, 761 Peralta Street, Oakland, said: "I will begin with myself first. I may say to the glory of the Lord that I have been much blessed by Brother Dowie's Missions. I have been attending them in Oakland and in San Francisco both. I was greatly pleased by his teaching, and at last I was even healed of heart disease that I have suffered with for 5 years. I don't look much as if I had been suffering from sickness, as you all can see; but I have felt very sick sometimes from heart trouble. I went to Brother Dowie and told him my case, and he laid hands upon me and prayed to the Lord, and the Lord healed me instantly. ["Praise God" from the audience.] I know that I am healed. I know the Lord has done it. I give glory to His name, and I will thank God as long as I live that I have heard the blessed gospel, and that I can believe in the Saviour, who has the merits to-day that he ever had; that He will not only save us from sin and death, but heal our bodies from all infirmities. We can trust the Lord in everything. He has made us and can and will heal us if we are sick.

"Now concerning the cases in Oakland who have been healed, I know them all. I know they are all true Christians so far as I can see. There is one case that has never given testimony in any of these meetings, a woman who has been healed wonderfully. It is Mrs. Soderstrand, who belongs to the Swedish Baptist Church. It was about six weeks ago, when the Mission was being held in the Opera House, a friend came to her house and they saw she was very sick, and she was expecting to die. I and my wife determined we would take a petition to Brother Dowie. So a petition was sent and she was prayed for in the Opera House. On the following Sabbath morning my wife went over to see her, and to her surprise found she was up, perfectly healed and attending to her duties. Prayer had been instantly answered. You can yourself imagine who did that; it was the Lord himself. Mr. Dowie has never seen that lady." (We added here that we had received her testimony in writing, and had read it at the Grand Opera House.)

Mr. Svenson continued: "Well, I know this lady perfectly, and that she is well. I know all these Oakland cases concerning whom this minister in Oakland has wrongly spoken. They are healed.

"There is another case of healing. A lady brought a little child 23 months old, that had been lame from the time it was ten months old, and when Dr. Dowie laid hands upon her it was able to walk. Do you remember that?" (Appealing to ourself.) "Yes," we replied, "the child was paralyzed for about 12 months and was instantly healed. How many of you saw that little child walk?" (About 20 persons in the audience rose.)

Mr. Svenson continued: "I can do nothing better than to recommend the Lord who made us all. He keeps us all. Oh, trust Him as a savior from sin, and also a healer in sickness. He will take care of you, spirit, soul and body."

Instantaneous Healing of 15 Years' Spinal Injury.

Mrs. Gerold, 823 Dolores Street, San Francisco, said: "I was in the Valencia Street car one day when I met a lady who said she had suffered from dyspepsia for twelve years, and could only eat a few things. She told me that she had gone to Dr. Dowie, who had laid hands upon her in Jesus' name, and that she was entirely cured, and she could eat what she wanted at any time, and had been doing it, and she knew she was perfectly cured. She told me that if I would have faith I could be cured. I have been a member of the British Aid Society, and I was so ill that I could not go any more to the meetings. My back was so painful it was not possible for me to go. I came here on Tuesday night last. I was very much bigoted. There was a woman there who was a Roman Catholic in her belief, and she was shaken by what Dr. Dowie said, and she at once gave herself to Christ. I felt a great deal of interest in her spiritual welfare, and was willing to do everything in the name of Jesus that I could for the welfare of other people. I came here again Thursday night and again on Friday afternoon. Then I asked the Doctor to lay his hands upon me. He told me at that time it was so late he would not be able to do it. On Friday night I came, and told the Doctor before everybody that I felt if he would lay his hands upon my back it could be healed. I knelt down and he did so, and I was instantly and perfectly healed. My physician had told me in April last that I must undergo a painful operation, but I refused, and I gave up taking medicine and looked to God. I always felt I would be relieved if I could only know God's way.; and now I am healed. My husband, who is present, knows that since Friday I have been an entirely different woman." (Calling her husband by name she said in a loud, shrill voice, "Stand up!" The audience laughed heartily and clapped their hands.) "Jesus done it all. I was told at dinner it was all very fine, this belief in Jesus, but that if my children were taken sick I would have to send for a doctor. I have two beautiful girls and a boy, and if they were taken sick this very minute I would not send for my old physician. I would go to Jesus. I was healed the moment Dr. Dowie laid his hands upon me and told me to look up to Jesus and leave my sin and weakness right there. I did it, and I am free."

Mr. Gerold, the husband of this lady, rose and in a very impressive voice said, "Doctor, I can only state that all my wife has said is perfectly true."

A lady rose voluntarily in the audience and announced that she was the one who met Mrs. Gerold in the car. She gave her name as Mrs Martinet. Said she lived on Twenty-eighth Street.

We added that the Roman Catholic lady who had been referred to by Mrs. Gerold, had found the Lord as her Saviour, and she rose up a witness to the fact. We also said that through her conversion a friend of hers had been brought to the meetings, and she had found Jesus as her Saviour.

Confirmation of Our First Case of Divine Healing in America.

Mrs. Brown, late of Sacramento, who was healed on June the 16th, and whose testimony has been frequently recorded, gave a very interesting account of her instantaneous healing. She said in closing: "When I came to see Dr. Dowie I came on a crutch, and I could not walk without it, but from the moment he laid his hands upon me to this time, I have been perfectly healed. Thanks to the Almighty, and to Mr. and Mrs. Dowie. I will be 69 years old Christmas morning, and I never felt better in my life."

Healing of a Presbyterian Elder's Wife and Family.

Elder Cadman, of the Presbyterian Church of East Oakland, said: "I feel very happy and glad." (Mr. Dowie remarked, "And you look happy too.") "I can testify to the healing power of Jesus. I don't think there was anyone in this city more prejudiced against this teaching than I was. I said two or three times to friends in our own church, and also to my father-in-law, that I did not believe in the teaching; that the days of miracles were past; that I believed we should use the means and ask God to bless them. I believed it, and I did so honestly. My father-in-law had been attending the meetings in the Y. M. C. A. Hall, and he urged me to go and hear Bro. Dowie. But I put him off, until, just to please him, I went, and it was the last night. It was just such a testimony meeting as we have here to-night, and from the testimonies there by the brothers and sisters who had been healed I dimly saw the truth of it. When Bro. Dowie went to Oakland I attended all through that Mission, and before I had attended many meetings I was a thorough believer in the doctrine of Divine Healing. So I went home and told my wife about it. There are many members of this church who know that my wife has been sick for a great many years. She felt, and so did I, that it was God's will that she should be so, and she bore it in that way; she just felt that it was an affliction that God had sent, and we must bear up under it and submit to it. We talked the matter over, and I showed her that sickness was not of God, but it comes from the devil; that Jesus came to destroy the works of the devil. She saw the teaching and the truth of it in a moment. She had never seen Mr. Dowie. I kneeled by her bedside on Friday night, and I put my hands on the back of her head, and asked God for Christ's sake to give my wife health and to strengthen her. She was troubled with extreme weakness in her back, and she just trembled like a leaf all over, and she said, 'Something has come over me.' I knew from the very expression on her face, and her look, that the healing had come, and I said, 'Nell, the Lord has healed you,' and she looked up with an expression on her face I shall never forget. And there we praised and thanked God. Just to show you the results, we had three little children; our youngest is a little baby only thirteen months old, and sleeps in a little crib alongside of its mother. In the night the little one would wake up, and I would have to get up and lift it out of the crib and take it to her, as she was not able to lift it. After she was healed she would lay on her side and reach out to that crib and take up the baby, which weighed twenty-five pounds, and bring it right to herself; and it requires a good deal of strength in the back to lift that weight in that way, out at arm's length. My wife has been able to do it right along, but never able to do it before.

"We have closed the medicine-box in our house. I had a box of medicines that cost us over $25—homeopathic medicines; we were doing all our own doctoring. We said, 'Now we will take the Lord for the children.' We had tests of our faith. One of our little children waked up in the night with croup. Dr. Fletcher was in the house, and she got up and came into the room, and wanted to give the little one medicine to relieve it, but I said, 'We won't do it; we will trust Jesus.' We knelt by the bedside, and I put my hand upon the child's throat and prayed. The little one went to sleep under the touch of my hand, and we just left it alone, and in the morning the child was all right. Just as simple as that. I tell you, dear friends, it is a reality. ["Amen," from the audience.] Do not trust to a physician, but leave it with Jesus, and He will honor your faith, and the healing will come.

"Brother Dowie said it required faith to testify for Jesus here. Well, dear friends, it does. But it does not now to me, because God has made my religion a reality. Before I used to worship God afar off. I was a church-member, but I never before realized Jesus as a present Saviour.

"I went to visit my father-in-law in Alameda just a little while ago, and as I was coming home, waiting for the train, I saw the Salvation Army at the Park Street Station, and I knew one of the members. There were two ladies and two gentlemen. Quite a large crowd had gathered around them. I stepped up to the Captain and I said to him, 'It requires a good deal of courage for those women to stand up there and testify.' He said, 'Indeed it does. It is not money that brings us here, but just the love of God and the salvation of souls.' Before I knew it, he said, 'Don't you want to say a word for Jesus?' I never thought that he was going to ask me to speak for Jesus in the street; and there were people who knew me there, too. I did not answer him for a few minutes. I just said, 'God help me.' I said, 'Yes, I will.' After the sister had got through I stood out there and gave a little testimony for Jesus. If anybody had told me a year ago that I would testify on the street with the Salvation Army, I would have thought I was going to be insane. My religion was just so deep. You want to bring your religion out into activity, and let people see that you are a Christian, and that you are working for Jesus."

Four Important Questions.

We said: "We have been teaching here for a whole month, and now desire to ask, first, Is there one single person in this building who doubts the *bona fide* nature and absolute truthfulness of these testimonies that have been given to-night?" (Many persons exclaimed, "No.") "If there is a single person, will that person hold up his or her hand." After looking over the whole audience, we said, "There is not one."

Secondly, will all who believe that the doctrine that we have been preaching for six months in this city is true—that is, all who believe that Jesus is a present healer—stand to their feet." Nearly the whole of the large congregation was immediately standing. (Mr. Dowie said, "Hallelujah; that is glorious!" "Thank God and Amens" from the audience.)

Thirdly, will anyone who believes to the contrary, that Jesus is not the healer, stand?

After looking all over the building and at the large audience filling it, we exclaimed, "There is not one. Hallelujah, the Lord has a victory."

Fourthly, will all here who have been healed through faith in Jesus just stand to their feet, and we shall try to count them."

A great many did so and we, with the assistance of Dr. Lane and Elder Cadman, counted, and found there were over two hundred persons on their feet. With great fervor we exclaimed, "Thank God for that!"

Instantaneous Healing of Sixteen Years' Internal Injuries without Human Touch.

Mrs. Gerans, 405 Turk Street, said: "Sixteen years ago I was walking through the street of St. Joe, Missouri, coming from Sunday-school, and the Catholic Christian Brothers were playing base-ball, so-called." (Mr. Dowie suggested in a little interruption that "unchristian" had better be put before the "brothers.") "I was struck by a ball in the stomach, and I suffered intense pain. I went to Boston, to Lakeport, New York, and a great many places. My father took me to different places, thinking that I could be cured. The last doctor I saw was Dr. Green, who lives on the corner of Turk and Taylor Streets, but he did not give me much encouragement. He thought he might 'patch me up,' as he called it.

"I heard about Brother Dowie, but I was afraid he was a Spiritualist. I was told not to go near him; that I would have to comply with all his doctrine and believe in his work. So I kept away from him. I was sick for a whole month and was not able to do anything, and I came to the meeting, and the first time I saw him and heard him speak I felt that was the true way to get healed; I knew there was no other source in the world for me to get healed. I finally gave up medicine and thought I might just as well die one way as another. I was very sick. On Friday afternoon, the 30th of November, I was sitting in the pew here and I became so sick I thought I could not possibly stay until the meeting was out. Brother Dowie said he was weary and he would let Mrs. Dowie speak for a while, and he sat down.

"I could not get hold of Jesus for myself; I was too bad a sinner, I thought; I was afraid the Lord would not hear me. I had prayed often to be healed, but I could not touch the hem of His garment. But I began with all the power of strength I had to pray that the Lord would help Brother Dowie that he could carry on this Mission. Sister Dowie was talking, and suddenly I went to sleep right in the pew. I never went to sleep in church before in my life. I don't know how long I slept, probably three minutes. I then straightened up (for I could not straighten up when I had those attacks before) and the pain was entirely gone. I was very much astonished. I was afraid to move for fear it might return. But the pain ceased, the sickness in my stomach was all gone, and I felt as fresh as if I had slept a week. I just felt like this:

"Now Jesus Christ has power on earth to forgive sins, and I want a wonderful blessing in my spirit. I felt that I had not the grace of God in my heart; that I had lived such a life that the Lord Jesus would not take possession of my heart. I would say the Lord has made me sick, and grumble at the Lord, and the blessing would fly away. I now feel that I have the indwelling power. I had felt so unworthy that I thought the Lord would not even use Brother Dowie for me. I went to see the Doctor twice, but he was so busy he could not see me. I am perfectly healed. I have had no sick spells, and I can eat everything I wish."

"I then asked: 'And you had other troubles besides of a serious nature?'"
"Yes, sir."
"You could only eat a few things?"
"A few things."
"Now this difficulty has all gone?"
"Yes, sir; on the 30th of November."
"And you are perfectly healed?"
"Yes, sir."
"What can you eat? Can you eat pickles?"
"I can eat pickles."
"Have you eaten pickles?"
"I have."
"Can you eat everything?"
"I can eat corn beef and cabbage."
"That will do, I think. I wanted a practical demonstration. Thank God. I know a good many details, not only of the serious injury caused by the baseball—and it was a *base* ball—but there were other troubles of a very serious character, and all were instantly and perfectly healed. You were sitting beside Brother Baker."

Mr. Baker said he noticed her coming in, and evidently in great agony, from the appearance of her face, and he called the attention of some ladies to her at the time.

Address by Rev. Dr. C. F. Lane, the Local Vice-President.

"Bro. Dowie has said that he has a new title, and we are glad he has. He is the President of the American Divine Healing Association; and this is a new name for me to be called. I am not ashamed of it, not ashamed to be identified with the American Divine Healing Association. I esteem it a great privilege, and, as I have said before, I have not words in the English vocabulary to express my gratitude to God and to Bro. Dowie for coming to America and to Sacramento, to this part of the world, bringing this beautiful gospel of Divine Healing.

"I was a poor, weak, sickly old man when Bro. Dowie came to Sacramento. I could scarcely walk a mile—about half a mile; was sickly and feeble. I had heart-disease. My food would not digest, even with all the medicine I was taking. From my brethren in the profession I sought counsel, and all they could give me, and all I could think of, seemed to do no good. As I said before in my testimony, I went to Sacramento to listen to Bro. Dowie's teaching. When he repeated the Lord's prayer, 'Thy will be done,' in speaking of God's will being done in Heaven and on earth and in us, I realized the beauty in that thought; that as there is no sin and sickness in Heaven, it is not God's will it shall be in me; that I might be healed and upheld, and have no sin and sickness. That was the thought, Bro. Dowie, that first entered into my heart. I always thought it was Father's will that I should be sick, and also my daughter. We frequently talked about it. And so we bore the sickness, and asked Father to help us bear it patiently.

"Well, we just went along, went along, praying and grieving and fretting, until I began to see it was not my Father's will that I should suffer sickness, and it was this blessed teaching of Bro. Dowie that enabled me to realize this: It was Father's will that I should be well and healthy, and have a strong body. So I just gave myself wholly to Him. I abandoned all medicine; but I am ashamed to say that I was not thoroughly confirmed in the teaching at first, and when I went back from Sacramento I just stumbled over a pill again. I had just got my eyes opened, but some way I thought I would just try another pill. But I felt so ashamed after I had done it that I would almost have given anything if I had never taken it. I was so ashamed and nervous I tipped over a chair, and I said the others will hear it and will know I have been taking medicine again. I have not taken a pill since, and never intend to take another one. I have just quit it altogether. I now believe I could walk six miles an hour, and I feel vigorous and strong, and, after toiling in these meetings for four weeks, listening to the sharp, clear voice of Bro. Dowie close to me, my head feels just as light and beautiful, and I sleep sweetly all night. Before I used to be rolling in the bed, distress in my stomach and burning and trouble in my head. Glory be to God, I am growing stronger all the time, and Jesus keeps me every moment. And now I am here, the local President of the Divine Healing Association in San Francisco.

"I am getting better in regard to my memory. It was so I could not connect my thoughts, but I am getting better in this respect all the time. I could not before get up in an audience and talk two minutes connectedly at a time, but my head is getting so much better that I am beginning to be able to quote Scripture.

"I am getting nearer to God all the time. And the best of all I believe Brother Dowie promises to pray for me; I believe he was praying last night; I believe you are all praying.

"Friends, we are going to have a blessed time, and God's people are going to keep on getting healed; and we are going to get Brother Dowie back here again. [Great applause.] We have just got the thing so beautifully arranged that Brother Dowie can't get away from us yet. We are going to pray for him, and he is going to pray for us; and when we have some pretty hard cases to heal we are going to write to the Doctor to help us out."

We then said: "Beloved friends, I feel if we were to keep you longer it would not be right. You have shown great patience, and although there are a large number here who have been healed and blessed who have not testified, and still desire to do so, it will be better now to close the meeting."

At this point we were interrupted by a fine-looking, intelligent, elderly woman, who rose from a front seat in the audience, and addressed me thus: "This is the first time I have had the privilege of listening to you, and I believe all that I have heard. Now I ask a great favor, if there is time, and that is that you will ask this kind audience to pray with you to God for a young lady who is deaf. She sits right here."

We instantly complied with the request, and a large number knelt. We prayed as follows:—

Prayer.

"We ask Thee, dear Lord, to bless all who have testified by speech or letter, or by silent witness. Enable them, dear Lord, to rest in Thee wholly for the keeping power. May they be kept by Thy power through faith unto salvation.

"And now we pray for this young lady who is present, and suffering from deafness, who asks to be restored to hearing. We trust she has faith to believe that she *will* be restored now. Many have been restored who have already testified, without any human touch; oh! grant unto her faith to rest in Thee now.

"And we pray for all those, dear Lord, that are sick ; for those who have been doubting Thy divinity. Oh! help them ; help the unsaved to find in Thee their Saviour and their Healer; help us all to find in Thee our all.

"Now let us go forward in Thy strength. Thou knowest, Lord, we claim to have done nothing, we have only been Thine agents, the power is Thine ; let all the glory be Thine.

"And now, Lord, this Mission does not close; the work will go on, and on, and on, and on. ["Amens" by the audience.] Let every church in this city get the doctrine. ["Amens."] Oh! that the ministers might preach it, so that thousands and tens of thousands, instead of hundreds only, might be healed to the glory of God. ["Amens."] Oh! may Thy ministers know with us that

> 'Thy touch has still its ancient power;
> No word from Thee can fruitless fall.
> Oh! hear us in this solemn hour,
> And in Thy mercy bless us all.'

"Thy word can heal us all. Oh! grant that everyone within these walls may be divinely blessed this night. We ask it in Jesus' name. Amen."

The audience then rose and sung the doxology with great fervor, and after the benediction was pronounced the meeting closed.

As our readers know, we had a very beautiful gathering of the friends of the Association on Christmas evening, two days after the above meeting, and after preaching in the First Baptist Church the following Lord's day, December 30th, we proceeded on the afternoon of Monday, the 31st, to San Jose, where we opened our second Mission. We continued there until the evening of Monday, January 14th, having had a most successful Mission, the report of which will follow in due course. But what we have given in this letter will be more than sufficient for one month. We will therefore hold over the report of the San Jose Mission until next mail.

We left San Jose on Tuesday, 16th of January, and opened our Mission in Hamilton Church, Oakland, Monday, January 21st, continuing daily until Monday last, February 4th. We resume the Mission in the same place on Monday, February the 11th, closing on Monday, February 18th. Reports of these meetings will also be given.

Report of a Praise and Testimony Meeting Held at the Centella Methodist Episcopal Church, San Jose, January 14, 1889, by Rev. John Alexander Dowie and His Wife after a Two Weeks' Mission, the Second Held in That Place.

[Reported by G. H. Hawes, 320 Sansome St., San Francisco, Cal.]

The meeting was opened by singing the hymn—

> "My hope is built on nothing less
> Than Jesus' blood and righteousness."

After prayer and the reading of many requests by Mr. Dowie, Mrs. Dowie read from the 35th chapter of Isaiah: "The wilderness and the solitary place shall be glad for them, and the desert shall rejoice and blossom as the rose," etc.

Announcements were then made in connection with the newly formed Branch of the American Divine Healing Association. Mr. Dowie then delivered an introductory address, in the course of which he said: "We desire to thank publicly our beloved brother, Pastor Gale and his officers, and the members of this church, for so kindly placing this building at our disposal.

"We also desire to thank the Rev. T. H. Lawson, and the officers of Wesleyan Methodist Church, who placed their church at our disposal for the first week of the Mission.

"And we wish to say that while we cannot continue longer here at present, we are thankful for the invitation extended to us to stay longer in your city.

"There are forty-one persons sitting around me who desire to publicly testify to their having received healing through faith in Jesus; and I wish to say a few words in introducing these witnesses for our Lord Jesus Christ. First of all, there are many of them whom I scarcely know except by sight, and some to whom I have scarcely spoken, excepting a very few words. In some cases they have been healed directly without any human touch. I give God all the glory when they are healed through my agency, but I am just as well pleased, and better in some respects, when they are healed without any human touch. Let God have all the glory.

"And now, beloved friends, it may be well first of all to introduce to you tonight

Some Who Were Healed in Our Last Mission,

And for this reason, that if I were to introduce first some that were healed today or yesterday or last week, some of you who are inclined to be hypercritical might say, 'These healings have not been tested; they may not be healed.' Well now, beloved friends, you can only take their own testimony at any time, and you can never be a competent judge as to whether they are healed or not, because you have never experienced their pains; you cannot see out of their eyes or feel with their senses; and therefore you have to rely upon your belief in their truthfulness, and their testimony must come to you upon their own word; and although there may be corroborative appearances, yet, after all, it is not upon the appearances that you can base the credibility of their testimony; they must be competent witnesses, and yet appearances go for something. Therefore tonight I think it is well to introduce first some of those who testified at the Testimony Meeting held in the First Methodist Episcopal Church, Dr. Jewell's church, last August. The first one I will ask to testify is our beloved Brother Lathwesen. You will remember that in that Mission he testified to his perfect healing. Dr. Bishop, who is still in sympathy with us, and who assures me he would have attended the meetings more had it been possible, testified that Brother Lathwesen was incurable, and all who knew of the case knew the same thing. The Rev. Dr. Jewell told you the same thing, and he was the one who first called my attention to the case. He said: 'I have a man, a member of my church, a beloved brother, who is down there at Pacific Grove dying, and, doctor, I do wish you could see him; I am afraid he is too far gone to be brought up.' Then Mrs. Lathwesen brought up a petition from Pacific Grove for prayer for him, and in that petition he wrote that he was daily expecting to be taken to Heaven, he was so ill and so sick. I said, 'Well, we will pray;' and I prayed and she prayed and we all prayed, but he did not get any better. Then she said to her friends, 'I tell you I will have to go down there and bring him up.' And down she went to Pacific Grove and she brought him up, and the first day he came into the meeting and heard the word, he was prepared by the Holy Ghost for the blessing. He was on that very same day healed instantly and perfectly of heart disease, I think of thirty years' standing, of spinal disease, and of a very serious cancerous tumor —everything disappeared. He was healed August 20th, last year, and here he is to-night to tell us that he has remained perfectly well, and has been able to do his work every day. He will tell you how many pounds heavier he is. The Lord bless him. Now, dear Brother Lathwesen."

Confirmation by Mr. Ch. Lathwesen of Healing of Spinal and Heart Disease and Cancerous Tumor.

Mr. Lathwesen, of 343 South Ninth Street, San Jose, stepped easily up the steps of the platform, and said: "My dear friends, I praise God with all my heart, that God, ever so merciful, He come down in such a great love after me, unworthy creature, and pick me up in mine great agony, in mine great sicknesses, in mine great—what shall I say—Oh! it is too much as I think about it. He relieve me of such a condition as I was in for thirty years. Many, many times I say to my dear wife, 'What I doing in this world; oh, what can I do? I don't see anything good in my hands, anything good in mine heart—what am I doing?' And she says, 'Wait, wait, you see a better time; nobody could do the work what you do, wait.' I get impatient, but I pray God give me patience. Many times I lift up mine poor hands and say, 'My God, remember me.' And He did. That I pray many, many times—I pray, 'Lord, stretch out Thine almighty hand before I die.' I am waiting, yes, I am waiting until last August I came in such a condition that God came down and stretched out His Almighty hand to me and cured me body and soul. Oh, what a God in Heaven; what a friend we got in Jesus! oh, what a friend we got in Jesus! What shall I say?"

Mr. Dowie asked him to tell how he suffered.

"Well, my dear friends, when I tell you the story of how I suffered, I have to tell you I lost my health when I was a little boy four years old; four years I had good health; was healthy in every way; then I fell in the water, and there I was in such a condition I was dead for two hours. I said many times unfortunately my poor father picked me up and rolled me so long I got my life again. Many a time I say unfortunately; but God had some work for me in this world. I suffered along and my parents called me consumptive. When I was about 32 years old then my heavy suffering commence, and now for the last thirty years I had an awful suffering; I wouldn't like to see a dog in the world suffer like I did; God forbid that I ever see such a thing. But I praise God there came a sweet time and a happy time ["Hallelujah!" from the people], and a glorious time, and God renewed this body, and now it is hearty and strong. The flesh on the poor bones was all gone; but since that time, about three weeks ago, I weighed myself and I gained twelve pounds since I was healed. Oh, what a God in Heaven! What a friend we have in Jesus. I thank God for the divine healing power; and I thank mine God in Heaven for this dear brother [turning to Mr. Dowie and shaking him affectionately by the hand], that he send him, and I was lucky to hear of him, and to see him and believe him. And now I am a hearty man. Praise God for it."

Mr. Lathwesen was about to leave the platform, when Mr. Dowie said:—

"One moment, dear brother; the other day a lady came to me and remarked that it had been said by a doctor in this place, who was a very kindly man usually, and supposed to be a Christian man, when visiting a patient of his, that this dear brother had never been healed and was just as bad as ever. She said, 'O doctor, you are entirely wrong.' But he said, 'I am right; I know better than you; I know all about the man.' 'Why,' she said, 'I am at Dr. Dowie's meetings with the man every day, and he is there every afternoon and evening, and his wife testifies, and he testifies, that he has not lost a single hour's work since he was healed, and that he is in perfect health, and he has gained twelve pounds.'

"I want to say that some persons imagined Dr. Bishop was the doctor to whom I referred and it was not. I do not know the name of the doctor, and if I did I would not tell it, because he apologized at once and he said, 'Well, I spoke believing what other people said, and I am ashamed of it.' Why should you repeat what other people say unless you have positive information direct?

"Now, Brother Lathwesen, have you been healed all the time?"

"Yes, sir, I am. Thank God for it." [Very emphatic.]

"All of the time?"

"Yes, sir."

"Able to work all the time?"

"Yes, and able to work as I have never done."

"Is there any appearance of the tumor?"

"No, it is all gone."

"You have got something else to fill up there now [referring to increase of flesh] and then the heart is all right?"

"Yes, sir."

"The spine is all right?"

"The spine is all right."

"You know he could not control his body at all. So far as you know you are a perfectly sound man?"

"Yes, I am."

"I bless God for it; the Lord bless you. Now we will have the wife come onto the stand; she can talk too, she has got something to say; she got healing in the last Mission, and got healing in this Mission. Come, dear sister."

Mrs. Lathwesen's Testimony to Her Husband's Healing and to Her Own Healing of Deafness, Paralysis, and Imperfect Sight.

Mrs. Lathwesen said: "I am very glad to testify to such a full house as is here and say what the Lord do for us. I say 'for us;' the Lord give me healing for mine own self—that I could tell—and got healing for mine husband too. Since mine husband is healed we have got a happy home; I never get sleepless nights with him now; he can lay down and go to sleep all night and get up in the morning and go to work. Before it was many times four o'clock before I ever shut my eyes just on account of him—he was so sick, and he would struggle in the bed, and I often thought this is the last attack he would get and I would find him dead in the bed. But, Brother Dowie, I can't find words to thank the Lord that he ever sent you as a messenger to San Jose. ["Thank God! Thank God!" from the audience.] The Lord keep you a good many years and send you to good many places to bring the good news that the healing power is just the same now as it was. I know it on mine husband; everything is gone; his whole body is renewed—I know that. If I go on the street often I meet twenty persons and even more, and they ask me, 'You believe that he is well?' and I say, 'I know it.' And they say it will not last a very long time. I tell them the Lord make him well, and He will keep him. I know that. I pray for that and mine husband pray for that, and Mr. Dowie prayed for it. And so the Lord keep him and that is five months; and when He keep him five months He will keep him so long as he has to live.

"And so we got a happy time. Always when I used to go down town the people would say, 'How is your husband?'

"'Oh, he feels very bad,' I would say. Then I would tell him and he would always feel so bad; and it got to be such an old story that I did not know what I should say. He suffer so much that I look up to the Lord often and say, 'O Lord, it is a little thing for you to relieve him from the pain.' Sometimes a sweat break out from the fever and pain; you don't know, you can't feel the feeling except you got somebody very sick mit you. They told me a few weeks ago that he was not sick—that he never was sick; that he only get it in his imagination. People used to say to me, 'Sister Lathwesen, if Mr. Lathwesen only would die I believe the people make up a collection and pay the funeral expenses.' [Laughter.]

"I was healed in the last Mission of mine hearing; I was so deaf I used to sit in the front seat at church, but I went out and I don't know anything about the preaching at all, but now I can hear anything; if I sit back I can hear everything.

"Then I got paralysis in my leg; I never speak very much of it; I thought if I speak too much my husband would trouble about it. So I keep it to myself—sometimes I speak to the women, and they say, 'You look out you get paralysis.' I say, 'Yes, what shall I do? I can't help it.' But the Lord relieve me of that.

"Brother Dowie was speaking about the spectacles and crutches for the eyes on Sunday, and I went with my spectacles in my pocket. But I never use them any more. To-day about twenty minutes before dinner I thought I have got to read a little if I shall testify to my eyes, and I read six chapters in the Bible without spectacles; and then I read here and there in Psalms, and everywhere I open the book I can read, and my eyes is so good. I thank the Lord for the healing power. ["Amens" from the audience.]

"O Brother Dowie, I am so glad the Lord sent you here; may he keep you for a good many years." [Mrs. Lathwesen, before leaving the stand, shook Mr. and Mrs. Dowie warmly by the hand, not forgetting the little son and daughter, who were close by. That she meant all she said, no one could doubt from the expression of gratitude upon her genial, motherly face.]

Additional Important Testimony of Mr. Ch. Lathwesen. Healing of Five Other Diseases, viz.: Catarrh of Lungs, Liver Disease, Kidney Disease, Piles and Tape-worm.

On the morning of Tuesday, April 2 (nearly eight months after the healing), Mr. and Mrs. Lathwesen called upon me at the residence of Mr Wm. Fruhling, San Antonio and Eighth Sts., San Jose, and Mr. Lathwesen, knowing that this edition of "First Fruits" was then in preparation, made the following statement in the presence of my host. He confirmed the same when I read it to the members of the San Jose branch of the American Divine Healing Association on the same evening in the First Methodist Episcopal Church, viz.:—

"I desire now to add, for the glory of God, the following to my previous testimonies delivered in San Jose, on August 3, in San Francisco on October 28, and again in San Jose on January 14, viz., I can now testify also that I was perfectly healed on August 20 of the following five diseases: Catarrh of lungs of 40 or 50 years' standing, liver disease of 44 years, kidney disease of 46 years, piles of 15 years, and a tape-worm from childhood. Some of these things were not pleasant to speak of publicly, but as I have ascertained that my last testimony is about to appear in 'American First Fruits' I feel it to be my duty to add these words. I remain in perfect health, working at my trade every day, and now, in my 63d year, I feel a stronger man than at any time in my life. I give God all the glory, and desire again to record my gratitude to Mr. Dowie as His servant."

CH. LATHWESEN.

Witnessed by Wm. Fruhling.

Confirmation of Miss Hudson's Healing of 15 Years' Rheumatic Gout and Inflammatory Rheumatism.

Mr. Dowie said: "Now, beloved friends, I am very glad to have that case. There are one or two more cases of the last Mission I would like to have testify.

"A lady came here with her brother, who is present here. Mr. Hudson, are you present here somewhere?" (A voice from the audience, "Yes, sir.") "You brought her from Canada, Mr. Hudson?"

"Yes, sir."

"I would like to say this dear lady was brought down from Peterborough, Canada, and he for her sake left his own beloved wife and child in Canada and came to California for the health of his dear sister. She had suffered for more than 15 years from chronic rheumatic gout, and inflammatory rheumatism. Her joints were in such a condition she had to make use of mechanical appliances to keep the bones from breaking; they were just as brittle as they could be; no oil in the joints. She was worn to a skeleton; only able to get about occasionally upon crutches, and in continuous agony for 15 years. She came here last March, I came here in August; she heard of the Divine Healing work; she came and listened to the teaching. One afternoon she came into the healing room and I laid hands upon her, and instantly she was on her feet and walked away without her crutches. She has walked to and fro ever since. She had been pining away for 15 years, until there was scarcely anything left of her to pine. She has been gradually gaining strength. I want to say that when I came down this time I looked at her from the platform in our first meeting, and I thought I knew that face, but I had to look at her two or three times in the audience before I was sure, for she had grown more fleshy, and she looked so much stronger, and so much fuller and ruddier in the face. I dare say you who saw her in the former Mission will say that too. I would like dear Miss Hudson to testify. I know she could not have used her crutches, for they have been in my care and possession since last August. I have a whole bundle of them."

MISS HUDSON STEPPED UPON THE PLATFORM

And said: "I am rejoiced to testify for Jesus; for His healing and keeping power. I have heard all over San Jose that I am worse than ever; that I am on my crutches and suffering more pain than I did before. I am rejoiced to tell you that I was never better in my life; for five months I have been in perfect health. I used to cry at night very often with pain; I now often cry in my bed for joy; I am in perfect rest after 16 years of suffering. I tried electricity for three years, and as for medicine I could not describe what I have taken—some of the most bitter medicine. I can never forget the joy that came in my heart when I heard that Jesus was a complete Saviour for spirit, soul and body. I was weary and anxious to go home, but it seemed as if I could not die, and then I wanted health; and when I heard Jesus would heal as well as save (I knew He had saved my soul), I accepted Him as my healer; and from that moment to this I have had perfect health, and I am thankful. Parties have told me it was magnetism, but I tell them different; I tell them I have found the right Physician at last; it is only Jesus that can heal when everything fails; there is power enough in Him; in Him we find a balm for every wound, a cordial for every fear.

"It is a wonder to me that so many of God's own children will not accept this beautiful doctrine. I thought the day after I was healed that everyone who believed in Jesus and were sick would surely accept Him as a complete Saviour. He is dearer to me this last five months than ever before. He sympathizes with us in all our experiences, and we can go to Him with all our little trials and troubles. Mr. Dowie told us Saturday night that 'there shall be no pain,' that the leaves of the Tree of Life are 'for the healing of the nations.' It rejoices me to know there is a leaf for every wound, and Jesus is the Tree of Life. I want every one of Christ's children who are suffering to fly right to Jesus. I have been so disappointed; my hopes have been so many times built up only to be blasted once more; but when we go to Jesus there will be no disappointments; He will be our Saviour and helper in every time of need. [Turning to Mr. Dowie] I can never thank you enough for being willing to come to San Jose for my sake, to teach me those beautiful truths; and though my heart is sad to think we may never meet again, I know I shall meet you on that other shore; I shall be waiting for you; I will be there to meet you." [Gives Mrs. Dowie an affectionate kiss.]

Mr. Dowie said: "I will ask her brother who brought her to California to tell the story. I never heard you speak before. Let it be a time of glorifying God. I know how glad you are."

Mr. Hudson said: "I am glad to be able to testify to the healing power of Jesus. I know my sister has suffered for 15 years; I cannot tell you how much she has suffered. I know now she is well.

"I have suffered a great deal from catarrh, but I feel I am healed from that. I think we have a great Saviour, and we can trust Him to heal us besides saving our souls. I am very thankful to Mr. Dowie for coming to San Jose to give us this teaching and that we are healed."

Mr. Dowie said: "Thank the Lord! you confirm all your sister has said about her case?"

"Yes, sir."

"She had suffered for 15 years?"

"Yes, for 15 years."

"And this was the last hope, to bring her to California?"

"Yes, sir. But the climate did not seem to have any beneficial effect upon her."

"Thanks be to God for His power. I thank you, brother, and I thank God you are healed too."

Confirmation of Mrs. Walker's Healing.

There was a dear sister at the last Mission came out of her bed and was healed. She writes me to-night. She is Mrs. Mary F. Walker, and she writes from the northwest corner of Third and Jackson Streets.

"I wish to testify, dear Dr. Dowie, that I have been healed through faith in Jesus. I never had any return of the trouble I had last July. My baby has been healed of severe illness, and my husband helped in answer to prayer.

"We are all so thankful that God has sent you and your dear wife to bring leaves of healing to suffering humanity. Yours in Jesus,
"MARY F. WALKER."

Mrs. Walker said: "I don't know how to express my gratitude to God for sending Mr. Dowie to us with these glad tidings; and I wish every Christian would embrace them."

Mr. Dowie said: "I am so glad that Mrs. Walker's sister and aunt have been brought to the Lord during the Mission, and that they are here to-night rejoicing in Him."

Instantaneous Restoration of a Young Lady's Impaired Sight without Human Touch.

Now there is another testimony belonging to the last Mission, although the dear sister did not testify at that time. A very sweet little case has come up. I will read the testimony, and perhaps the young lady, who is a member of Centella Church, will add something to it.

"137 North Tenth Street, San Jose.

"Dear Sir: I wish to give God the praise for having healed my eyes, which were so affected as to render me unable to read, write or sew, or engage in any similar occupation. The circumstances in brief were as follows: I had been having my eyes treated for 18 months by a prominent oculist, Dr. Simpson, and although they were improving he gave me no hopes of a perfect cure, and said I would have to wear glasses many years.

"But thanks be to God I learned through your teaching that Jesus was the great healer. I went home in prayer, and he answered my prayer by healing my eyes instantly, giving me a perfect sight. This was at the time of your last Mission in this city. Since then I have attended school every day and have had no trouble with my eyes whatever. Glory to God. Yours in Christ,
"Belle Bowman."

"Now let us see you. I think all know you."

Miss Bowman stepped upon the rostrum beside Mr. Dowie, and said: "I feel that I never can be thankful enough to the Lord for what He has done for me. I had suffered so much and so many times I felt the pain that I had in my eyes was almost unbearable. I had been treating for 18 months, and still the doctor gave me no hope of going to school and studying. Very often I would ask him if he did not think that after a while I could go without my glasses, but he never said yes. I never really had any hope of going without them; I supposed I would always have to wear them. The doctor said they could be made stronger so they would probably give me no pain, yet they would be weak, and I would not be able to see well with them.

"When Dr. Dowie held his last Mission here my parents went to hear him, and they would come home and tell me how good it was, and would explain to me what he had told them, and I felt that I must come and hear him; that if I could just hear him I would be healed. I went one afternoon feeling that Jesus would heal my eyes, and He did heal me. I had been wearing dark glasses for two years, and I took them right off, and I said, 'I know they are all right now,' and they were. About two weeks after that I started to school. I had not been for two years. I have been going to school every day and have not had a bit of trouble since. I never can be thankful enough to Mr. Dowie for teaching me that Jesus is my healer."

Mr. Dowie then said: "I never touched the dear maid; did not know she was healed until I came to the city on this last Mission. Now where is the magnetism in that? Some folks call it animal magnetism, and I am the animal that did it. If that is the case, I want you should pay the animal. Where is the animal magnetism, beloved? I didn't know the dear maiden at all; I didn't know she had been healed until this Mission; but like many others she followed the teaching and she said, 'Of course he is right; Jesus is the healer,' and looking to Jesus only, she took off her spectacles and she saw clearly. Who did it? You can't talk about its being imagination; Dr. Simpson didn't think he was treating a case of imagination."

"Dear Mr. Bowman, will you add a word?—the father of this young sister. He is a prominent member and office bearer of this church."

Mr. Bowman said: "I feel that it is only necessary to corroborate what my daughter has said. There is one thing she might have added to the last of her testimony, which would prove that she has used her eyes to a great extent; she has stood at the head of her class. So you see the necessity of her using her eyes a great deal. Before that time she could not go to the well for a dipper of water without having her glasses on."

"I have heard Dr. Simpson tell her myself that he had no hope that she could get along without wearing some kind of glasses. I believe in giving a man credit for all that is due to him. Her eyes were at one time very seriously affected, and they were comparatively improved at the time she went to this Mission in last August, but not so she could use them. She got out her books at that period a number of times and attempted to study, but her eyes would pain her so she would have to give it up. So we know her eyes were affected seriously at the time she went to the Mission; and we know she has never said one word about their troubling her since. I know one time when she was going out in the sun, her mother suggested that she put her glasses on, and she said, 'Do *you* wear glasses when you go out?' Her mother said, 'Of course not,' and she replied, 'Then *I* don't need them.'"

Mr. Dowie said: "Where is that mother? I think you had better stand up and confess your sins. Corroborate the dear daughter's testimony—just a word from you. It will be nice to get the mother's testimony."

Mrs. Bowman said: "She had a shade she used to wear, before her healing, over her eyes in the evening, and one morning as we were going out in the hot sun, I said, 'Hadn't you better take your shade along to shade your eyes?' She looked at me and she says, 'Do *you* need a shade for your eyes?' I said, 'No; my eyes have not been bad as yours have been.'

"'Well,' she says, 'if *you* don't need it, *I don't.*' So that is all about the glasses."

Mr. Dowie then said: "Thanks be to God. How many of you know Belle Bowman, and know how she suffered with her eyes? Just stand. [A number stood up.] Her pastor knows it. Brother Gale, just add a word; you happen to be on your feet."

The Rev. Mr. Gale, pastor of Centella M. E. Church, said: "I need not corroborate at all sister Belle Bowman's statement, for all who know her know that she would not dissemble in the least ["Thanks be to God," from Mr. Dowie], not in the least, everybody who knows her, knows that. I know that since my pastorate began in this city, that many times she had to be in a dark room, not permitted to have any light at all, her eyes would not endure it. Thank God that he has heard her prayer and healed her. [Mr. Dowie exclaimed, "Thank God! Thank God!"]

"She was a teacher in our Sunday-school; she tried to teach, but had to give it up because her eyes were so bad. And the boys whom she taught felt very badly; they said, 'We want Miss Bowman to teach, we don't want anybody else.' Thank God she is now healed, and now teaches her class in the Sunday-school."

Mr. Dowie said: "Will all those who have been healed in their eye-sight in this Mission, please stand—who have got power to see? [Several rose.] There is quite a number who have been healed in their eye-sight in this Mission.

"I will ask this sister to speak."

Another Case of Restoration of Imperfect Sight.

Mrs. D. A. Brown, 52 South Second Street, said: "I want to speak a word, dear friends, for Jesus; nothing that I have done for myself or anything done for me, just Jesus. Last summer in July, at the camp-meeting—and there are a good many here to-night whom I saw there, and who know my eye was very bad. I went with it all tied up. It was all swelled up. Brother Newton held a Healing Meeting. I went up to the meeting, and the second day I felt that I was healed, and I took the cloth right off and went home; I never put it on again. The eye has been gradually healing ever since; but still I wore spectacles.

"Last Thursday Brother Dowie spoke about taking away 'the crutches from our eyes,' and the next morning at 11 o'clock I read a few verses in my Bible and went up into the closet and I prayed, and as I came out I picked up my Testament, and I said, 'How well I can read.' I never could see so well before. I went down-stairs and told my husband; I went rejoicing; I said, 'Praise the Lord, Jesus has healed my eyes.' And I read a few verses to him, and said, 'Just see how well I can read in this Testament without my glasses.' He handed me a paper, the *Youth's Companion*, which, as you know, is quite fine print, and I read a few lines off without my glasses. I have not had them on since. I praise God for it all. Now the same day I found some pills in the house, and just the looks of them made me sick to my stomach; and I threw them in the stove. I said, 'That is the last of medicine that goes down my throat.'

"I praise God for all he has done for me. My head and eyes never felt so well as they do to-night. I give God all the praise; and I also thank Brother Dowie for his wonderful teaching, and know I have been greatly blessed. May you be successful wherever you go."

Healing Instantaneously of Fifteen Years' Disease of a Young Man.

"Now there are to be other classes of healing. The first person healed in this Mission is a brother, Charles P. Grant. He is a native of the State of Maine, and has been in this country about two years; is working upon the corner of Julian and Fifteenth Streets. He was healed in the first days of the Mission, when the Lord opened his understanding as to the Scriptures, and he sought and received healing of fifteen years' trouble."

Mr. Grant said: "I have had suffering more or less all my life. I think it was on New Year's night you spoke on the 'Two Chains.' That night I was healed through faith in Jesus. I am a native of New England. I came out to this country partly for my health, and I thank the Lord I got it. Last summer working in the orchards I felt pretty tired, not fit either to live or die, that is about the way anybody feels when they are sick; the curse is on them. I wrote to my sister something about it; I felt so that I never would get well unless by a miracle. When you opened your Mission here on New Year's eve, that convinced me that Jesus was the Healer; and on the next night when I retired I asked Him in full faith with all my heart, soul and spirit and body, and He came in a bright, shining vision, that was GLORIOUS! THAT WAS GLORIOUS! UNSPEAKABLE! I can't doubt the divinity of Jesus Christ—I could not. He said He had all power to restore and to heal the sick and unfortunate of my class, and, alas! there are many such. I don't know, but I think that the full effects of the Divine Power was on me for about fifteen minutes. I was pretty near transfixed. When it went off I just jumped up and I shouted 'GLORY!' I was so full for I was healed and blessed. I have to thank you Mr. Dowie."

"Do you feel perfectly well?"

"I do."

"How many years did you suffer?"

"About sixteen years from dyspepsia, and the result of other troubles. The doctor said I had passed through enough for any man to pass through. Pretty nearly enough to lose my reason."

Mr. Dowie continued: "He suffered all these years as many young men suffer. The Lord be thanked; He has put him perfectly right."

Mr. Grant said: "The Lord says His word shall stand forever; not one jot or tittle but shall be fulfilled." ["Hallelujah!" from Mr. Dowie.]

Remarkable Conversion and Healing.

"I am empowered to testify on behalf of Mr. Chapman, of Polhemus Street, between Santa Clara and San Jose. The story is an exceedingly interesting one; I would like to state it just as it has been stated by himself publicly in this place this afternoon. He has been at the meetings from 11 A. M. to-day, and as he is an aged gentleman, he has gone home with his dear wife; he has given me permission to speak for him.

"In this last Mission, about the middle of the month of August, 1888, at the First Methodist Episcopal Church, out of the many hundreds of petitions I received, there was one asking me to pray for an unconverted husband; the letter said that he was an open blasphemer, far from God, and that the writer, his wife, loved him dearly, and mourned that he was an alien from God. The petition was very touchingly worded, and amongst other petitions I laid it before God. A few minutes passed and we were engaged in other exercises, when a letter was handed up to me to this effect (I have it somewhere among my papers): 'It is supposed that a Mrs. Chapman is in your meeting; will you please break the news to her as tenderly as you can, that her husband has been thrown from his buggy and has been picked up for dead; blood is running out of the left ear, and he is lying unconscious, and it is feared he will die before she reaches home. Will you break it to her so she may not be surprised?' I asked if Mrs. Chapman was in the meeting. It was the very same Mrs. Chapman whose name was at the bottom of the petition for prayer for this husband. The lady rose in the meeting. How many of you were there and saw her stand up—will you please rise? [Quite a number stood up.] Thank you. Well, I went down to see her. I asked the people to sing a hymn, and I went down to see Mrs. Chapman, and I said: ' Sister, I have got some news; was this your petition for your husband's conversion?'

"Yes, sir."

"' Well,' I said, ' the devil is trying to kill·him; the devil knows that I have been praying in faith for his conversion here this afternoon, but I have just heard that he is thrown out of his buggy and picked up for dead. Now don't be troubled, he is not going to die, he is not going to die, don't be troubled.' She looked at me. I said: ' You go home, sister, it is all right, we will keep you up in prayer before God; he is not going to die. You will find him unconscious, but I exhort you in Jesus' name to *hold on*.'

"She went home. The next day they told me he was unconscious, still we held on, and said he was not going to die. The third day he was unconscious still, but during that day he woke. Now, let me go back into the history of the case. He had been ill for over two years, and on crutches nearly all of the time; seven months of that period he had been in bed suffering, and unable to turn himself without aid. But he would not hear the Name of Jesus mentioned in his presence, nor allow anyone to pray. His wife said she used to crouch behind the bed and pray silently. At the time of which we have been speaking, when he was hurt, he was in a condition that he could be lifted into his buggy and drive into town and attend briefly to his business, and then go back again. He had been doing that on the day he was thrown out and picked up in the condition I have described.

"When he was aware that we had been praying for his conversion within a few minutes of his being thrown out of his buggy, he said: ' The prayers of that man of God and of the people of God have been answered, and I owe my life to the mercy of God and to their prayers; and now if God will have mercy upon me I will seek His face.' And he set to work from that time to seek the face of God, and he prayed without ceasing, until it seemed as if his reason would go, that God would have mercy on him, ' such a sinner.' One morning he woke up with a consciousness that God had had mercy on him. No human minister was there to teach him, The HOLY SPIRIT alone ministered to him.

"And now he has been waiting for me to come down here to San Jose, and he has been at all our meetings. He had been upon his crutches until the other day, when he was there. It was last Wednesday, he was sitting there, and I asked a dear little Swedish woman who has been healed in this present Mission to stand up and testify to her healing, one afternoon. She did so. I then said, ' Now you say you were crippled—let us see how you can walk.' She had not been able to walk without limping, 'for years, but rose and walked rapidly to the front of this platform. I then said, ' Go round the church.' She then laid hold of this aged Swedish sister sitting here [indicating], and said, ' You, come too.' And this sister, who had been suffering from eighteen years of sickness, rose, followed this poor woman, and in doing so was healed instantly. Quite a number of other people in the meeting began to say they were healed. Presently I saw Mrs. Chapman talking to Mr. Chapman, and I said, ' In the name of the Lord Jesus, Brother Chapman, you rise up.'

" I had been speaking about the paralytic man in the 9th chapter of Matthew, and Brother Chapman just rose, left his crutches behind, and walked up and down the place, and upon legs with which he had not walked for two years. When he was thrown out of his buggy, his previous injuries were aggravated by the concussion, and the knee-cap split; but he is now in such a condition that he can walk about, and can take off the harness from his horse. He left his crutches behind him, and he was here to-day walking without them.

"All who saw that scene will you please stand? [Many rose; Mr. Dowie counted them and said, "There are thirty-two."] Thank you. Now that scene happened in the presence of many witnesses who have stood before you, and is no fable."

Healing Instantaneously of One Afflicted for Eighteen Years.

"Now I would like the dear aged lady who was healed that afternoon while we were speaking of the paralytic man, to whom Jesus said, 'Take up thy bed and walk,' to testify. I was so full of faith, and so were the people on that afternoon, that I told quite a number of folks to rise in Jesus' name, and they did it and were healed."

An aged lady rose and gave her name as Marian Neilson, residence 306 East Clay Street, San Jose. She talked the English language very indistinctly, and it was difficult to report much that she said. But she was very earnest and eager to tell about her healing, and caused a great sensation among the audience. She expressed her thanks that the Lord had taken away her pain, which was very great; one trouble was rheumatism. She spoke of Mr. Dowie's remarks about the paralytic man, and how she had been healed and relieved from pain afterwards. She turned around and said, "I thank you, Mr. Dowie; I thank you, Mrs. Dowie."

Mr. Dowie asked, "Are you quite well?"

"Yes, sir."

"How many years were you sick?"

"Eighteen years."

"And you are now quite well?"

"Yes; just in a moment my pain stopped, and I can go where I want to now."

Mr. Dowie exclaimed, "Thanks be to God. Look at her happy face. Let her husband tell the story. You stand up, dear brother."

Confirmation by Her Husband.

"My wife has been sick about eighteen years, since I lived in Iowa; she had been sick there nearly all the time, sometimes in bed. Then we lived in Tacoma, Washington Territory, and I have been here about eight months. She was sick up there all winter long; I had three doctors there, she had awful sickness there, and then I went down here for health, and she felt some better since she came here; but she had pain and she was sick; she had pain in the body all over. I said, 'We will go to Dr. Dowie and try to get healed.' She was very sick last month and now she feels all right. I see myself she feels better. I can sleep good now, and I can use my arms all right. She had rheumatism and great pain."

"You know she is well? Does she sleep well?"

"Oh, yes. She never could walk up town before, but she can do it now all the time."

Mr. Dowie said: "Hallelujah; and you got a blessing?"

"Yes, I feel a great deal better, too; I know my head is better, and I will praise God for what He done for me and my wife. I feel very glad to know Jesus saved my soul. I am free and clean; He took everything away. We have been children of God for about twenty-two years. ["Thanks be to God," from Mr. Dowie.] I know Jesus is the same now as He was before."

Mr. Dowie said to him, "You send that news to Sweden. Thank you. God bless you."

Healing of Twenty Years' Heart Disease and Many Troubles.

"Now I have got a little testimony here, written by Mrs. Nellie Hatfield, of 48 North Third Street, San Jose: 'For twenty years I have had heart disease, and sharp pain; had other disease in connection with heart trouble; was very feeble, and it seemed as if it would cease altogether, and that death was near. I also had trouble with the stomach. My food did not assimilate, and my body and limbs were swollen. I had difficulty in working, I suffered much pain in my head. A week ago Sunday night I was taken with pain in my heart, and instead of using former remedies I prayed to the great Healer, and the pain all left me and I slept. Wednesday night I felt the pains in my stomach, and I went direct to the Saviour and He completely cured this poor, pain-inflicted body. In the morning when I rose I was all healed; the swelling in my body and limbs was all gone, and I am now perfectly well and free from all my former complaints. I want to give God all the glory. MRS. NELLIE HATFIELD.'

"Just rise and confirm that testimony, dear sister."

Mrs. Hatfield responded: "I can't express, hardly, the gratitude I owe to God, for I can't tell the suffering I passed through. A year ago I lost my little boy, four years old. I had then this heart trouble, and after he died it seemed much worse, and I had those spells frequently, and the doctor would come two or three times a day. He said sometimes he did not think I could live five minutes; that it was not possible. Those spells seemed to come on faster and faster; I used to have them nearly all the time. My heart did not beat right, and my stomach was in such a condition that eating a small piece of bread would distress me, and I could hardly endure it; I was nervous, and could not walk a block without being tired out. One Sunday I thought I would come up here; but I was afraid to go out, for I had those spells so often. I never dared go alone. The Sunday I came here to the meeting I was taken with this pain in my heart when I got home. I had been taking medicine, and the more medicine I took, it seemed, the worse I felt. So I took it to Jesus, and I felt better in a little while. The next morning I got up and I says to my husband, 'I am being healed; I feel it in my heart.' He says, 'Ain't you kind of nervous? I think you are.' I said, 'No, I feel it, I KNOW IT!' That day I felt so well I thought I would go to meeting in the afternoon, and I came to the meeting; I felt I could walk so fast. Then I felt so well I went back at night. The Wednesday following I was here at this meeting, when this lady who has just testified was healed. I went home that night, and after I had retired this pain came into my stomach, and I said, 'What shall I do?' just like that. My husband said, 'You said you was going to take it to Jesus.' I prayed to God to take it away, and it was not five minutes until it left, and when I got up in the morning I felt perfectly well.

"When I used to go out with my husband I would be half a length behind him, and now he says it is all he can do to keep up with me. I am so happy, I feel like singing all the time; and I do thank Brother Dowie that he brought this news to this place, and so many have been blessed through him."

Confirmation by Her Husband.

"Will that dear husband tell us about the healing of his wife?"

Mr. Hatfield rose from the back side of the building and said: "I can say that all my wife has said is true. I will add more to it. For a year not only regularly did she take some remedy before she went to bed, but many a night I have had to get up and go for a doctor. I made up my mind the doctor was not doing her any good. We give her everything we could think of; she was taking pills and everything else. So this night she was speaking about (I don't like to get up nights out of bed and strike a fire and heat water, and make ginger tea, and all these things), I said, 'You just take that to the Lord; I don't want to get up.' ["That's candid," by Mr. Dowie.] So I just plagued her a little. She said, 'I won't touch medicine. I am just going right to the Lord.' I was just getting ready to light the lamp and I said, 'How do you feel now?'

"'Well, I feel pretty well,' she said, 'I am going to sleep.' Then I went to sleep. I told her the next morning when we got up that she had better be a little bit careful about eating, and see if you are healed or not. (I am ashamed of that now.) She said, 'I do feel it; I DO FEEL IT!' I said, 'It is all right, but wait a little while.'

"She spoke about walking and being behind; she always used to be behind this way, but now it is turned around, and I am behind this way. [He illustrated the two positions quite graphically, and greatly amused the audience.] So it is a great benefit to us; great benefit to me. I am praying for grace so that I will be able to keep alongside of her."

Mr. Dowie said : "I saw you both coming along to this meeting to-night, at a good swing in front of me."

Mr. Hatfield added : "I am expecting the Lord to just put me right alongside of her, and to keep up with her."

Confirmation of Healing of Spinal Disease.

Mr. Dowie said: "I want little Miss May Jackson, of Saucelito, who was healed in our Mission in San Francisco, of spinal complaint, to say a word. She is gloriously healed."

Miss Jackson said : "I would like to say a word for Jesus and tell what He has done for me. I suffered for ten years with spinal disease. I have been treated by the best doctors, and in the Surgical Institute in San Francisco, and the doctors all said I would have to wear braces all my life, and not only a back brace, but a leg brace. I have suffered a great deal ; I have been so I was unable to turn over in bed, and I could not move myself. I have always been told that Jesus sent the pain and I must bear it well for His sake.

"I heard Mr. Dowie in July last, and I at once accepted Jesus as my Healer. I heard him on a Sunday, and then on Thursday, in the meeting, while Mr. Dowie was praying—he did not lay hands on me—just all kneeling down, I felt the Lord was going to heal me; and I said, 'I will touch Christ.' Then I felt a strange feeling go through me, and I put my hand to my back and the curvature had gone down wonderfully. Since then the Lord has been healing me wonderfully all the time, and I have had no pain whatever. Before that I was so weak at times that I would have to lie in bed for days at a time. I thank God all the time for what He has done for me. He has not only been my healer, but He keeps me ever since. And I want to thank Mr. Dowie too."

Mr. Dowie then turned Miss Jackson around so that her back was to the audience, and he said: "Her back curved outwardly, now you see it is back, in an opposite way. [To all appearance her back was perfectly natural.] The dear young sister has been taking care of my little daughter at her home, and she is her father's housekeeper, and she can take care of the whole household; she took good care of my little girl. She is a very happy little lady, as you can see, and she is able to tell what the Lord has done for her."

Our Perplexity.

Mr. Dowie said, with an air of perplexity, "There are so many here who have been healed, that I shall have to ask some to give short testimonies. We have a number of most interesting cases."

Healing of Ten Years' Asthma, Catarrh and Gravel.

Mr. Dowie then called upon Mr. F. X. Lussier, 352 South First Street, and said : "Our brother came just as he was on the eve of undergoing an operation of a serious character. He felt that he must come and hear what we had to say, and he has been healed, and ever since has been able to enjoy splendid health. I believe he is a member of this church."

Mr. Lussier said : "I have been sick for ten years; have had asthma, catarrh and gravel. I decided to come to California for the benefit of my health, but could not get rid of my troubles. Last week (Tuesday) I went up to see the doctor (Dr. Bishop) and he said it would be necessary for me to have an operation. I was going to have it done but my wife objected to it. I met Brother Bowman that day, and he told me I better go and see a Dr. Christ. I believed in Christ, of course, but I did not have any faith to get cured by Him. But on Sunday afternoon I came here, and Dr. Dowie asked me if I believed in Christ, and I said, 'Yes.' Mr. Dowie laid hands upon me and prayed. I felt healed. That night I went to bed and slept all night, and the next morning I felt better, and I have been gaining from that time till now. I thank God for His healing."

What I See—What I Hear—What I Feel.

Mr. Dowie then called upon William Fruhling, corner Eighth and San Antonio Streets, to testify, who responded as follows (speaking very fervently, with a strong German idiom, evidently with deep feeling.)

"The first thing I want to say is *what I seen*, and the next thing *what I heard*, and the next *what I feel*. I got about three points. ["Hallelujah, a good arrangement," from Mr. Dowie.]

"The first thing is I see Brother Lathwesen. I know Brother Lathwesen since came in town here, and he stay, I guess about a week or two in my house when he came here, which was about fourteen or fifteen years ago. And the next thing I been with him last August in the Pacific Grove, just about pretty near a month right together. Brother Lathwesen was so he could not walk very little, about half a block. I got my buggy and I thought I drive him around once in a while, but he could not stand even that. Then Brother Baker went down there (he live there), and I heard that Brother Dowie was down here, and the people get healed here. So Sister Lathwesen went down here, she thought so long as we staid there he would be safe, she was generally afraid to leave him alone. Then Mrs. Lathwesen sent word that he shall come right away down to the meeting, that he would be healed. Well, I and my wife was a kind of afraid, we knew how he was, he was just in such a state that we thought every moment it would be the last of him, because he went this way. [Illustrated by going through a series of violent muscular contortions.] He sit on a chair, and sometimes it seemed as if the chair would tumble right over. So my wife said, 'We won't say nothing this evening, for fear when he hears it, it will be the last of him.' So we waited till the next day, and then I sent word to Mrs. Lathwesen that she should come right up. That was on Wednesday; on Thursday we thought we would stay a week longer, and then we thought we go down, so went on Thursday. Sister Lathwesen came on the train and we went back with her and Mr. Lathwesen. On Saturday morning I heard that Brother Lathwesen got healed. Well, I tell you it was just so to me as if the mountains there had been moved, because I know in what kind of state he was. I know how he had been the last few days. It was just terrible. But the Lord change his condition altogether.

"The next thing is, I knew Mr. Chapman, who was so wonderfully saved and healed; I had a good deal to do with him, I know what kind of a man he was; I had been talking to him a good many times about Christ. But he was one of the greatest infidels I think I ever saw. It was about Good Friday, two years ago, there was a servant there, a German girl, and she came to our church, and so we promised to go there and see her; and so it was Good Friday, and me and my wife went there to see her; he was not at home, and his wife neither. This girl was there and she was distressed in her spirit, and so we talked with her a little, and after that we prayed with her, and she got converted in his parlor. The same Good Friday the girl got sick and she wants to leave, because she could not stand the work, there was a great deal of hard work, and she asks us if she could come to our house for a few days, and we tell her she could. One day I went down there to get a trunk, and Mrs. Chapman was there, and there happened to be another girl there just in her place. But a few days before I got the trunk I saw her, and she was a German girl, and I had been asking about her soul (because I was German too), and so I tell her about the church and that she could come there. We talked German. Mr. Chapman said, 'Now you don't come any more to my house, you get our girls to go away.' But it was not our intention at all.

"The next point, that is myself. I have been troubled this last four or five years. The first thing I had pneumonia and lung fever, and the next thing I had bronchitis, and sometimes I could not speak without coughing very much, and now I tell you I been going out this last week in the rain and the fog, and the Lord keep me. This morning when I was getting up I had a pain in my right side and in my lung and I thought I get another spell, and it seem to me the devil just had me and there was a kind of temptation. But I bless the Lord He just came in and the pain went away, and my lungs stuck right out here somehow or another [illustrating], and I feel just so happy. [Much laughter.]

"The next thing is, I praise God for His salvation. I know the Word of

God from my youth up, and I tell you I never experienced more light and more glory in the Word of God than I do to-night. The most precious thing in the Word is salvation, it is so true, it is just so light. I tell you that is the greatest blessing what a man can ever get when a man can read the Word of God and know what it means, for the salvation of the body, soul, and spirit. May God bless you all."

Forty Healed, Prepared to Testify.

Mr. Dowie said: "I thank Brother Fruhling for his testimony. Now I want short testimonies, there are more than forty persons here prepared to testify who have been healed; if anyone who has been saved feels like saying a word, please rise and do so." A gentleman rose. Mr. Dowie asked, "You have been saved in this Mission?"

Saved and Healed.

He said he had, and continued as follows: "That is one thing to be thankful for, I have been a good ways off from the Lord, but I felt seriously troubled about it. I did not hear Brother Dowie when he held his Mission here before, but I happened to come in last Sunday a week ago, and he made a strong impression upon my heart, and I said, 'O Lord, please forgive my sins.' My wife had told me, 'Now, when you go, let God heal you too.' Well, I had faith to be healed, and thank the Lord He has healed me in one way. I had an unfortunate habit of smoking; my wife has often said, 'I think we will have to put your pipe in your coffin, you could not get along without it.' I had it in my pocket when I came to church and I tried to get it out twice on the way, but the Lord seemed to possess me and I shoved it back again. When I got home, do you know I longed to smoke, but the Lord says, 'No, you shall not do that,' and the Lord has kept me this week.

"I will tell you another thing He has healed; He has healed my heart."

Mr. Dowie asked if he had smashed up the pipe, to which he said:—

"I keep it as a memento, if I should throw it away I might be tempted of the devil to buy another one. I will keep that to keep me from smoking; I have no other use for it.

"Another thing I can praise God for, I feel like I was a hundred pounds heavier and stronger, not alone in body, but in spirit. ["Hallelujah," from Mr. Dowie.] I can go on the street and carry myself upward. I praise the Lord from morning till night, and when I go to bed I sleep sound, and I have not done that before. This is all I have to say." [The gentleman gave his address as 57 Webber Street, off South Seventh Street, San Jose.]

"Is There a Doubting Thomas Here?" Not One, Brother!

Mr. Dowie said: "I would like to hear a few words from Brother Folsom. I am deeply indebted to the brother for all his kindness in connection with this Mission."

Mr. Folsom said: "I can't add anything to this testimony, it is overwhelming; can you ask for any more, are you not satisfied? *Is there a doubting Thomas in the congregation to-night?*"

Mr. Dowie took this occasion to ask all who believed the Lord Jesus Christ was the Healer, to stand to their feet, and nearly the entire audience rose, and he exclaimed, "Thanks be to our God."

He then said: "Those who do not believe the Lord Jesus Christ is Healer, will they just stand to their feet?"

Mr. Folsom said with great emphasis, "*Not one, brother!*" "They dare not stand up. I am like the brother here, the Lord in these meetings has done more for my soul and to lift me up than He has for my body, but He has done wonderful things for my body. Is there one in this house, is there one that has heard all of this that does not humble himself and get lower and look upon Jesus as his complete Saviour—not a half Saviour? This to which we have listened is a whole gospel, not a half gospel. Is there one word in it which you cannot receive? Has there a word been preached here but what Christ preached when He was on the earth? When the question came up here before the officers of this church whether or no Brother Dowie should be asked to hold meetings, there was not a dissenting voice. How glad I am that was the case.

"Now, when Brother Dowie goes away, this healing does not go away, this power does not go with Brother Dowie, he has only taught us the lessons where we could find this healing. And there are so many here unsaved that *these meetings are going to continue.* Come and be saved. ["Amen," from the audience.] Come to Christ, and then you can find the healing right here just as you have through Brother Dowie. Now these meetings are going on to-morrow night; come in; come everyone who don't know Christ and seek Christ and be saved, and then you can claim Him to heal your body. And, oh, how grand it is to have a Saviour that comes down to save the soul and heal the body and make us all complete!

"Now, while He has done great things for me bodily, He has done more for me spiritually. I see faces here all around me that I met in meetings fourteen months ago, and they know how I stood then; to-day I can't tell how much nearer Christ is to me. It is wonderful, and I am enabled with the help of Christ to do more in one day than I did in weeks. Here are sisters and brothers around me who met me in the First Church, now come and receive this Saviour as Healer, as a perfect Saviour.

"Now, Brother Dowie wants me to say something for my wife; He has done wonderful things for my wife, not only this time, but when we went to the other Mission she was wonderfully helped; it come in like a flood and partially overwhelmed her. She has been holding on as well as she could. And now she has been attending these meetings right through, until about Saturday, when she was taken suddenly ill. Sunday she got very bad, very bad, so that the pain, she said, in her throat seemed just like needles that went through her, and almost stopped her breath. To-day noon I told Brother Dowie, and he went over with me. She was lying on the lounge partially dressed, in easy clothes, a morning gown. She could not speak aloud, only in a whisper, and suffering very much. Brother Dowie talked to her a little while and laid hands on her, and immediately she was relieved, and there was only just the least feeling left. Her throat was so sore this morning that she ate nothing, but she rose at once after Brother Dowie prayed and laid hands on her, and went with him to the table this noon and ate a hearty dinner—one or two eggs and bread and butter, and drank some hot water, and this evening she is quite comfortable, but a little weak. So the Lord has done much for my home in the way of healing, but more spiritually.

"Accept this Saviour! I would ask every unsaved one to accept this Saviour that can heal spirit, soul and body. ["Hallelujah," from the audience.] He can raise you on a higher plane.

"[Turning to Mr. Dowie] I thank you for all your kindness to me and mine. But understand me, you have only pointed us to Christ." (Mr. Dowie said, "We give him all the glory.")

Trying to Close the Meeting.

Mr. Dowie said: "I do thank God for the dear brother's testimony. Now, beloved friends, I want to get to the meeting of the new Branch which we are forming here of the American Divine Healing Association, which we hold at the close. I will just ask all who have not testified just to stand to their feet—all who have been healed through faith in Jesus, rise! There are more than thirty standing who have not testified." [A gentleman back in the audience said he would like to say a word, and was allowed to do so.]

"Pray for Me!" The Cry of a Man Seriously Injured and God's Answer.

Mr. James O. Mitchell said: "I would like to say a word on this Divine Healing. I was under great doubt about it. Last Saturday a man was telling me about his own healing. Well, at the time I doubted it. He referred me to Dr. Bishop as to how ill he had been, and I went to Dr. Bishop and asked him about it, and he said the man was very sick and he did not expect the man would ever get out of his house again. This man has testified here to-night.

"There is another case I saw. A man, to-day, hurt his back at a house where I was, from falling, and I took him and put him in a wagon and took him home; he was in great pain. He went to bed, and was not there five minutes when he says to his wife, 'Pray for me.' That man jumped out of bed and said he was well, and we started off and walked two miles; fifteen minutes before, he could hardly walk at all. This man is a well man, healed through faith in Jesus."

Reasons for Being Particular.

The man who was injured was present, and Mr. Dowie called upon him to state his case, which he did. He gave his name as William McElanon, living at 77 Union Street. As the name was peculiar, the reporter asked for the spelling of it twice, and Mr. Dowie said to the audience: " I will tell you one reason why we are so particular. In Oakland, lately, a minister went to investigate some case of healing, and he said in a Pastors' Meeting in San Francisco, that he tried to find the first person mentioned in pamphlet 'American First-Fruits,' and he could not find the person at the number given, which was 160 Broadway; he said there was no number there, that it was out in the water. Now if that minister had been candid, he would have asked if there was any mistake. The correct number was 860 Broadway, and because of the printer's mistake, he read a paper charging that the healings were false. We are going from here to Oakland, and we shall prove *his charges* false, by the evidence of the people themselves, who will re-affirm their healing publicly. So we try to be careful and get the exact address."

The Words of the Man Himself.

Mr. McElanon testified as follows: "About ten o'clock this morning, I went out on Third Street, for Brother Clinton, where he is building a house, and I went up on the porch, and the railing was just fastened up, and I leaned against it and I went right over, falling about five feet, and struck on the small of my back across a piece of timber. I could not get up. They took me up and put me in the wagon; I could hardly walk, and could not move without pain. I ate a little dinner and went to bed. I asked the Lord to help me, and I began to feel better. I said, 'I know the Lord will cure me,' and I cried, 'Pray for me,' and then jumped right up. Now I have no pain; only at times, when I stoop a little, do I feel the slightest effect of the accident."

Mr. Dowie asked, "And this accident happened this morning?"

"Yes, sir."

"And you had heard our teaching?"

"Yes, sir."

"And you believed it?"

"Yes, sir. Brother Clinton took me home, he can tell about it." [Pastor Gale spoke to Mr. Dowie, and said the speaker was a member of the church, and Mr. Dowie so announced.]

Confirmation by One Who Carried Him Home.

Mr. Clinton was then asked to speak; he rose and said, after giving his name as J. E. Clinton: "I took him home from the building. He was assisted to the wagon with considerable difficulty. We drove him home. The riding in the wagon hurt him very much. When I got to his house we took him out, and I turned around and went away. I know he was quite seriously hurt. I see him now here, healed."

A Good Closing Testimony.

Mr. Dowie, with a good deal of enthusiasm, said: "Thanks be to God; that is what I call a good closing to the Mission. Here is a brother attends the meeting, he is a child of God, he listens to the doctrine, he is not sick, but suddenly an accident occurs, and instead of sending for surgical aid or medical treatment, the man calls upon Christ for help, and he jumps out of his bed and is quite well. Under ordinary circumstances a man falling like that might be ill for weeks and months, but here he is to-night. Praise be to the Lord Jesus; He is physician and surgeon and everything; He mends and keeps His people. Hallelujah to His name. We will give Him all the glory.

"Now, beloved, I would just like my dear wife to say a word or two; will you just allow me to ask her to say the closing words of the Mission. Come, dear. Mrs. Dowie will say a word."

Mrs. Dowie's Closing Address.

Mrs. Dowie said: "It gives me very much pleasure to hear all the beautiful testimonies this evening. I am sure we are all very grateful to God for His goodness, and that He has shown in this place that He is not only a Saviour from sin, but He is the Healer of our diseases as well; that we can take all our sins and all our diseases and lay them upon Him.

"I think at this late hour and after hearing all this beautiful testimony, you do not want to hear anything further from me to-night. I feel my heart is very full, and it has, indeed, been a joyful meeting; it has been joyful to sit here and listen to all that we have heard. God has confirmed His Word. The scenes we have witnessed here have been just the same wherever we have preached this gospel. This healing is indeed Divinely scientific—not that which is falsely called 'Christian Science'—but we know it is scientific because wherever it is preached we see exactly these results; we see the lame walk, the blind see and the deaf hear, and to the poor this gospel is preached. As one dear sister said, who is not here to-night, but who has testified in these meetings, she said when she first came to the meetings and listened to the Word, she could not understand everything (she was a Swede), but she listened. She said somebody told her when she first came that she would have to be perfect. 'I knew I was not perfect; but when I listened to the teaching that Jesus was the healer, that He was healing the sick; and when I heard it was to the poor the gospel was preached, I knew I was poor, and that was for me; I knew I was lame and sick all over in body, and the Lord Jesus made me to see that this healing was for me.' And she went home and asked the Lord to heal her, and he took away all her pains and all her sickness and healed her perfectly. That is the dear sister who was used to help this dear old lady here (Mrs. Neilson) to her healing; she said to her, 'Jesus did it for me, you come and He will do it for you too; He did it for me, He will do it for you.' We just have to go and tell others what Jesus has done for us and what we have seen Him do for others, and tell it in such a way that the people can't help receiving it; they must be convinced that 'Jesus Christ is the same yesterday, to-day, and forever,' that His words are true when He said, 'Lo, I am with you always, even unto the end of the world.' Jesus Christ is here to-day healing by His Spirit, and He dwells in the hearts of the believer, and He can fill these temples of ours and tabernacle with us; He fills our spirits, souls and bodies, and He leads us by His beautiful Word, and 'faith comes by the hearing of the Word of God.'

"We are so rejoiced that our dear Saviour is lifted up. He said, 'If I be lifted up, will draw all men unto me.' And He is lifted up as the Healer as well as the Saviour. As in the wilderness the brazen serpent was lifted up and the people looked upon it and were healed, so it is with Jesus; when He is lifted up before the people they see Him as the Saviour and also as the Healer.

"I am pleased to have been here to-night and to have had such a beautiful meeting; I thank God for it, and I just say to you all, God bless you; may He be with you all, and may you never forget this beautiful teaching as long as you live, for Christ's sake."

Mr. Dowie then spoke briefly and closed the meeting.

[Dr. Holmes handed to me the following note during my visit to San Jose, relating the incident narrated on pages 36 and 37 of "First-Fruits," and asked me to give a place in this edition.]

"SAN JOSE, Cal., Jan. 2, 1889.

"I desire publicly to say that the statement in Mr. Dowie's pamphlet, 'American First-Fruits is correct, for I was an eye-witness to the incident. I had just spoken to Mr. and Mrs. Dowie as they passed out of the church, her hand grasping his arm, and they had walked but a few feet when Mr. Dowie slipped and fell, and so great was the force of the fall that he was suddenly wrenched from her arm and fell with great force on the asphaltum sidewalk. I stepped to him immediately, and took hold of him and helped him up, and he and one or two others called on Jesus for help. That help seemed to come immediately. He looked at first somewhat pale, but, after standing a short time, he started for his hotel, accompanied by his wife and one gentleman. I went part of the way with him. This was almost night, and when the usual time came for services, the church was filled, and some said, '*Now is the time to test his faith and doctrine.*' Many were agreeably surprised to see him come into the church and conduct the services as usual, except that he did not use the arm that was dislocated at the shoulder. He did not seem to have any pain while speaking. The services that night lasted till nearly 11 P. M., and then he retired to his hotel. I saw him next day and he was apparently as well as usual. S. HOLMES.

Extracts from a Report of a Praise and Testimony Meeting Held in Oakland, California, in Hamilton Church, by Rev. John Alexander Dowie and Wife, after a Two Weeks' Mission, Monday Evening, February 4, 1889.

[Reported by G. H. Hawes, 320 Sansome Street, S. F.]

The meeting opened with singing of hymn 162,—
"My hope is built on nothing less
Than Jesus' blood and righteousness."

Mr. Dowie then said: "During this Mission we have had a very large number of requests for prayer; I suppose with those received to-day, about five hundred or six hundred petitions for prayer within the last fortnight, and God has very graciously answered in many cases.

"We are now at the end of this fortnight's Mission, but, as you know, it is the intention of continuing at the close of this week for still another week, but as the present Praise and Testimony Meeting had been announced, we felt that the program should be carried out, although we usually hold the Praise and Testimony Meeting at the end of a Mission."

Prayer was then offered by the Rev. Dr. C. F. Lane, and Mrs. Dowie read Isaiah 35

A Reply to a False Accusation.

Mr. Dowie, after making certain announcements, said: "Now, beloved friends, it must be very clear to you that it is not advisable that I should speak myself at very great length, nor do I think it necessary, further than to say a few words concerning the testimonies about to be given by the scores of persons around me on this platform who have been healed through faith in Jesus. I have taken no pains specially to get any person to testify; I have invited no one individually or separately to come and testify. Everyone who sits upon this platform to-night is here voluntarily, and what they have to say is entirely of their own free will. I do not dictate a single word of their testimony, and I am not responsible for a single word they say; they are themselves responsible before God. And I want to state clearly, and so that no one will misunderstand me, that *I have healed no one*, neither in this or any other Mission; those who have been healed have been *healed by the Lord*. We give Him all the glory and ascribe to Him all the power. 'Thine, O Lord, is the kingdom and the power and the glory.'

"I am informed that a public attack was made upon the work in the Oakland *Evening Enquirer*, in this city, by a Baptist minister named Fleenor. I have been told that person has said that many of those who testified in the Oakland Mission held here before, could not be found. There are none so blind as those who won't see, and no one will find such difficulties in finding people as those that don't want to find them. It has been a very remarkable fact that this gentleman has failed to find persons who are healed, and yet these very persons are here to-night to testify to their perfect healing, and say that the statements made in 'American First-Fruits,' pages 18-26, are true in every particular, and these are the statements which have been falsely disputed by this person. Mrs. H. P. Penniman informed me herself, the other day, and her sister, Mrs. Captain Gove, that they at once wrote to the local paper, the *Evening Enquirer*, stating that the assertion made by Mr. Fleenor concerning her case was not true; and they also wrote to the San Francisco *Chronicle*, stating that every word in 'American First-Fruits' was true. But not a line of that letter appeared in either paper. This proves that they publish falsehoods on purpose, and that they desire to suppress the truth.

Exposure of the Falsehoods of a Minister and Editor.

"Again, in the case of the dear girl, Annie Burkmann, of Oakland (pages 55-56 'First-Fruits'), who has been attending most of our meetings in this Mission, but is unable to be here to-night, it was stated that her testimony was not true. She was healed of blindness in the left eye, of fourteen and one-half years' standing, and she remains perfectly restored, although Mr. Fleenor dared to deny the fact. I took the pains to ask Annie Burkmann to go down to the office of the Oakland *Enquirer*—the paper in which this statement was made—and her friend, Mr. Wilson, and our Brothers Svenson and Pereau, went down with her at my request, a few evenings ago. She showed herself to the editor, and he examined her and her friends and admitted that she had perfect sight in the left eye. 'Is that so?'" said Mr. Dowie, addressing the gentlemen he had named.

"Yes, sir," was the immediate answer of all.

"And he took your names and addresses and said he would contradict the false statement made by Mr. Fleenor, in his columns, but he never put a single line in his paper?"

"Yes, sir."

"You will all see, then, that is an illustation of the animus of our ministerial enemies and of the fairness of the local press. You see I don't complain without just reason concerning the absolute unfairness of the local press and of the San Franciscan press, in this matter; they persistently publish falsehoods, and never published a truth when they got it.

"There are a number here who were

Healed in the Last Mission in Oakland,

and who will give their *viva voce* testimony; you will hear the living voices of those who spoke on the last occasion and were healed.

"I am told that the case of Mrs. S. Ransome, mentioned in the pamphlet as residing at No. 9 Fourteenth Street, is a mistake, and that it should be 709. That is just a little mistake in transcribing, possibly not the reporter's, it might be the printer's, and it escaped correction in reading the proofs. She says it is stated in Mr. Fleenor's paper that she can't be found. If he had asked us, we would have helped him to find her.

"This lady was healed of heart disease, and perhaps it might be well for her to just repeat her testimony as to whether she retains her healing. Her case is given on page 22 of 'First-Fruits,' and is headed,

'Instantaneous Healing of Heart Disease Without Human Touch.'"

Mrs. Ransome rose from the platform, and said: "My name is Mrs. E. Ransome, and I live at 709 Fourteenth Street. I can be found there. I stand here as a witness for Jesus. I came to the First Presbyterian Church when Mr. Dowie was here before, and I took about the third seat from the stand; I had not spoken to any person, and no one had spoken to me. But when he offered up prayer, I prayed to the Lord that if there was anything wrong with my heart that it might be put right (for I had an idea that it was not right), and I prayed earnestly that He would put my heart right. Then all at once such a throbbing took place that I thought I must cry out for help; it was all I could do to smother it. But all at once when Mr. Dowie stopped praying, it stopped. I can praise God that I have been healed and been kept ever since. I feel almost young again.

["Thank the Lord," from the audience.] I thank God and no one else; for Mr. Dowie never put his hands on me, never spoke to me, nor touched me. To God I give all the praise. If anyone wants my testimony they can have it either in private or public."

Mr. Dowie asked: "Were you suffering a long time from heart disease?"

"Yes, sir. Many times I had considerable trouble in going up a flight of stairs."

"And that had been quite a number of years?"

"Yes, quite a number."

"And you have been in perfect health ever since last August?"

"Yes, sir."

"Healing of Hip Disease of Ten Years' Standing."—Page 22.

Mr. Dowie then said: "Miss Josie Colienour has testified publicly that her testimony is correct. I believe in that case the *Enquirer* did publish what she said."

[A lady in the back of the audience, named Mrs. Thompson, here spoke up and said, "She is at Woodland at present. I had a long talk with her mother and she told me the girl had spinal and hip disease, and ever since you prayed for her she has not had one particle of it. Before that she could not sleep at night."]

Mr. Dowie said, "Mrs. Thompson, of Orange Street, Oakland, once a member of Mr. Fleenor's Church, confirms the testimony."

"Healing of an Eight Years' Decrepit African Sister."—Page 54.

Mr. Dowie then called upon Mrs. Williams, a colored lady, to confirm her previous testimony, saying: "Dear old aunty is young again. What is your address, aunty?"

"459 Sixth Street, near Broadway, Oakland."

Mr. Dowie—"She testified in the Mission at the Grand Opera House, that she was instantaneously healed of long-continued trouble. I believe she is known to hundreds of persons in Oakland as one who was almost an imbecile, unable to earn her living or do anything for herself. She tells us she was instantaneously healed."

Mrs. Williams said: "Stand up for Jesus. I can say that I was like the woman that is spoken of in the Scripture that had an affliction, I think for eighteen years, and Jesus loosed her from the bondage of Satan. I have been troubled from the crown of my head to the soles of my feet with neuralgia, and I couldn't wear shoes on my feet. The doctor that attended me if he were here would testify, but the night I testified in San Francisco he died.

"The first time I heard this gentleman, Dr. Dowie, was in San Francisco, I prayed that this man of God might come over to Oakland. I put such trust in the Lord Jesus Christ that I said there would not be any man or woman get any relief in Oakland if I didn't. Mr. Dowie came and I didn't know it. Then somebody said, 'Mr. Dowie is here.' And I said, 'Where is he?' 'At the First Presbyterian Church, corner Fourteenth and Franklin Streets,' they said.

"I went and dressed myself, and after a hard time walking I got there, and knelt down and prayed, and Mr. Dowie came beside me where I was, and he laid hands upon me. The next morning I got up and I did what I have not done for eight years; I went out and earned my dollar and a half, washing. I said I would go in faith in the Almighty and His Son Jesus Christ. I mean to testify for Him like Moses of old. ["Hallelujah!" from the audience.] I did my work; was there at half past six and never stopped till nearly six at night, and the lady said, 'Auntie, ain't you tired?' 'No, ma'am, I am working on the strength of Jesus Christ,' I said. I did my work and I came home like a little child, tickled to death, and showed my dollar and a half. 'Holy Moses, see what I can do; I have earned a dollar and a half,' I said. I had been sick for eight years.

"Brothers and sisters, I have one request to make, Don't fight this servant of God, for the arm of Jehovah has come down upon him. God has said, 'Touch not my anointed and do thou my prophets no harm.' No, 'it were better for you that a mill-stone was hanged around your neck and you were cast into the depths of the sea, than that you should trouble one of these little ones.' Remember when you are troubling God's people you are troubling the great Jehovah. But I must sit down, for I would talk here all night if I didn't."

[The African lady spoke with a great deal of life and earnestness, and greatly interested as well as amused the congregation. Mr. Dowie said: "Auntie can walk as well as talk, and is quite young again."]

"Confirmation of Previous Testimony."—Page 22.

Mr. Dowie continued: "Amongst those who testified at the last Mission was Miss Wilcox, who had been ill for about twenty years of various infirmities. She came into the meeting on crutches; laid down her crutches when she laid down her sins, and she walked away at once perfectly free, and she is here again to-night to testify. Some folks can't find her, we have found her for them. Will you give us your present address?"

Miss Wilcox said: "743 Minna Street, but I cannot be found there in the day-time; I can be more readily found at 1237¾ Market Street, any evening of the week."

"Now, dear sister, just briefly tell what the Lord has done for you, and how He has kept you. We want to confirm previous testimony first of all. It is given in the pamphlet, on page 22."

Miss Wilcox then said: "All I have to say is to the glory of God and the praise of his Son Jesus. I was twenty-eight years a sufferer. I was given up by physicians in Iowa, Illinois, Kansas, and also in California. I was troubled with various diseases. I received an injury when I was eight years old which has followed me all my life until seven months ago. Praise the Lord. For four years and four months, I might say, I was on crutches, and when I was not on crutches I was in bed. I was on my crutches two years, eleven months, and four days. The Lord has healed me and given me strength to walk. I received strength to walk at the end of the third lecture I heard Brother Dowie deliver, through his prayers and my own; I threw myself wholly on the Lord and asked Him to make me perfect, and He has done so. He is not only able to heal our bodies, but to keep us healed, and to keep us under all circumstances. Praise His name for what he has done for me."

"Restoration of Hearing of One Who Had Been Totally Deaf in Right Ear for Eight Years."—Page 22.

Mr. Dowie said: "Mr. Rudens testified in the last Mission, and he is one of those that 'can't be found.' He lives at No. 11 Telegraph Place, San Francisco. He was here this afternoon and confirmed his testimony."

Mr. Rudens was not present, but another party said: "I had a talk with him last night and he said his healing remained as perfect as at the time he received it."

"Healing of a Minister from Dyspepsia of Eight Years."—Page 23.

"I want two or three more of these cases; is the Rev. Mr. Green present? He is pastor of a German church in this city."

[Mr. Green was not present, but a gentleman in the audience spoke up and said he lived in the same house with him and he knew he was perfectly healed. Mr. Dowie then said that Mr. Green had been attending the present Mission, and had said his healing remained the same as was stated in the pamphlet.]

"Healing of Eczema from Birth in a Little Boy."—Page 24.

Mrs. Stacy testified concerning her little boy; she says that the testimony given on page 24 of this pamphlet is exactly correct.

"Healing of Five Years' Internal Troubles."—Pages 24 and 59.

"Mrs. Margarita Johnson, do you confirm the testimony given in this pamphlet?"

"Yes, sir."

"This is a very remarkable case. She was sick for five years and had seen ten doctors, and was in a very bad condition. Will you now kindly confirm your previous testimony, Mrs. Johnson?"

Mrs. Johnson said: "I have removed from 1068 Twenty-fourth Street to 1723 Eighth Street. I want to say the Lord is my Healer, first my Saviour and then my Healer. I was sick for six years with internal diseases, and I seen many doctors in Minneapolis and St. Paul. Then my friends tell me I better change climate, and three years ago I came out here; but everything failed. I saw many doctors, but there seemed to be no hope for me. For three months before I see Mr. Dowie, I could hardly leave my bed; I lose my appetite and I could hardly work at all. Mr. Dowie said the Lord is willing to heal as well as to save. I felt I wanted to be free from my sickness, and Mr. Dowie laid his hands upon me and I was healed; that was on the 18th of July; then I felt my disease again on the 23d of July, and I ask God to help me that I could rise up again; and in the night at twelve o'clock I felt the Lord healed me, and I felt a beautiful blessing, and I went to sleep; and while I was lying there I heard a voice, 'Satan desired to have you, but I have prayed for thee that thy faith fail not.' I ask the Lord that nothing should happen to me again. I felt free from disease, but I felt as if I was bound with a chain around my feet, and as though I could hardly walk. And I asked the Lord to help me and that I should be relieved. Then I got a bad cold and I lay sick again. I opened the Bible, and I read, 'Ask and it shall be given; knock and it shall be opened unto you.' I asked the Lord to heal me perfectly, to make me whole, spirit, soul and body. I was lying there and I heard him say, 'Peace, be still;' and I felt just like someone touched me. I felt perfectly free, and He seemed to be so close I wanted to touch Him, and I put out my hand and said, 'Lord, can I touch you?' And I felt something like a stream pour all over me, and I felt so happy; seemed as though I didn't have the same body I used to have; and He has kept me ever since. I give God all the glory, and I am thankful that Mr. Dowie came here." ["Amens" from the audience, and "Praise the Lord," from Mr. Dowie.]

"Healing of Ten Years' Chronic Neuralgia and Spinal Injury." Page 60.

Mrs. Pereau, Bristol St., West Berkeley, then testified: "I am glad to be able to glorify the Lord. I was a great sufferer from neuralgia for ten years; it had become chronic. It affected my spine and I was not able to lay on my back. Dr. Selfridge told me there was no cure for me. So I suffered on until Dr. Dowie held meetings at the First Presbyterian Church, Oakland, and I went there and heard the teaching. I took Jesus as my healer, and, the Lord be praised, I am healed ever since."

Healing of Cancer in the Tongue.

Dr. Dowie said: "There was a very remarkable healing of cancer in the last Mission held in Oakland, and I shall ask the lady to give her testimony; her testimony was not given publicly in Oakland, but she gave her testimony at the Central Presbyterian Church in San Francisco on December 23d last. The lady had a cancer in her tongue; I laid hands upon her in the First Presbyterian Church in this city. I have examined her tongue (and any physician can do so) and it is perfectly well. The lady says she is in perfect health. I would like Mrs. King to give her testimony."

Mrs. King said: "I reside at 1265 Center Street, Oakland. I am glad to-night to testify to the power of Jesus. ["Thank God," from Mr. Dowie.] He can do to-day just as much as He did eighteen hundred years ago. ["Hallelujah" from the audience.] I suffered with a cancer on my tongue for five years. The last Mission, through the teaching of Bro. Dowie, I accepted the healing power, and He has healed me, spirit, soul and body. While I have use of this tongue I shall give Him the praise. ["Hallelujah" and "Amen" from the people.] It is a great thing to stand and testify to this power, and it is what we are here for; to stand up for Jesus, and Him only. I give God all glory and praise.

"And there are other things; my eyes are better; I have new sight in Jesus; new hearing. Praise his name to-night. He wants no sickness, no cancers, no disease there. Oh, what a glorious thing it is to be a child of God! I am nearer to-night to Him than I ever was in my life.

"Brethren, do not persecute this blessed work. Oh, Jesus is here to-night! Give Him all the glory." [The testimony of this lady created great interest and enthusiasm, and there were constant expressions of approval from the audience.]

Mr. Dowie said: "May I ask you the names of the doctors who diagnosed and treated your case?"

"Dr. Darrin, he attended me two months; then Dr. Miller, who is our family physician; then Dr. Dohrman, and Dr. Sienna."

"And they all pronounced it cancer?"

"Yes, sir."

"And now you are perfectly free?"

"I am perfectly free."

"We will praise the Lord for that. I think we might have a Song of Praise. Let us sing, 'All hail the power of Jesus' name.'"

[The entire congregation seemed to burst instantly into song, and all seemed imbued with enthusiasm and spirit.]

End of Confirmation of Oakland Testimonies.

Mr. Dowie then said: "I don't think you wish to have any more confirmation of previous testimony given in the last Oakland Mission. Are you all satisfied? [Cries of "Yes, yes."] Very well. These living witnesses and their emphatic testimonies are God's answer to our false accusers, and I will not waste another word upon them."

Healings During the Present Mission.

"I think now we will take up some new healings of this Mission; that will come down very close. The first of these was that of a dear sister who was saved in this Mission. She is quite competent to tell her own story. I will simply introduce Miss Pereau, 1212 Seventh St. Miss Pereau is a public school teacher in your city; a teacher in the Cole School, I think. She had been compelled to leave scholastic duties on account of the state of her health, but is now entirely healed, and will shortly return to her duties."

Remarkable Instantaneous Healing of a Lady Teacher.

Miss Pereau, an intelligent young lady, who has lived nearly if not all of her life in Oakland, read her testimony, which was as follows:—

"For the past fourteen months I have been an intense sufferer from severe stomach disorder, which rendered me totally unfit to perform my duties as teacher in the public schools of this city, and compelled me to obtain, at the opening of the present school term, a leave of absence from the Board of Education.

"I was unable to digest or assimilate any food, with the exception of a small quantity of bread and milk, and at times suffered acutely from the effects of that.

"I consulted some of the best physicians in regard to my case, and tried many compositions in the form of patent medicines, but was unable to obtain even temporary relief. Our family physician, Dr. R. L. Hill, of this city, pronounced my case nervous prostration of the lining of the stomach, produced from overwork.

"Last Monday I sought and found Jesus as my Saviour; and on Thursday last, in Dr. Dowie's meeting, I accepted Him as my Divine Healer. Dr. Dowie laid hands on me that afternoon, and bade me in the name of the Lord to eat a good meal, which I did a few hours later, Dr. and Mrs. Dowie being eye-witnesses, as they dined at the same table. I ate turkey, vegetables, peaches and cream, cake, and an orange, from all of which I felt no ill effects. I ate a hearty breakfast the following morning, and have been eating my food heartily ever since. *I was instantaneously and perfectly healed*, and by the grace of our Lord and Saviour Jesus Christ I will remain so." ["Amen," "The Lord bless you," etc., from the audience.]

Mr. Dowie said: "This lady is well known in connection with the public schools of this city, and the case was just as she says; it was instantaneous healing; it was perfect; and it has every appearance of being permanent. She was healed last Thursday night; it is now Monday. I had promised to dine with her brother at West Berkeley that night, and she was there. We found a very nice dinner waiting for us. I said to her, 'Now you are healed. In the name of the Lord Jesus Christ you are to eat a good dinner.'

"'Why,' she said, 'I have only eaten bread and milk, and not even able to take that sometimes, for fourteen months.'

"I said, 'You must eat a good dinner in the name of the Lord Jesus Christ.' Her brother carved for her the turkey, and I said, 'Now eat.' She looked at me, but she went at it. [Laughter.] It was quite pleasant to look at her; she ate a splendid dinner; she took peaches and cream—the cream was nice and rich; she ate bread and butter, and partook freely of things she could not touch before. The next morning she ate a hearty breakfast with the family; I saw her eat eggs and drink coffee. This dear young lady has friends who know all about her case; I see two or three of her relatives present. We are very glad to have this witness; for she is an illustration of how Salvation and Healing follow each other; and her decision is leading many to Christ.

A Representative from San Jose.

"A dear sister has come to us from San Jose, who was healed down there only a few weeks ago, and her healing is rather remarkable. She brings tidings from the San Jose Branch of the Association, which is composed of over one hundred members. They meet every week in the parlors of the First Methodist Episcopal Church, and our dear friend and brother, the Rev. Dr. Jewell, is a warm helper in the Association. There are a number of very earnest friends there. I want to give her an opportunity to-night to tell of her own healing and of the healing of others whose cases are well known and reported in this book."

Healing of Twenty Years' Heart Disease and Other Troubles.

The lady referred to was Mrs. Hatfield, residing at No. 48 North Third St., San Jose, and she rose from the platform, and said: "I am only too glad to tell you what Jesus has done for me. For twenty years I suffered from heart disease. I had the leading physicians in Council Bluffs, Iowa, and from Omaha, Nebraska, and in Southern California, Anaheim, and in San Jose; none of them ever helped me. A few months ago a physician was called, and he did not think I could possibly live five minutes; he did not have time to give me medicine, but injected morphine over the heart. One doctor in San Jose said I had a tumor in the stomach, or a collection of water, he could not tell which. My stomach was bloated, and I could not eat; I was living on prepared food, and my food would not assimilate without a great deal of assistance. I had neuralgia in my head nearly all the time, and it affected my eye-sight; I could not read fine print at all, and spectacles were of no benefit; there seemed to be a blur before my eyes. The best I could do was to read coarse print a little at a time. I could not sing at all. It seemed that bloating of the stomach, or whatever it was, affected my singing. I used to sing in the choir, and I could not sing at all, even at home.

"The doctor had forbid my going out into any crowd; said it was not safe; I had spells when I would fall wherever I was. One time I was standing in the door and I fell right out on the ground. I was afraid to go to church; had not been for two months; I was afraid I would be taken ill there.

"The first Mission Brother Dowie held in San Jose, in August last, I seemed to receive a great deal of faith from his teaching that others could be healed, but not myself. When he held his second Mission there last month, I had not been out of the house for some weeks, only just a little ways, but I prayed to God that He would give me strength to go and hear Brother Dowie; I thought I would like to hear his teaching once more. I had no idea I would ever get well. I could not go but a little ways before I would be all out of breath, and my hands would shake if I took a paper in them. It was just from my heart; it never beat regularly at all.

"It was four weeks ago last Sunday I came home from the Centella M. E.

Church, where I had heard Brother Dowie's teaching, and I told my husband there were so many people being healed I believed I could be; 'I am going to give myself up to Jesus for healing; I can't live but a short time and I will trust Jesus while I live.' I knelt down and prayed to God for my healing, and I went to sleep and slept very quietly, which I had not done for weeks. The next morning when I arose I seemed very strong; I could walk and not get tired, and I was so happy. I said to my husband, 'God is going to heal me;' and he said, 'You are a little excited.' I said, 'No, I have the witness within.' I went to church twice that day and had to walk about eight blocks. I ate a hearty breakfast that morning. I attended the meetings until Sunday evening; I had company then and could not go. I retired about 10 o'clock and I was taken with a severe pain in my stomach, and I went to God with it again. And as I prayed the sinking feeling passed off, the bloating in my stomach went down, and all at once it seemed that before my eyes the words came, 'He giveth His beloved sleep.' I dropped to sleep in an instant, and the next morning when I awoke I was so happy. I sprang out of bed and I said to my husband, 'I am healed; just look at my stomach.' I could lap my clothes way over on my stomach. Now I can eat, I can walk, I can work, I can do anything. Thank God for what He has done for me.

"I don't see how people can doubt Jesus when He has done so much for so many different ones in this part of the country. I do praise His name for what he has done through Brother Dowie in our midst."

"In San Jose during the last Mission there was a Frenchman, a Mr. Lussier, who had asthma, and he had something seriously the matter with his throat, and lungs, and other troubles. There had been a council of physicians and they gave him no hope of recovery; and they had decided to perform an operation the next morning. A brother told him about Brother Dowie's meetings and asked him to go down there, and he went and was healed. In our meeting the other night he got up and testified that he was now well; he could go anywhere and felt perfectly well.

"Then there was a sister, Miss Hudson, who attended our church in San Jose (the Baptist Church,) she had rheumatism; she was so crippled that it was only once in a while she could go to church, and then on crutches. Some of the time she had to be carried, for she could not walk at all. The physician said her bones were all turning to chalk. She could not move her arm up at all. I saw her one day go into Brother Dowie's meeting on crutches, and I saw her come out walking without them, and she is walking now. I saw her just before I came up, and she was walking all around, goes to church, and she seems perfectly well—only she can't run, as I can, for my bones have not turned to chalk. But she is getting strong and improving fast.

"Then there was Brother Lathwesen. He had a cancer in the stomach, heart disease and spinal troubles. He was shaking all over, his arms would go this way [indicating], and his foot would go that. He was the worst-looking object I ever saw. I thought he looked more like a mummy than anything else, and I said to myself when he came into Dr. Dowie's meeting last August, 'What will come next?' He was so bad it didn't seem possible that anything could be done for him. He came out of that meeting well, and is well now. He attends the meetings down there now, and he can run just as I can. He is perfectly well. I saw him only the other night. For thirty years he had suffered in this way."

Mr. Dowie remarked: "You tell me that you bring greetings from a great many healed."

"Yes, sir. The last day you laid hands on sixty-one, I believe, I don't know how many of those were healed, but there were a great many healed in their eyesight and other troubles.

"I am only too glad to bring the news from the Association in San Jose, and to say in regard to myself that I can see, and sing, and run, and do anything, for all which I give God the glory."

Restoration of the Sight of the Left Eye of a Twenty-Six-Year-Old Lady, Which Had Been Blind from Birth.

There is a remarkable healing in this Mission, which I am very thankful to be able to present to the glory of God. It is this little lady here whose name is Ada Aspengren. She told us her left eye was totally blind from birth. She is twenty-six years old; she does not mind my telling her age, and it wouldn't matter if she did. I had the joy of seeing her give herself fully to the Lord. I then laid hands upon her and prayed. The left ear was affected, and the left side of her head seemed to be involved. I saw there was an obscuration upon the left eye, which was quite blind, but the film has entirely passed away. Any person looking at her eyes would only see that the pupil of the left eye is a little more dilated than the other. She can cover the right eye up and see with the left one very well. I will just ask her to close her right and tell the time indicated by my watch, which has stopped, I find. [The lady did so, looked at watch, and promptly replied, "Half past four."]

"That is right. That eye was totally blind, and I know it, because I tested her. When she closed her right eye she could not see anything, she could not tell whether I was holding up a piece of white paper or black cloth, she could not tell me anything about any object I held up. Now she can readily tell any object."

The young lady rose from the platform and said: "I am so thankful to the Lord that He opens my eye, when I heard the teaching of Brother Dowie. I was born blind in my left eye and deaf in my left ear. I bless the Lord I can see now and I can hear. I shut my right eye and I can see you all sitting here in the seats, and I am so thankful to the Lord. I cannot speak very good English, so I can't say very much."

Mr. Dowie said: "You are doing very well." [Responses of "Hallelujah," from the audience.]

She continued: "I praise the Lord for everything He has done for me. He bless me a great deal. I can hear pretty well now in that left ear."

[Mr. Dowie stood off at some distance, and in a moderate tone said, "God is love," and she immediately repeated it after him, having the right ear closed.]

Mr. Dowie said: "She can both see and hear, and we cannot add very much to what has been shown and said. I am very grateful for the blessing."

Healing of Serious Internal Trouble of Three Years.

Mrs. Stafford, of Oakville, near Toronto, Canada, rose and testified. This lady spoke so low the reporter could catch only a few words; Mr. Dowie, realizing she could not be heard, said when she closed: "This sister said that for three years she had a very serious malady. She came to this State to see if she could get any relief. She was attending our meetings and became violently ill; then her dear sister sitting by her side came and told me that she feared her sister was dying. But she had received the doctrine and would not take any medicine; she wanted me to go and see her, and I did so, and laid hands upon her, and she received the healing instantly, and was so well she was able to come to the meeting that afternoon, and has been coming ever since."

Healing of Tumor, Dropsy, Etc.

"I would like to have her sister say a few words, Miss Black, of Rockford near Chicago, Ill." [This lady also spoke low, and it was difficult to hear all she said.]

"I have been attended by a Mrs. Dr. Wilson. She told me she thought she could help me. My trouble was tumor. I came to Oakland the 1st of July. Staid until the 26th of September, when we went to Oregon; staid till December, and then came back. I was some better, but had dropsy. She told me she could help me. I could scarcely walk, and it seemed as though something came up in my throat and choked me. I went to Mrs. Murphy and she gave me remedies. I took the remedies two days, and then came down to Dr. Dowie's meetings, and was healed. God is my healer.

"'On last Saturday afternoon my sister was healed. The doctor laid hands upon her and she received healing.

"The dropsy is all gone; I have no symptoms of it now. And the choking is all gone."

Restoration of Sight After Twelve Years' Blindness.

Mr. Dowie said: "I wish to mention a case of great interest in this neighborhood, that of Mrs. Castro, the wife of a Spanish gentleman, Don Victor Castro, of San Pablo Ranch, near Berkeley. She is well known in this whole country-side, and is here to-night; has been attending this Mission with her dear husband, who is perhaps 'the oldest inhabitant' of California, since he was born nearly seventy years ago at the Presidio, near the Golden Gate, long before this city had any existence, and before the stars and stripes waved over this State.

"Mrs. Castro was thrown from her carriage about twelve years ago and became blind in consequence. She suffered also from rheumatism. She has asked me to-night to speak for her, and has said she would answer my questions which I might put to her.

"She came to the Mission held in the Grand Opera House in October and November last. I had the joy of seeing this lady, then quite blind, standing up in the Opera House amongst those who were seeking a perfect salvation in Christ, and she gave herself to the Lord fully. A day or two afterwards I had the privilege of seeing her in my private rooms. I laid hands upon her and instantly sight was restored. The sight has been increasing steadily since. And I think I am right in saying that the rheumatism has all gone?"

"Yes, sir."

"And she is now able to see. Her friend, Mrs. Dr. Smith, of 1002 Adeline Street, Oakland, who sits by her side, just told me that Mrs. Castro said, 'What beautiful wall paper!' as she went by one of the stores to-day. I will just ask Mrs. Castro to stand and confirm this testimony, that her sight is now restored."

The lady did so, saying, "Yes, thank God."

"I think Dr. Smith knew the case?"

Dr. Smith replied, "I do."

"And you know she can see?"

"Yes, sir. Many times she has passed her hands over my wife's face when visiting her, and said, 'I would like to be able to see you,' and now she can—I KNOW SHE CAN."

"I may say that this striking case has led to many happy results. I pray God just to perfect our sister. The sight is increasing steadily. The disease was one that oculists could not touch. I think, doctor, I am correct in saying this?"

"Yes, sir," replied Dr. Smith.

"I think she was one of your patients?" observed Mr. Dowie.

Dr. Smith replied, "I was the family physician."

"We give God all the glory," said Mr. Dowie, "and pray that this interesting case may have far-reaching results, and lead many to find in Christ their all, as our sister does."

Instantaneous Restoration of Defective Sight without Human Touch.

Mrs. Wixom, of 1778 Eighth Street, Oakland, said: "Dear friends, it rejoices my heart to-night to be able to say a word in praise of my Redeemer. Brother Dowie knows nothing of the healing which I am referring to. It occurred about two weeks ago. I attended a meeting where this sister, Mrs. Burlingame, was in charge, who was also healed in Dr. Dowie's Mission, and she asked several to read the Scripture lesson, and they all refused, then she came to me. To refuse such a request is something I never did, to refuse to do anything for God. I sat beside the sister and she handed me the Bible and asked me to read the 103d psalm. I never thought of my eyes being not able to read fine print, or to write a letter for some months. I had hurt my eyes sewing on black dress goods. She handed me a book and it was a blank; I could scarcely see anything. I thought to myself, What shall I do? tell the sister I can't read? Then it came to me to ask the Lord to give me my sight. I knelt in prayer and the book was open before me, and I asked the Lord to give me my sight, and that I might read His word in the Spirit. We arose and sung a hymn, and I took the Bible and read distinctly; my eye-sight never was better. I had almost forgotten to tell about it, because the Lord has been so good to me a great many times.

"On last evening this dear sister who sits by my side was at our house, and I picked up the *Herald of Holiness* and read aloud about a case of Divine Healing. I held the paper out at arm's length and read it very readily. My mother, who is present, was at the Mission when Sister Burlingame asked me to read the Scripture lesson, and my mother said, 'How is she going to read without glasses.' I told her, however, to ask the Lord to give me sight, and He did so. Praise His blessed name. I have believed in Divine Healing for twenty years, but never had the joy and pleasure of hearing the doctrine preached until Brother Dowie came. I have been a very earnest listener to the doctrine." [Mr. Dowie exclaimed, "Thank God, I am very much pleased."]

Confirmation by Her Mother.

"Where is the mother of Mrs. Wixom? I think she ought to give her testimony."

Mrs. Sturgis, of 1778 Eighth Street, Oakland, an aged lady, rose from one of the side pews in front, and said, with a good deal of vigor and earnestness: "I confirm my daughter's testimony. My testimony is that the Lord Jesus is able to save spirit, soul and body. In my own experience I have found it so. Every day I feel I am created anew in Christ Jesus. I have seen the time when I was always sick; now I am never sick, but always well. ["Thank God," from Mr. Dowie.] I had consumption, and I have had almost everything you can mention. Now I don't know even weariness. I am sixty-eight years of age, and Christ is my all.

Confirmation of Restoration to Sight of the Boy Born Blind.

Mrs. Richville, the mother of the little blind boy healed in the first San Francisco Mission, said: "My little boy received his sight on the 4th of July, and he is improving steadily right along. I now live at 353 Fourth Street, San Francisco. When I took him over to Berkeley the last time, he looked out of the window when we were on the train, and was able to read the letters painted on the fences—the advertisements. He could read them very readily. He is improving right along. I give God the glory. I feel it is my mission on earth to tell the story of how Jesus gave sight to my son born blind.

"I was wonderfully healed myself. I was sick about a week ago and I sent up for prayers to the little Mission on Market Street. I was healed in fifteen minutes; I was healed perfectly and have not been troubled since. I had rheumatism between the shoulders. I don't know what I had done to let the devil get such a hold on me, but he let go pretty quick, when I left it all with Jesus."

Healing of Broken Ankle and Rheumatism.

"I live on Foley Street, Alameda. I give God the glory. I was saved at the Grand Opera House. I came on crutches, suffering from rheumatism and a broken ankle, and I left my crutches behind me, and the Lord has kept me ever since, and I shall always have Him for my great physician."

Healed of Fifteen Years' Sufferings.

Mrs. Gerold, 823 Dolores Street, San Francisco, said: "I attended three meetings of the last San Francisco Mission, when I was healed. When I went there I could hardly lift my hand. It didn't take but three meetings to find out Jesus was my healer. I have remained perfectly healed ever since, and I hope to continue so. I feel perfectly thankful and satisfied. I was fifteen years suffering with this disease; but I am perfectly healed."

Instantaneous Healing in the Open Meeting.

Mr. Dowie said: "I would like to mention the case of a lady sitting at my right. It is a case of instantaneous answer to prayer under very serious circumstances, openly in the Mission. She was sitting here with her husband on Monday night last when I was speaking, and my attention was directed to her at once, for I saw her turn ghastly pale. I watched her, for I am accustomed to see quickly signs of anything serious. She gradually sank until her head lay upon her husband's shoulder. From the look of her face I feared she was dying. I instantly gave out a hymn, which the people sang, and went to her. With her husband's help she was carried into the room back here. She was in a most serious condition, one of complete collapse; her heart had almost stopped. We called upon the Lord, and laid hands upon her. When she was restored sufficiently, I went back to the platform and continued the meeting, and Mrs. Dowie took the case in hand and continued to pray with her. She had a very peculiar deliverance. The pain went away from the region of the stomach, and then she was able to bring up water, and in a moment she realized that she was perfectly healed.

"Her husband was sitting by her side unsaved, but our dear brother, when he saw his wife healed, came right out and knelt down at the Lord's feet, and found salvation. [Many expressions from the audience of "Praise the Lord," "Thank God," etc.] I will ask the lady herself to speak."

Mrs. F. W. Wetmore, 565 Eleventh Street, then said: "While I was listening to Mr. Dowie's lecture a violent pain took me in the stomach. I do not know what the cause of it was. Anyhow, I thought I could overcome it by listening intently to what he was saying, but I could not, and fell forward. My husband said, 'Can I help you?' I said, 'No. I am in such great pain I can't move now.' With that the light seemed to be going away from me, and darkness came upon me. I thought I was being led somewhere, and I knew the minister had something to do with me. He left me and continued his discourse, and Mrs. Dowie prayed with me, and quite suddenly the pain left me. I have been free from pain since that night."

Confirmation by Her Husband, Who Was Saved and Healed through the Incident.

Mr. Dowie asked her husband if he would not corroborate the testimony. He readily did so, and said: "I will state that I was sitting alongside of her, but partly turned away from her, listening very intently to what Mr. Dowie was saying. I noticed he was looking in the direction of my wife, and it caused me to turn round, and I saw she was very sick. We took her into the back room and Mr. Dowie prayed with her and laid his hands on her, and remained with her a few minutes, and then came back and continued his discourse. Mrs. Dowie remained with her. She was suffering everything but death. Finally she threw off a little water, and she got up and said, 'I have no pain at all; I am entirely healed, and I thank God for it.' Who could help loving a God and a Jesus that would do such a thing?" ["Hallelujah" and "Amen" from the audience.]

Mr. Dowie asked, "You gave yourself to Christ that night?"

"I did."

Eighty-Eight Witnesses Ready to Testify to Their Healing.

Mr. Dowie then said: "I feel if we were to continue to add testimony to testimony we would scarcely strengthen what you have already heard. I will ask all those who have been healed through faith in Jesus to stand." [Eighty-eight persons were counted.]

An Attempt to Introduce the "Christian Science" Imposture.

At this point a lady asked the privilege of speaking, and spoke of her healing in such a manner as led Mr. Dowie to inquire if she was not a believer in so-called Christian Science. She replied that she was. Mr. Dowie firmly forbade any testimony from that standpoint, saying that Christian Science was neither scientific nor Christian; that it denied the divinity of Christ, denied the existence of sickness and sin, denied the Atoning Sacrifice, denied the personality of the Holy Spirit, and was antichristian.

Believers' Baptism and Divine Healing.

A lady asked the privilege of giving a short testimony, and said: "Twenty-five years ago I was lying at the point of death. For four years I had been an invalid. One night as I lay resting the Lord spoke to me and said that if I would be baptized I would be strong for the work. I did not know just what that meant. I had been a Christian eight years but had not been baptized with water. So the next Sabbath I went forward at the command of my Master and was baptized, and I went down into the water sick, trembling, lifeless almost, and I came forth well by the power of God, and for the last seventeen years I have been in the Mission field at as hard labor and as much of it, I suppose, as any gentleman engaged in missionary work. Blessed be God for His power, and for His keeping power. I am so glad to-night to know that the Lord is my perfect healer. I have no other physician."

Singing of Doxology.

Mr. Dowie then offered the following

Prayer.

"Father in Heaven, bless the meeting that is just closing; bless the testimony that has been given to the power and the willingness of Thy dear Son to heal all diseases. We bless Thee for the blind that have received their sight, for the lame that have walked, for the deaf that have heard, and for the cancers and the diseases that have been perfectly cleansed.

"We thank Thee, O Lord, that these are but a few of a great many, and that the witnesses now to Thy power to heal are rising up in all parts of the country.

"Give us, dear Lord, in the resumption of the Mission, greater blessings than we have ever had in this Mission. Grant that Thy servants who have received this truth may be enabled to show by their grateful lives that they are nearer to Thee than ever before, and more earnest in the salvation of their fellow-men, more and more determined to glorify Thee in their spirits, souls, and bodies, which are Thine.

"Hear us, Lord, and forgive anything that has been said amiss. In Thy great compassion look upon those who are being led astray by Modern Spiritualism and Christian Science falsely so-called, and these many forms of error that are contrary to the truth of our Lord Jesus Christ. Help us, O Lord of grace, to withstand evil in every form, and to maintain the standard of simple faith in a living Saviour.

"And now, Lord, accept our gratitude, and help us to carry these beautiful Leaves of Healing to many sin-sick nations. We pray Thee that we may be spared to do this. I ask Thee, dear Lord, for myself, for my beloved wife, for my Secretary, and for my dear little children, the little pilgrim band who are carrying this Mission from land to land. Raise up many to help; and may the Branches of the American Divine Healing Association in this State be Bands of earnest Christians, helpful to all portions of the Church of the living God.

"Again we pray that Thou wilt bless us each individually; keep us very close to Thee, and may we ever be faithful in following only Thee. We ask it for Jesus' sake. Amen."

Mr. Dowie then pronounced the Benediction, and the meeting closed.

Extracts from a Verbatim Report of a Praise and Testimony Meeting Held by Rev. J. A. Dowie and Wife in Hamilton Church, Oakland, Cal., Monday Evening, February 18, 1889.

(Reported by G. H. Hawes, 320 Sansome Street, San Francisco.)

[The large platform was crowded to its utmost capacity by those prepared to testify, and scores besides were seated in front and on each side. The building was quite filled with a large and intelligent audience.]

Prayer.

"May the words of our mouth and the meditations of our hearts be acceptable in Thy sight, O Lord, our strength and our redeemer."

Hymn 162.

"My hope is built on nothing less
Than Jesus' blood and righteousness."

Mr. Dowie then delivered a short address with reference to the work and the future arrangements for Missions. In the course of his remarks he said: "We have placed before the Lord in our meetings to-day a very large number of petitions for prayer—I think about fifty petitions, from various parts of the world; some have come from Switzerland, some from Sweden, some from Australia and New Zealand, and from all parts of the continent. Our average number of letters is over one thousand per month, and apart from any meetings or other work, the attention demanded by this vast correspondence taxes every power the Lord has given us.

"I would give public thanks to my God that for Jesus Christ, our Saviour's sake, He has given us the help of the Holy Spirit in these series of meetings, which for eight months we have conducted in this State.

"Although we shall meet with the friends on one or two public occasions, this is the last Mission we shall have for several months. We have it under consideration whether we shall stay the remainder of the year upon this coast. It is the desire of a very large number of friends that we should. I would like to-night to commit that matter to God, that I may get sound judgment; I want to do what God wants me to, for

"Whilst place we seek or place we shun,
The heart finds happiness in none;
But with my God to guide the way,
'Tis equal joy to go or stay."

"I just feel like that about it. It is very pleasant to stay on this coast; but there are invitations to hold Missions throughout the Middle and Eastern and Northern and Southern States of your country, and from Canada, from Great Britain, and they are beginning to ask from Australia, 'When are you coming back here?' And so we have these invitations. I thank God for these fields. We have calls from Asia and Africa, and from all countries in Europe, and we do feel that the Lord is linking us with His saints who are holding up this Banner and Seeking for the Light, in all parts of the world. I mention this at the very beginning to-night, for I want to beseech God to give us wisdom, even while engaged in this work, that we may be able to come to some right conclusion in the course of a week as to whether we shall stay for a year longer on this coast or not."

After Mr. Dowie had read the petitions and offered prayer for each, his prayer was closed in these words:—

"And now we ask Thee to bless us in this closing night of the Mission. Grant that Thy Holy Spirit's Power may rest upon all who are here, and that great grace may attend every word spoken in Thy name; we ask it for Jesus'. sake."

Mrs. Dowie then read the 67th Psalm: "God be merciful unto us and bless us, and cause His face to shine upon us."

Concerning Finances.

After making announcements for meetings of the Association, etc., Mr. Dowie spoke a few words; he said: "I would like to say now that the free-will offerings which will now be taken up, are in the nature of thank-offerings, and in case anybody thinks we are making a great deal of money out of this matter, I want to say that *no charges have been made of any kind; that no person who has ever been healed has been asked to give a single cent of money;* that the poor have been treated just as kindly and as lovingly and as patiently as the rich; there has been no difference, but as a matter of fact, it is the poor comparatively who have argely been blessed. Thank God there are some who have been blessed who are in other circumstances. I would like to say here that I have borne the entire responsibility of these Missions since I came to this country, with the solitary exception of the Mission held in the Grand Opera House, which was undertaken by friends. The expense is not inconsiderable. I cast the whole matter on the Lord, and the Lord sustains and provides for me. He has done it already spiritually and in many ways. I only wish I could spend ten thousand lives upon the work; I give him all I have, spirit, soul, and body, and time and talent. We work night and day, and this gospel is without money and without price in the fullest sense of the word. ["Amen" from the audience.]

"I just say that because these free-will offerings are to cover the expenses of the Mission. Remember, it is not for my sake, but for the work's sake; and for the work's sake it ought to be fuller and richer and freer than it has been. I am talking for Christ. The Lord will bless, and, I have no doubt, perfectly take care of his work. I think it is due to myself that I should make this statement."

The hymn, "Jesus, lover of my soul," was then sung, and a collection taken up.

One Hundred and Sixty-Three Witnesses Stand Up Prepared to Testify to Their Healing.

Mr. Dowie said: "Now, beloved friends, I would like before we ask anybody to witness with their lips, that everyone who has been healed through faith in Jesus Christ our Lord, will just please rise to their feet, and I will count them.

"There are 163 persons. [Exclamations of "Praise the Lord," and "Amen."]

"I would like very much that every word of testimony be directly given and in the simplest language, and that no one shall give any glory to me, but that all glory shall be given to Him from whom all power has come—to our Lord Jesus Christ."

Healing of Cancer in the Tongue.

Mrs. King, an elderly lady, said: "It is a privilege to-night to testify for Jesus and Him only. This is a large congregation, much larger than I have ever testified before. I praise God He is with me to-night. He has given me a new tongue and a new song in my mouth to sing praises unto Jesus; and I am the daughter of a millionaire to-night, and that is the great King up there. Oh, praise his name!

"For five years I had a cancer on the side of my tongue, and I had four doctors: Dr. Darrin, in the city, on Stockton Street; Dr. Miller out in the Mission, San Francisco, on Valencia Street; Dr. Dornin and Dr. Sienna. The more I doctered the weaker and the worse I grew.

"When Dr. Dowie came here, under his doctrine I received Jesus for my healer, and He has healed both soul and body. Praise the Lord. There is glory in my soul. The Scriptures tell us to testify to God, or worse may befall us. I am going to testify while I have the use of this prattling tongue for the glory and honor of my God and Saviour. He is a wonderful physician; He is my keeper and He is my physician. Not another drop of medicine shall touch my lips. I give Him all the honor and glory to-night."

Mr. Dowie said: "There were two large holes in her tongue, and the disease was entirely beyond all human power to heal. I have examined her tongue myself, and it is perfectly healed. One tonsil was cut away because of the disease."

Instantaneous Healing of a Lady Who Came on Crutches.

Mr. Dowie said: "These crutches [holding them in his hand] belonged to Mrs. Hierlihy, of 2110 Alameda Avenue, Alameda. Her husband is the proprietor of a large planing mill, corner First Street and Broadway, Oakland, and therefore is well known to many in your city. She has been here all day since 11 A. M., and until a late hour this afternoon. She found it necessary to return home, and asked her friend, Mrs. Wixom, of 1778 Eighth Street, to testify for her.

"I may say that as far as I know the case she has been on these crutches for some time, and been ill for twenty years, off and on, and been in bed and unable to be about for several months. It is comparatively recently that she has been able to get upon these crutches. She was healed instantly and perfectly, and can go about freely without crutches.

"We received the following petition for prayer from Mrs. Hierlihy, to which her healing is a direct answer.

"'ALAMEDA, Cal., Feb. 12, 1889.

"'DEAR MR. AND MRS. DOWIE: I want you to pray for me. I have been very sick for five months with a fever. I cannot stand up, nor walk a step without the aid of crutches. I regret very much that I could not attend your meetings. I have suffered for many years with a painful knee, which has quite crippled me in the last four years. Do pray that I may be healed, God is my Father, Christ is my Saviour. Yours sincerely, MRS. N. J. HIERLIHY.'

"Mrs. Wixom knows more about the case than I do. I believe she is your old friend?"

"Yes, sir."

"You know these crutches?"

"I did not know them, but I saw her leave them."

"You know who they belonged to?"

"To Mrs. Hierlihy. She is an intimate friend of mine, and she has been very ill for some time. She has had, amongst other troubles, a very bad knee; it was swollen so badly that she was crippled and could not walk upon it. Recently she had a very severe illness that confined her to her bed for several weeks, and her life was despaired of.

"She heard of Brother Dowie's meetings, and was very anxious to come. But she said it seemed as if the adversary kept her from going, until this past week, when the way was opened, and she was brought in a buggy. She came in on crutches and with the assistance of several persons, and could scarcely get here, she was so feeble. She was healed instantly, left her crutches and walked out to the buggy, and got into it alone without any assistance. She came here again to-day, and her husband told me she ran away from him, got out of the buggy, and came in herself, when he didn't know it.

"She wished me to testify for her to-night. She was obliged to go home. I am very glad to say she has taken Jesus for her physician, and she is greatly blessed in spirit, which is better than all. Praise His name."

Mr. Dowie asked, "You believe she is free from her disease in every way?"

"Yes, sir. She was sitting on the front seat during the meeting, and she rose up and walked, and I said to some friends, 'Look at her; she used to limp so badly, and now see how nicely she walks.'

"I am sure she has been ill for several years—I don't know how many."

Mr. Dowie said: "We give God the glory in this case. The sister has been daily testifying by her presence here, and staid till late this afternoon, but had occasion to go home."

Confirmation by Annie Burkmann of Her Restoration to Sight after Fourteen and a Half Years' Blindness in Her Left Eye.

Mr. Dowie said: "At our last Testimony Meeting here, on February 4, I said that some very wicked and very false statements had been published in the papers of your city, regarding the cases of those healed in the first Oakland Mission. I referred especially to a statement published in the Oakland *Evening Enquirer*, that a number of the persons who were alleged to have been healed through faith in Jesus had only a mythical existence, or their testimonies were false. We proved the falsehood of the charge on that occasion, and silenced the *Enquirer*. We shall still further prove its wickedness this evening. Now, let all those upon this platform and in the audience who were healed in the first Oakland Mission please stand." Fifteen persons stood, and amongst them Miss Annie Burkmann. Pointing to the young lady, Mr. Dowie said: "Miss Annie Burkmann's case was specially attacked. This dear girl's case is mentioned on pages 55 and 56, in the little pamph'et entitled 'American First-Fruits,' and a Baptist minister named Fleenor has dared to say it is untrue. My stenographer sitting here to-night, Mr. G. H.

Hawes, of 320 Sansome Street, San Francisco, took down all the testimonies exactly as they appear in the "American First-Fruits," and he is a professional stenographer. He reports here to-night in a professional capacity. He reports continually in courts of justice, commissions, and in all kinds of important positions, and Mr. Fleenor dared to say that these testimonies were false. Amongst those he said were false is the testimony of this dear girl. We intend this evening to go fully and publicly into this and other disputed cases, and show once more that the little pamphlet states the simple truth. Miss Burkmann, where do you live now?"

"813 Peralta Street, Oakland."

"This lady is sixteen and one-half years old, and was blind in the left eye for fourteen and a half years. She had disease in both eyes. She has had her sight restored. Mr. Fleenor dared to say that testimony was false, a lie, in effect, and that her sight was not restored. I took the pains to ask Mrs. Pereau, Mr. Svenson, Mr. Wilson and others to go down to the editor of the *Enquirer* with this girl and show him her eyes. He examined her eyes and said that she could see perfectly. He took the addresses of the persons who came with her and her own testimony, and said he would put the matter straight the next morning, and he has never said a word about it. [Laughter.] Now that is fairness on the part of the local press publishing falsehoods, and then saying they will tell the truth, and, by failing to do so, telling another falsehood. They rob God of His glory. I convicted them publicly a fortnight ago in this hall, but they still remain impenitent, and still spread false statements concerning these cases. Is that so, Brother Svenson?"

"Yes, sir."

"The editor said he would 'straighten that out'?"

"Yes, sir. We are all witness to that, besides Annie Burkmann herself."

"I want you to see we are not complaining of the persistent falsehoods of the local press without a great deal of reason, and we will never allow it to lie with impunity. [Cries of "Amen."] I care not a single farthing for all that the press can do or say. God is in this work, and He is stronger than all the force of a corrupt newspaper press." [Fervent "Amens."]

"Whereas I Was Blind, Now I See."

Miss Burkmann then said: "To-night is just four months ago since I first could tell the time on a little watch, and now I can read medium print perfectly well, which I never did before. I give all the glory to Him who did it."

Mr. Dowie held the face of his watch before her and asked her to tell the time, saying the watch had stopped. She said, "Twenty-five minutes past eight." This she did with the eye that had been blind, covering the other completely. He then asked her, "That was the eye that was perfectly blind for fourteen and one-half years?"

"Yes, sir."

"And now is the disease out of both your eyes?"

"Yes, sir, they are perfectly well."

"And they were diseased all your life?"

"Yes, sir, except one and a half years."

"Who gets the glory?"

"God."

"Thank God. That will do."

Her Brother Testifies: "What She Has Told You Is True."

Mr. Svenson said Miss Burkmann's brother and sister were present, and asked Mr. Dowie to have them stand up.

Mr. Dowie did so, saying, "We will have this matter out with the editor. I like an open fight with God's enemies. JESUS IS CONQUEROR."

The brother and sister came to the platform from the audience, and turning first to the brother, Mr. Dowie said: "Are you the brother of this girl?"

"Yes, sir."

"How long was she blind?"

"Well, I could not tell you. I know she was blind from her childhood."
"And you know she sees?"
"I know she sees."
"What is your name?"
"Gus Burkmann"
"Where do you live?"
"813 Peralta St.'
"Tell all you know about your sister's case."
"Well, I can't tell anything more than what she has said. *What she has told you is true.*"

Her Sister Says: "All that Annie Has Said Is True."

Mr. Dowie then turned to the sister and asked: "What is your name?"
"Christine Burkmann."
  Where do you live?"
"1428 New Broadway. All that Annie has said is true. I know she was blind in her left eye since she was one year and a half old, and now it is all gone; the Lord has given her her sight. I remember when she got the trouble, because I had her in my arms. Now she can see and her eyes were pretty bad." [Cries of "Hallelujah" and "Glory to God."]

Her Swedish Friends Confirm the Testimony.

Mr. Svenson, of 761 Peralta Street, Oakland, who knows Annie Burkmann well, said: "Remember that in this case she is old enough to speak for herself; she knows what God has done for her, and that is all we need to hear. But now her brother and sister testify also to the truth of her own statement, and if anyone is not satisfied with that testimony, we can't help it. If you cannot believe now from what you have heard in this case we cannot convince any man at all."
Mr. Dowie said: "Thanks be to God."
Mr. Svenson continued: "She knows that she has been blind and now sees."

Confirmation of "First-Fruits" Reports.

Mrs. Pereau, of West Berkeley, said she confirmed her testimony given in "American First-Fruits."
Miss Johnson confirmed her testimony given at the Praise and Testimony Meeting held two weeks previous.
Mrs. Leveritz confirmed her testimony as recorded in "American First-Fruits."
Mrs. Stacy confirmed her testimony regarding the healing of her son as given in "American First-Fruits."
Mrs. Ransome confirmed her testimony as given in "American First-Fruits."

John Ashworth's Case.

Mr. Dowie then said: "There was a little mistake made in 'First-Fruits.' The address of Mr. Ashworth is given at 160 Broadway, and Mr. Fleenor said, that would be out in the water; there was no 160 Broadway. Any candid, honestly disposed man could have seen that was a mistake of the printers, but not so Mr. Fleenor. He and other ministers, I grieve to say, made merry over the mythical John Ashworth, whose home was under the water, and Mr. Fleenor and his friends made merry in public. It was 860 Broadway where this young man lived. He is now absent in the country, where I know not, and I cannot produce him here; but we have his written testimony, and there are scores now present who heard him deliver it last August."

[Although we did not know where to find John Ashworth, God did, and in answer to our prayer, and through the columns, as will be seen, of a friendly little weekly newspaper, John Ashworth came to light within three weeks of the meeting. The following letter from him speaks for itself, both as to his healing, its permanence, and the spiritual results of the Lord's work. Surely it is our

Lord Himself who thus enables us to put His enemies to shame. Alas! that they should be those who profess to be of His own Household.]

"RIVERSIDE, Cal., March 8th, 1889.

"DEAR MR. DOWIE : I have the pleasure of writing to you again. Recently, someone sent me two papers from Oakland. They were published in San Francisco, and called The *San Francisco Vindicator*. Who sent them I do not know, but I read them over and was pleased. They gave accounts of another Mission you have lately had in Oakland, and of its success. But, as usual, I read how you had been attacked by the Oakland papers. Nevertheless, that does not alter my faith in your good work. My faith is twenty-fold stronger than on July 18th, 1888, on which date I was healed, and I am enjoying the same excellent and perfect eye-sight to-day. Spectacles, after fourteen years' wearing, have been entirely abandoned. To my mind, since then (July, '88), I have had new life given to me. Somehow I have a peace that never entered my mind before. I do not have to meet trials and temptations in the same way that I had to meet them before this wonderful blessing came. Temptations and trials are now only pleasures to me.

"What I once loved, I now hate, and what I once did hate I now love. Somehow I have a spirit that gives me more understanding of the Bible. These last six months I have learned more of the Bible than in all my short life put together. Where I was once weak in all details of life I am twenty-fold stronger. Life is a pleasure to me now. Words of expression cannot give my gratification to Christ, and my whole heart and soul are glad. I feel like St. Paul,—I have to say, 'Lord, what wilt thou have me to do?' I have prayed for you and your missionary work continually, and wondered many a time where you were. May the Lord bless you and Mrs. Dowie in your work. Believe me,

"Yours sincerely, JOHN ASHWORTH."

Healing of Many Years' Dyspepsia.

Mrs. Newton, 1269 Cypress Street, Oakland, said: "I am perfectly healed of many years' suffering from dyspepsia. I bless the Lord for it. I took Him at His word." (Mrs. Newton spoke so low it was difficult for the reporter to hear her, but he understood her to say that she had been healed of neuralgia before Mr. Dowie came.)

Healing of Ten Years' Heart Disease.

A lady rose on the platform and gave her name as Mrs. T. E. Sprinkle, 1305 Peralta Street, Oakland. Mr. Dowie did not seem at first to know much about the case, and said: "I really do not remember what many are healed of, even although used in the cases. I have seen so many hundreds of persons healed that I do not recall the cases until I have looked at them for a few moments."

Mrs. Sprinkle then said: "I suffered with heart disease. I feel to thank the Lord that I am perfectly healed, spirit, soul and body. Two doctors treated me for heart disease,—Dr. Darrin, in San Francisco, and Dr. Grissell. Now I am perfectly healed."

Mr. Dowie asked Mrs. Sprinkle how many years she had the difficulty, and she answered, "Ten."

Confirmation of Healings After Eight Months.

Mr. Dowie asked those who were healed in the first San Franciscan Mission to please stand. A large number did so; and as this was the last Testimony Meeting likely to be held in the immediate neighborhood of San Francisco for some time, Mr. Dowie deemed it profitable to show the permanence of these Divine Healings by giving a few of those mentioned in "First-Fruits" an opportunity of again witnessing for Jesus.

Mrs. Ritchville said she confirmed the testimony regarding her own healing and sight restored to her boy, who had been born blind, as given in "American First-Fruits," pages 10 to 12 and 48 and 49, most emphatically. She added that her boy's sight was improving all the time. [Cries of "Bless the Lord."]

Mr. Edwards testified that he was healed without human touch in the first Mission.

Miss Foster said: "I confirm my previous testimony (recorded in 'First-Fruits,' pages 14 and 15). I was wonderfully healed on the first day of the first Mission in San Francisco."

Mrs. Edward Leach said, upon being asked if she confirmed her previous testimony (recorded in "First-Fruits," pages 57 and 58), "Indeed I do. The Lord keeps me all the time."

Mrs. Chambers was asked if her mother was continuing in perfect health (referring to Mrs. Brown, who was healed of a bone felon.) She replied that her mother remained well, and was in Sacramento. This healing is recorded on pages 4 and 5, page 39, and pages 46 and 47 of "First-Fruits."

Dr. Dowie said regarding this case: "This was the first case healed through us in this country. She has repeated her testimony frequently. She was incurably ill at Sacramento; she came down to San Francisco, with great difficulty, on a crutch, and was saved and then healed instantly. Her daughter was restored to God at the same time, and she now wants to confirm her mother's testimony. [Turning to Mrs. Chambers] That is all true?"

"Yes, sir. She had a bone felon in the ankle, and it is entirely healed. She says that it is her best foot. She would have been glad to have been here to-night, but it was inconvenient for her to make the trip down here. She wanted me to testify for her."

Healed After Twenty-Eight Years' Suffering.

Mr. Dowie then referred to the case of Miss Wilcox, as follows: "On the 2d of July last this sister, after twenty-eight years' suffering, at the hall of the Y. M. C. A., was instantly restored to God, and left her crutches, which we have in our possession to this day."

Miss Wilcox said: "I confirm my testimony, which is in 'American First-Fruits.' (Recorded on pages 13, 23 and 50.) It is all true. My present address is 426 Fulton Street. I can be found there if anyone wishes to call upon me."

Mr. Dowie said: "Let us see how you walk." [Miss Wilcox, looking strong and vigorous, walked with no difficulty whatever, causing a great degree of interest in the congregation, and there were many fervent exclamations.]

Miss Wilcox continued: "For four years and four months I was afflicted with this last trouble. But the disease was of twenty-eight years' standing, which caused the ulceration of the ankle. It broke out in different places. When I was twelve years I had hip disease, which caused one leg to be shorter than the other; but after I had received strength to walk, and had been walking two weeks, the short leg became longer than the other, and, as near as I can remember, on the 26th of September last it came in its place the same as the other."

A Leading Lawyer Says, "The Evidence Is Enough to Convince Any Court."

Mr. Dowie then said: "All who saw this lady come up on her crutches, lay them down and rise up and walk, please stand. This was a public healing. [A number stood up.] Nineteen witnesses. Is that enough, Mr. Galpin? You are a lawyer."

Mr. Galpin, a lawyer of excellent standing of San Francisco, immediately responded from the audience, "Yes, sir; enough to convince any court."

Mr. Dowie said: "Now you see the Law confirms this Gospel. I have a good lawyer on the subject." [Laughter.]

Remarkable Healing of a Young Lady's Arm.

"I want some of the cases now that have been healed in this Mission. Miss Nettie Johnson, 1331 Union Street, San Francisco, will speak first. I will first of all ask her to show you her arm."

[Miss Johnson exposed her forearm, showing on the under side a scar three or four inches long and half an inch wide, red, and plainly visible to the audience.]

She said: "I was in Memphis, Tenn., a year ago the 13th of this month, and a piece of woodwork fell on my arm and broke it. I did not leave the place until hot weather commenced, and the bone decayed. I went to Dr. Taylor, on Geary Street, and he said I would never have the use of my arm from my elbow up—that I could never turn it. He took me to a skeleton, and showed me just exactly how I would be affected. I had it operated on, and sure enough after it had healed pretty well I could not turn it at all. He said I would have to give up my music.

"I came here to Mr. Dowie, and he laid hands upon my arm, and instantly I tried that movement and I had it. [Exclamations of "Bless the Lord."] It has given me no pain, and I have practiced on an average five hours a day on the piano ever since." [Great enthusiasm in the audience, and fervent exclamations.]

Mr. Dowie asked: "Have you now fully given your heart to the Lord?"

"Yes, indeed."

"How long did it take for the Lord to heal you of that which the doctors said would be a life-long infirmity?"

"About half a second. About four inches of the bone had been taken out. The nerves that run into two of the fingers were cut, and when I tried to use those two fingers I had no control of them at all; now I have a perfect control of them."

Healing of an Internal Cancer.

Mrs. Boillot, 1123 Greenwich Street, San Francisco, who had testified in previous Missions, repeated the story of her healing, and also that of her baby, in an eloquent manner, which deeply impressed the large audience. This case is given fully at page 42 and pages 64, 65.

A False Shepherd, or a True Shepherd? How the Lord Settled the Question.

Mrs. Boillot said: "My baby was very sick at the beginning of the Mission in the Grand Opera House, and I would not go to any doctor. I prayed for the baby, but that time it seemed the prayer would not be answered. I heard that Mr. Dowie was preaching, but some of the Christians with whom I was in fellowship told me that he was a 'false shepherd,' and that the sheep ought not to follow the voice of a stranger. So I kept away. But the Lord called me all the time, 'Go to Mr. Dowie with the case. Go to Mr. Dowie with the case.' And I struggled with the Lord for many a day. The child got worse and worse, and three days and three nights it did nothing but cry and scream all the time, and no food would agree with it. Prayer did not amount to anything, and all the time I heard, 'Go to Mr. Dowie with the case.' At last I yielded to the Lord."

Mr. Dowie asked, "Didn't you think I was a very bad man?"

She replied, "I don't feel worthy to tell the truth about it.

"I sent in a petition for prayer at the Grand Opera House on the 17th of October last, asking you to pray for my baby, and saying I would pray at eight o'clock. I knew the time you were praying, for I saw a change in the face of that child. I said to the little girl, 'They have been praying for you, and I have been praying for you, and now you go to sleep.' The baby wanted to cry as usual, and I said, 'Now you go to sleep, for the prayer must be answered.' And the baby fell asleep, and it slept until eight o'clock the next day. The next day I gave her just the same food that never would agree with her, and her stomach supported it beautifully. The child was changed, the food was not changed, and it has been well ever since.

"I saw that Mr. Dowie was the servant of God. I am not worthy to stand up to-night, and I must say, if he likes it or not, he is the servant of the God most high, and the Lord has given us great grace in bringing him over here. I have received such a blessing in my soul, through the Divine Healing doctrine. I can say that I trust the Lord, and I can never express my thankfulness and gratefulness. I hope Mr. Dowie will forgive me that I ever thought he was a false shepherd; but I have seen he was not a false shepherd. The Lord led me through deep waters to see it, and I give Him the glory."

Mr. Dowie: "Ezekiel 34:4, and the words of our Lord in the ninth and tenth chapters of John, show clearly that one striking characteristic of 'the false shepherds' is that they oppose the ministry of Divine Healing. Of course we fully forgive our sister. It was at no time her willful sin that she thought evil of us. She was deceived by professing Christians, who will have to give an account to God for their sinful conduct, in making and spreading falsehoods concerning the work of the Lord in which we are engaged."

A Lady Teacher Confirms Her Testimony.

Miss Pereau, of 1212 Seventh Street, and of the Cole Public School, Oakland, with much earnestness and clearness said: "I deem it one of the greatest privileges that I have ever enjoyed in my life to be one of the number who stand before you to-night to glorify Jesus not only as my Saviour, but as my Healer, for He not only saves us from sin, but He redeems our mortal bodies according to His own promise.

"I was a great sufferer for fourteen months or more from an affection of the stomach—a nervous affection I think it was. I would not attempt to give it a name, because the different doctors I consulted gave it different names, and likewise treated it differently. Dr. Hill, of this city, called it nervous prostration of the lining of the stomach, brought on from overwork. Whatever it may be called, I know that I suffered very intensely from it, and for fourteen months I was unable to digest or retain anything on my stomach whatever, with the exception of a small amount of bread and milk, and the bread had to be very stale, and the milk with very little cream on it, or it would make me very sick.

"I know there are many people that think a little stomach disorder don't amount to much; but if you had suffered as much as I have, you would think differently. But to let you know just exactly how bad it was, I will say that I could not take anything that had any saccharine matter in it, or anything greasy. On one occasion, when Dr. Hill treated me, he gave me those little pellets made of sugar and water, medicated, and the amount of sugar those little pellets contained made me deathly sick, and he had to give me medicine in liquid form. A short time before I was healed I accidentally, in eating a little piece of dry bread, got hold of a little scrap of butter, which I did not notice on the bread, and which, if I had known, I would not have eaten the bread. I suffered three days intensely from the effects of that small amount of butter; I don't think there was more than you could spread over a nickel. [For foreign readers let us explain: "A nickel" is a 5-cent piece, about the size of an English sixpence.] I was perfectly prostrate, and I could not raise my hand to my head, broke out in a cold perspiration, and had to lie down, and the effects did not wear off for three days. This will give you some idea of the bad condition of my stomach.

"It is three weeks ago to-day that I accepted Jesus as my Saviour right here in this building. I had never given myself up entirely before that day to become a thorough Christian. On the following Thursday I accepted Jesus as my Healer. Dr. Dowie laid hands upon me here in this building and prayed. He laid hands on more than sixty others on the same occasion. He just touched me—no rubbing—and took his hand away instantly. He afterwards told me to eat a good, hearty meal in the name of the Lord. I felt considerable apprehension when I heard that; but he was going to dine at the house of my brother with me that evening, and I felt that I must do it, because I knew he would see me. I just prayed that I would be healed, if I had not been already—of course I could not tell, because I had not eaten anything—for I wanted to be healed before I sat down at the table, because I knew he would make me eat. So we sat down to the table, and the Doctor had me served to everything that was on the table, and the food was very rich. The Doctor said, 'You eat now.' [Laughter.] I ate a large piece of turkey, and you know that turkey is the hardest meat there is to digest, next to pork anyway. I might say here that the last meat I had eaten before that was some beef-steak. My mother took a very nice piece of beef and scraped it, taking just the fine meat, and put it between two or three slices of bread, and made a little sandwich and heated it all through, without a particle of grease about it. I ate that, and it made me very, very sick. I saw then that I could not eat any more meat; I did not attempt it either after that. I could not eat oysters, or soft-boiled eggs, or any of those things that are considered a light diet. Besides turkey I ate potato, rich gravy, all the butter I wanted on my bread, dressing on the turkey, drank coffee, and wound up with peaches and cream, cake, with a thick frosting of sugar on it (before that I could not have eaten a particle of sugar), and an orange. But better than that, I have gone right on eating. I know there are a great many who think that I might have eaten *at the time*, because the Doctor was beside me and inspired me with faith and courage; but the blessing continues all the time, so *that* idea will not stand. The next morning the Doctor took breakfast at the house, and he saw me eat fried eggs and drink coffee. The other morning I ate a large piece of fried salmon. Now I can eat everything."

Mr. Dowie said: "I think on account of your illness you had to retire temporarily from your position?"

"Yes, sir," she replied, "at the beginning of the present school term I asked for and obtained a leave of absence for sixty days; I thought if I was better at the end of that time I would go back, but it looked very doubtful. That time has not yet expired; I will go back when it has expired, well and strong, which I did not expect when I took the leave of absence."

Mr. Dowie exclaimed, "Thanks to God; I am very glad."

[This young lady has returned to her duties as teacher, full of strength and hope, and is now an active Christian worker.]

Healing of Eighteen Years' Infirmities and of Thirty-Four Years' Total Deafness in the Left Ear.

"Now that is a very late case; now we will have one that is older." [Mr. Dowie called on Mrs. Gerold, of 823 Dolores Street, San Francisco. She rose from a back seat of the crowded rows of persons on the platform, all prepared to testify to their healing. Mr. Dowie asked her to step to the front. She said:—]

"I am very thankful to be able to come out and let the people have a look at me. I was sick for eighteen years when I went to the Doctor. When I told him about my disease he asked me if I was fully converted, and if I was willing to take Jesus as my healer. On that very day I did both. I think it was the Saturday before Christmas, and it was the happiest Christmas I had on earth. I was instantly healed. I attended only three meetings when Mr. Dowie laid his hands upon my back. My husband and my children used to help me get off from my chair; they had to lift me up. When I was in the street-cars I used to be very much embarrassed, and they would say, 'Madam, can I assist you to rise?' I had a great deal of pain. I had spinal trouble and was often unable to lift my foot from the ground. When I went upstairs my children would lift up one foot and place it on the stair, and then lift up the other, and I used to get upstairs in that fashion. Since I was healed I have remained perfectly well. I have no pain in my back or anywhere else.

"I had been deaf in my left ear ever since I was three years old; never heard anything in that ear. Mr. Dowie asked me on the evening when I first testified at the Central Presbyterian Church, San Francisco, if that was my address on a card I had given him. I was sitting below him in front of the platform, and he spoke in a low tone into my left ear, and although I had a big piece of cotton in my ear I heard what he said in that ear, and I had never heard anything with it since I was three years old, when it was made deaf by scarlet fever. I am now thirty-seven years old.

"I give all the glory to God, because if He hadn't healed me, I would not have been healed, although it was accomplished through Mr. Dowie's agency."

Mr. Dowie said: "That healing of the deafness of thirty-four years is a very interesting matter."

Healing of Twenty-Four Years' Spinal Injury and Ten Years' Affection of Vocal Cords.

"I will ask Mr. Hugh Craig, of Piedmont and of 312 California Street, San Francisco, to say a few words concerning the healing of his family, and to confirm the testimony he has already given publicly. ["First-Fruits," pages 50 and 51.] Mr. Craig is the President of the newly formed Oakland Branch of the American Divine Healing Association. His testimony may be of special value in Oakland, now that he is occupying so important a position in connection with this work."

Mr. Craig stepped up to the front from the body of the church, and said: "I wish to indorse the testimony of Mrs. Craig and myself, which you will find stated at length in 'American First-Fruits.'

"We got acquainted with Mr. Dowie and his family upon his first arrival here, but we were very shy and very chary about taking to ourselves the doctrine, and only after hearing him repeatedly in the First Presbyterian Church did we see the truth at all clearly. Upon the first occasion that I took Mrs. Craig she was not able to stay at the meeting, and I had to take her home in about an hour. Her affection of the spine had been so bad for some twenty-four years that she could not sit for any length of time. After a visit from Mr. Dowie at our house, and prayer and laying on of hands, Mrs. Craig's affection of the spine was perfectly healed.

"She had another affection of the vocal cords from which she had suffered ten years. For this trouble she had been under treatment of Dr. Liliencrantz, of Oakland, and Dr. O'Toole. She has been entirely healed of this trouble. She has been well of both these affections since July last. Mrs. Craig is here. We are well known to many people in Oakland and in San Francisco. We give the glory to the Lord Jesus Christ. We appreciate the visit and the teachings of Mr. Dowie, which have been a great blessing to my family."

A Local Doctor Accepts Divine Healing.

"I have now the pleasure of mentioning two sisters; one of them is the wife of a beloved Christian doctor of medicine in this city; and it is a great joy to me that Dr. G. S. Smith is a member of the Council of the Oakland Divine Healing Association. He has now fully accepted this doctrine of healing through faith in Jesus. I believe that is so, doctor?"

Dr. Smith replied, "Yes, sir."

"I have had the joy of being instrumental in the healing of dear Mrs. Smith and her sister, Mrs. Bancroft. Dr. Smith lives at the corner of Adeline and Tenth Streets, Oakland.

Healing of the Doctor's Wife.

Mrs. Smith said: "I may say that for the last ten years I have never been what one might call a well woman. I am naturally active, and I have gone about when really I was not able to. My husband knows better than anyone else, perhaps, what I suffered. I suffered a great deal more than I ever said anything about. About three months ago I was very ill, and I was five weeks on my back, unable to be up.

"I have known Jesus for twenty years as Saviour, but not as Healer. It is a blessed thing to know He is the Healer of His people, and that He always will be. I have never felt so well as I do to-night, and I expected to be under the doctor's care for six or eight months more. I have been so for twelve months past; and for two years at a time I have not been out of the doctor's hands, you might say, although I am a doctor's wife. I have had the best of care and the best of treatment. I have had the consultations of the best doctors of San Francisco, and yet I never was well. But now I do not expect to be sick any more. I thank God that in my spirit, soul, and body I feel refreshed and blessed. I am very glad to be able to testify to the help I have received. I shall trust the Lord to keep me, and will trust Him as my healer for the rest of my life."

Healing of the Doctor's Sister.

Mrs. Bancroft, Dr. Smith's sister, then spoke as follows: "The Lord has blessed me in body, and He blesses me in soul and spirit. I have known the Lord for thirty-three years as Saviour, but I have never known Him before as my Divine Healer. I have suffered for three years from internal gout of a very dangerous character; I have been several times at the very gates of death within the last two years in California. I believe that the Lord has healed me.

"The other day I was at the meeting here and I had a very severe attack of this pain; it was after Brother Dowie had laid hands upon me in the name of the Lord. But Satan, to try me, had sent me, in this meeting, a very severe attack of pain. I went to Brother Dowie and told him about it; he took my hand and pronounced a benediction in the name of the Lord, and the pain went away immediately. I look to the Lord for the future as my Healer.

"I want to tell you, also, that I did not want to be healed; it was greatly against my will. I looked upon disease, and especially of my disease, as a sort of means to get to Heaven by. I never wanted to live long since I have been a Christian; I never wanted to be an old woman; I never wanted to see my dear ones taken from me one after the other and I be left behind. I looked upon my disease as a sort of balloon to carry me to Heaven; and I was mad when I heard about Brother Dowie; I didn't like Brother Dowie, because I did not want to think that he could be instrumental in healing me. But after the Lord showed me how He was willing to heal me, and how I could be healed, I thought I ought to be healed, and He made me willing to be healed; and so He has healed me. Now I am willing to live ["Thank God"], willing to live for Jesus; I hope to live for Jesus and to work for Jesus with the strength He has given me, and trust Him to keep me. And I want to die for Jesus if it is necessary." ["Thank God," "Glory to God," from the audience.]

Mr. Dowie said: "I may say that our sister, Mrs. Bancroft, and Dr. Smith, are the son and daughter of that very eminent man of God, the Rev. George Sidney Smith, D. D., F. T. C. D., late of Dublin, Ireland. I have great joy to think God has used me to other members also of that family. I am so glad this work is going all over the world in so many ways, and these testimonies will give joy to many hearts in the beautiful Emerald Isle, a land which God will yet most richly bless, and which we hope to visit, for many there are desirous of hearing this doctrine from our lips."

Saved and Healed.

A lady giving her name as Mrs. Wallace, Todd St., Lorin, said: "I have been saved, and I have been healed of a severe kidney trouble."

Saved, Healed, and Working for Jesus:

Mrs. Rodenbeck, of Alameda, said: "I want to praise the Lord for what He has done for me. I was a great sinner, but I am rejoiced to testify for Him to-night. I have been on crutches; I had a lame instep for thirteen years, so that I could not walk. Praise God, He has strengthened that and I have the full use of my instep. I am going to testify for Him whenever I can. He has given me strength, and I am going to work for Him. He has saved me and healed me, and I have work to do, for my family is not saved."

Mr. Dowie asked: "All who saw this sister come in, and saw her leave her crutches behind, rise." Quite a number did so.

Two Little Boys Tell of Their Healing.

A little boy rose on the platform, and in a clear and earnest voice said: "I was sick and the Lord healed me."

Mr. Dowie asked him what his name was, and he said, "Albert Peterson," and that he lived on Oak Street, Alameda.

Another boy rose and said the Lord had healed him. This was the son of Mrs. Pereau, West Berkeley.

Restoration of Voice.

Jane Bray, of 787½ Stevenson Street, San Francisco, said her voice had been restored, and also been healed of another trouble, the name of which the reporter did not catch.

Restoration of Sight and Hearing to One Born Blind and Deaf in Left Eye and Ear.

Miss Ada Aspengren, of Sutter Street, Oakland, then stepped forward, and said: "I am very thankful to the Lord that He healed me, and for what He has done for me. He blesses me, spirit, soul, and body.

"*I was born blind in my left eye, and was deaf in my left ear.* I can see now well, and hear well too. There is something else, I didn't tell Brother Dowie about; that was something I had in my breast for about two years. It gave me a cough, and it was worse in the morning. That is all gone; the Lord took it away. I ask Him to, and He took it. I leave all the sickness with Him, and He is willing to take it."

Those who knew this lady were asked to stand up, and Mr. Svenson, Mr. Wilson, Annie Burkmann, Mr. Sparman, Mrs. Smith, Mr. Cadman, and several others stood up.

Healing of Nine Years' Spinal Disease.

Mrs. Wilcox, 236 Kearny Street, San Francisco, said: "I am very glad to testify to what the Lord has done for me. I was healed in the Central Presbyterian Church in San Francisco. I had had spinal disease and internal diseases which kept me very much of an invalid. For nine years I had worn a brace—a spinal brace—and could not go without it, and finally I was enabled to take it off in the strength of Jesus, and I have not put it on again, and don't intend to, God being my helper. I am trusting in Him. I thank Him. I have been brought very much nearer to Him than ever before. I have had such a blessing spiritually, and He has done so much for us in our family."

Healing of a Daughter.

Mrs. Wilcox continued, "I am living with my daughter and she was not able to go to that mission in the Central Presbyterian Church, as we could not both leave home at the same time. I told her of this beautiful teaching, and she took it to herself, and before she attended any of the meetings she got considerable of a blessing. She had catarrh for a great many years, and it was very serious, and scrofula showed itself at times in different ways. It was very serious. She has taken the Lord as her healer, and she is improving very much; she is almost entirely healed. The last week she had a swelling in the upper part of her eye-lid on the inside, and there was a bunch as large as the end of your finger. She had great confidence that through faith and prayer it would be taken entirely away, and we prayed earnestly for it. The swelling gathered and then discharged terribly; but I want to tell you that she has not had one bit of pain in that eye, although it was shut from the swelling. You would think to look at it that it was a very painful thing. She came over here on Friday and Mr. Dowie laid his hands on it and prayed, and the next day it began discharging, and I never saw anything discharge so. But it has been perfectly wonderful that every of bit pain has gone out of it and she has been able to sleep, and able to go on with her work. She could not see out of that eye. It is really wonderful what this teaching will do in the family.

Our Little Children Have Been Made So Happy About It.

"If they get hurt they just ask Jesus to take it away, and immediately it is done. They have been sick with fevers, very high fevers, and they have been cured of colds. We give all the glory to God. I wish that everybody could take Jesus as their Healer. I am so sorry that we cannot convince all of our Christian friends that Jesus is just as willing to take all our diseases as our sins."

Healing of Many Years' Dyspepsia.

Mrs. Martenet, of Twenty-eighth Street between Mission and Howard, San Francisco, said: "I never had the courage to testify before. I had nervous dyspepsia for many years. I can say that I have been healed entirely. I have also had a number of accidents lately to me, which I have been healed of instantly by prayer. I was healed in the Grand Opera House Mission by laying on of hands. I thank God I am able to testify to-night."

Healing of Rheumatism, Inflammation of Eyes, and Pneumonia.

Mrs. Rudens, 11 Telegraph Place, San Francisco, rose in the audience and said: "I cannot go away without testifying what the Lord has done for me. I got healed first in July; I had a stiff rheumatic arm, and I could not straighten it out, and I had awful pain.

"In the last two or three weeks I had a very bad cold and inflammation of my eyes. A week ago I came over here and Mr. Dowie laid hands on me, and the same night the swelling left my eyes, and my eyes got quite well. Last week I had pneumonia and I thought I would die; I was very bad. I went to Bro. Holmes' meeting on Market Street, and they prayed for me there, and there was such a power there; and when I went home the pain all left me, and I have had no pain since. I praise the Lord."

Healing of an African Young Lady.

At this point a bright, intelligent, young colored lady rose in front of the audience and said she had been healed that day, and that her name and address was Miss Gertie Smith, 1013 Seventh Street, Oakland.

Mr. Dowie said: "I laid hands upon a large number that were healed to-day. I do not call at these meetings for the more recent testimonies as a rule; I like to place on record those that have stood for a while. But this lady has come forward of her own accord, and I am very glad to have her testify. She is one of over one hundred and fifty persons on whom I laid hands during this day for healing. We have had all-day meetings, and have not left the building since 11 A. M."

Miss Smith said: "I have been sick ever since a child eleven years of age, and I have doctored a great deal and with many doctors, not only in this city but in other places. I have found no one to help me only Jesus, and I found Him to-day. It has been difficult for me to walk for the past three or four days; but to-day I came here and I found Jesus, and He healed me soul and body, and I went home and buttoned up my shoes, which I have not done for three days. I feel that I am a new person. I have no pain whatever, and I have given my spirit, soul and body to Jesus." ["Thanks be to God," from Mr. Dowie.]

Mr. Dowie said: "She had internal troubles; it was a very severe case. Dr. Lane has just informed me she was converted with more than twenty others at the close of our meeting here this morning. And now I will ask that brother, who has been assisting us largely in our Salvation after meetings during several months to say a few words. He is the President of the San Francisco Branch of the American Divine Healing Association, and is well known and highly esteemed amongst us."

Another Doctor's Testimony.

The Rev. C. T. Lane, M. D., said: "I was just thinking that the time will surely come by and by when the people of Oakland will not be unbelievers in Divine Healing.

"I scarcely know where to begin. I am not going to say very much. You who have known me for the last three months, know that it is pretty good testimony just to look at me. About three months ago I would have had to sit at the further end of the building to listen to Brother Dowie, for I could not bear the sound of his voice if I was near him when preaching. To listen near a preacher would affect my head and my heart, and I would be very nervous. Now I have been here all day since this morning about 11 o'clock in this meeting right along, and I am stronger and feel more vigorous to-night than when I came this morning. I think that is pretty good testimony.

"I have not words, dear friends, to express the thankfulness of my heart to

God for what He has done for me. It is marvelous what the Lord Jesus hath done, and what I have seen Him do through the agency of Brother Dowie. The lame have walked that came in on their crutches; the blind have seen, and all kinds of diseases have been healed. The Name of Jesus has been preached, and I have realized that there is a power in that Name which I never knew before. Jesus Christ seems to be nearer to me now than any time in my experience since I gave my heart to God when I was sixteen years of age. I realize He is present all the time to save, to heal and to keep. He keeps me every moment.

"I am expecting we will see greater work done in Oakland when this unbelief passes away. And it is passing away. The people are beginning to realize that Jesus Christ is the healer of His people. I realize it in my heart, and I thank my Heavenly Father that I ever listened to Brother Dowie, and that the Lord sent him to this Coast. I have not words to express the joy of my soul. ["Thank the Lord," from Mr. Dowie.]

"Not only has He healed myself, but my dear daughter. Our home is a house of rejoicing. A few months ago it was a home of sorrow, and of pain and grief, but now we rejoice all the day long, having Jesus with us as our healer."

Saved and Healed of Paralysis and Concussion of the Spine and Brain in a Remarkable Manner without Human Touch.

A gentleman arose from his seat in the audience and came to the platform. He was a middle-aged man, and appeared to be in excellent physical condition. He first gave his name and address as F. W. Wetmore, 565 Eleventh St., Oakland. He is a member of an old and prominent family in Oakland.

He said: "About three months ago while in Bakersfield I was working on a scaffold, and it broke down with me and I was hurt. I had paralysis, and concussion of the spine and brain—so Dr. Adams, of Oakland, tells me. I suffered everything. Of course everybody knows a person who has an injured spine has something pretty serious. For three weeks I never shut my eyes; I could not sleep. They telegraphed for my father to come down there and get me. I was at Visalia at the time when they telegraphed for him. He brought me home and Dr. Adams came to the house to attend to me. He cupped me several times, but my flesh was dead; I had no feeling at all; he would cup me and I never would feel it; could not tell from the feeling when he did it. After that I began to have a little life, and to feel it.

"When this Mission was first started I came to the meetings with my wife, and it was about all I could do to get here; I suffered so much the first meeting I attended that I was unable to hear what Mr. Dowie was preaching. The next night my wife thought I had better come again. I did so, and did not feel so bad and was able to hear what was said. I attended the Mission regularly every night. My wife was taken suddenly sick here three weeks ago to-night, and Mr. and Mrs. Dowie went into another room with her and prayed for her, and she was healed instantly, and I came right out and gave myself to God. I was converted that night. ["Thanks be to God," from Mr. Dowie.]

"Two weeks ago last Thursday night I began to lose my pain. I had never been free from pain, but from the night I was converted my pains began to grow less and less all the time. But two weeks ago last Thursday night I was in my room and we were ready for bed and we were praying, and I got right up and told my wife that I was cured. I will tell you how I knew I was cured: I felt the pain gradually leave my body, and I felt so light and so good, and I told my wife I felt just as if I wanted to go right through the house and shout for joy.

"I give God the credit. But I want to say that if it had not been for Mr. Dowie I never would have been cured. There are a number of people who think these things are done by human magnetism. I will state that Mr. Dowie never laid his hands upon me, except to shake hands. I asked him to pray for me in the open meetings, and he did so. The day before I was healed I could not lift twenty-five pounds off the floor, but now I think I could stand a pretty good tussle with any of you. I could not lift my foot upon a chair like that [easily placing his foot upon the seat of a chair] without taking hold of it and lifting it up. I am now strong and hearty. Last Saturday I worked half a day, and all day to-day. I went out to Temescal and laid the foundation for a little cottage there. While the laborer was getting ready, I just took his hod and filled it up with bricks a number of times and carried it around and dumped it where I was going to work. I think that will prove that my back is all right."

Mr. Dowie: "Thank God. That is a good testimony with which to close our long series of Missions during the past eight months. We lay it and all the others, with adoring love and gratitude, at Jesus' feet, saying, 'Thine, O Lord, is the Kingdom, and the Power, and the Glory, forever, Amen!' Let us sing with all our hearts the grand Doxology to our Triune God."

The audience then sang with great fervor:—

> "Praise God from whom all blessings flow
> Praise Him all creatures here below,
> Praise Him above ye Heavenly Host,
> Praise Father, Son, and Holy Ghost."

Mr. Dowie then offered the following:

Prayer.

"Father in Heaven, we thank Thee for the mercies of this beautiful day; for Thy condescension and love in using our words, in using our hands, and also in showing that Thou dost heal without any human touch.

"And now for many dear ones who have been healed we pray, and for the multitude that know Thee not as their Healer. We pray also for those who have been blessed and are being perfected. May Thy Mighty, Holy Spirit bring them out perfectly, and may they more and more be filled with Thy love. May they manifest Thy glory and live for Thee.

"May these testimonies, which we humbly lay before Thee now in the name of Jesus, all glorify Thee. We have no glory in this matter, excepting to glory in the Lord.

"And now dismiss us with Thy blessing, and use us in the way that Thou seest best. Lead us right on in this work, and establish it trhough the wide world, for Jesus' sake.

Benediction.

"And now, beloved, abstain from all appearance of evil; and the very God of peace Himself sanctify you wholly. And I pray God your whole spirit and soul and body be preserved entire without blame unto the coming of our Lord Jesus Christ. Faithful is He that calleth you, who also will do it. The grace of our Lord Jesus Christ, the love of God, and the fellowship of the Holy Spirit abide in you, bless you, keep you, and all the Israel of God everywhere forever. Amen."

TALKS WITH MINISTERS ON DIVINE HEALING.

TWO ADDRESSES, DELIVERED BY THE REV. JOHN ALEXANDER DOWIE, AND MRS. DOWIE, B INVITATION OF THE CONGREGATIONAL CLUB, AT THEIR MEETING, HELD IN THE PARLORS OF THE Y. M. C. A., SAN FRANCISCO, MONDAY, DECEMBER 17, 1888.

[REPORTED BY G. H. HAWES, 320 SANSOME STREET.]

The parlors were crowded with an attentive and earnest audience, principally consisting of ministers and officers of Congregrtional Churches in and around San Francisco. The Rev. J. A. Cruzan presided, and after preliminary business had been disposed of he introduced the Rev. J. A. Dowie and Mrs. Dowie.

Mr. Dowie spoke as follows:—

"BELOVED FRIENDS: I am glad of this opportunity to speak to you. If I were to place before you the text most in my mind, it would be the words contained in the eighth chapter of Matthew, sixteenth and seventeenth verses: 'When the even was come, they brought unto Him many that were possessed with devils; and He cast out the spirits with His word, and healed all that were sick; that it might be fulfilled which was spoken by Esaias the prophet, saying, HIMSELF TOOK OUR INFIRMITIES, AND BARE OUR SICKNESSES."

DIVINE HEALING NOT "MIND HEALING" NOR "CHRISTIAN SCIENCE."

"I am glad this subject has been placed before you in the two words, 'Divine Healing.' I have nothing in common with what is called Mind Healing, nor that 'opposition of science falsely so called,' called Christian Science, and I do not like the term, Faith Healing. 'We are saved by grace *through* faith and not of ourselves; it is the gift of God! We are kept by the power of God through faith.' While faith is a very precious grace, yet it is only the medium of the communication of God's infinite love and power, and we must never put it in the place of God Himself. Therefore I am glad the subject is expressed in the words Divine Healing, or 'Healing through Faith in Jesus;' not healing BY faith, but THROUGH faith; through faith in Jesus, by the power of God. As this doctrine is presented by us in our teaching it covers a large field; and however diversely it may be put, and however variously it may be illustrated, it, after all, comes to two points.

TWO CARDINAL DOCTRINES.

"*First*—That 'Jesus, the Christ, is the same yesterday, to-day and forever,' and being so, He is unchanged in power and in will. If His words, 'Lo, I am with you alway, even unto the end of the world;' are true, and they are, then He is as much present in power and in spirit to-day as when He stood in the flesh upon the earth. This being so, we have ever presented in our teaching that He is able, that He is willing, that He is present, and that He is longing to heal His people as in the days of His flesh.

"*Second*—That Disease, like Sin, is God's enemy, and the devil's work, and can never be God's will. Peter said in the household of the Centurion Cornelius, Acts 10:38: 'God anointed Jesus Christ with the Holy Ghost and with power; who went about doing good and HEALING ALL THAT WERE OPPRESSED OF THE DEVIL, for God was with Him. Nineteen centuries ago 'all manner of sickness and disease' was healed by Jesus, and as 'all' whom He healed 'were oppressed of the devil,' it follows logically that all sickness and disease is still the devil's work. When Jesus heals He is not undoing the work of the Father, but the work of Satan. The will of God is to heal now, as it was nineteen centuries ago, *all who believe.* Now in teaching these two points

CHRIST IS THE HEALER, SATAN IS THE DEFILER,

We are accustomed at some considerable length to put them before the eyes and the minds of the people as effectively as we can. We do this with the aid of diagrams. Here is one which we call 'The Two Chains.'

GOOD	EVIL
JESUS ○	SATAN ○
SALVATION ○	SIN ○
HEALING ○	DISEASE ○
LIFE ○	DEATH ○
HEAVEN ○	HELL ○

"The Chain of Good begins with Jesus—from all eternity the eternal Logus, who was God, and in the beginning with God; the 'Lamb of God slain from before the foundation of the world'. Then follow what He hath given to His people, Salvation, Health, Life, Heaven.

"Then the Chain of Evil is Satan, Sin, Disease, Death, Hell. Jesus and Satan are opposed; salvation and sin opposed; health and disease opposed; life and death opposed; heaven and hell opposed. The point is, Has Christ delivered us from 'all the power' of the enemy? We teach that He has, and, therefore, that salvation extends to the body, and that His 'saving health' is a Gospel of Salvation and Healing which must be proclaimed 'among all nations.' Therefore we teach

'THE REDEMPTION OF THE BODY;'

(Romans 8:23) and that the 'Life also of Jesus should be made manifest *in our mortal flesh.*' 2 Cor. 4:11. We make the bold assertion of the Apostle Paul, namely, 'If the Spirit of Him that raised up Jesus from the dead dwell in you, He that raised up Christ from the dead shall also quicken *your mortal bodies* by His Spirit that dwelleth in you.' Romans 8:11. This 'redemption of the body' was never taught by Jesus as something belonging to the hereafter. He taught that this was to be the continuous work of the Holy Spirit in all the ages. How plain are His words, 'He that believeth on me, as the Scripture hath said, out of his belly shall flow Rivers of Living Water.' The Rivers were to flow from the Bodies of Believers, and they did. The Bodies were to be Fountains of Divine Life; for it is written, 'This spake He of the Holy Spirit which they that believe on Him should receive; for the Holy Ghost was not yet given, because that Jesus was not yet glorified.' See John 7:37-39. But the Holy Ghost having been given, the Body becomes the Temple of the Holy Ghost and the Temple of God is to be clean. So that redemption extends not only to the spirit $\pi\nu\epsilon\upsilon\mu\alpha$, and the soul $\psi\upsilon\chi\eta$ but to the body, $\sigma\omega\mu\alpha$; Christ's redeeming work extends to the entire being, spirit, soul and body. Therefore, Divine Healing, the restoration by the Holy Spirit, through faith in Jesus, so long as we 'abide in Him,' is provided for us through all our earthly pilgrimage. When our pilgrimage ends, though we may be old and worn, we shall 'lie down in peace and sleep,' and neither Satan, nor sin, nor disease, nor death, nor hell, shall have any dominion over us, if we let Christ set us free.

"Now in presenting these truths it seems to us that we are

STANDING UPON THE ROCK OF ETERNAL POWER.

We have no teaching outside of the word of God in this matter. We do not present our theories. This ministry is continously the ministry of the Word of Life. We hold fast to Jesus' words: 'It is the Spirit that quickeneth, the flesh profiteth nothing. The words that I speak unto you, they are spirit and they are life.' We believe that 'Fools, because of their transgression, and because of their iniquities, are afflicted,' not because God afflicts them with foul disease. There are many such to-day whose ' soul abhorreth all manner of meat; and they draw near unto the gates of death.' But we also believe, as God's word teaches us, that when 'they cry unto the Lord in their trouble, *He* saveth them out of their distresses.' We do not believe that He does this by pills and potions and plasters, but 'HE SENDETH [Revised Version] His word, and HEALETH THEM, and delivereth them from their destructions [or pits].' See Psalms 107:17-20. These are four wonderful verses.

"And so the whole Mission is

FIRST OF ALL A TEACHING MISSION;

and the whole ministry, as we are enabled to present it, is based entirely upon the word of God. We therefore present that word as fully as we can, always remembering that this was the way in which Christ carried out His great earthly Mission. He did three things: He taught, He preached, He healed. Matthew 4: 23 and Matthew 9:35 have exactly the same phraseology: 'Jesus went about all the cities and villages, TEACHING in their synagogues, and PREACHING the gospel of the kingdom, and HEALING every sickness and every disease among the people.' Teaching came first, Preaching next, and Healing last. That is the divine order in which it was ever put, and the Kingdom of God can only be extended by that Threefold Ministry. Alas, that preaching should be considered the beginning and end of the Christian ministry in these days! A true minister should not only be a divinely ordained preacher, but a divine teacher and healer, as in the church of the first century.

"We have found in connection with this, that as the beautiful Gospel of Divine Healing is placed *after* Salvation, we have

A BLESSED OPPORTUNITY OF PRESSING CHRIST'S SALVATION

upon the people who come to listen. We tell them that they must not attempt to 'touch the hem of His garment,' and that they cannot get into contact with Him at all for physical healing until they have spiritually owned Him as their Lord and their God. We remind our readers that it is written, 'Bless the Lord, O my soul, and forget not all His benefits, who *forgiveth* all thine iniquities, who *healeth* all thy diseases.' Psalm 103 : 2 and 3.

"Forgiveness first, and Healing second. Jesus put it in the same manner: 'Son, be of good cheer, thy sins are forgiven thee,' preceded, 'Arise, take up thy bed and go unto thine house.' Matthew 9:1-7. The leper must first be a true worshiper at Jesus' feet, ere he can find in Him a merciful healer. Matthew 8:2-4. So we have taught that God requires saving faith on the part of those who come to seek Him for healing. There must first be a surrender of the spirit, and a reception of Christ as the Saviour from sin, and that is the *sine qua non;* a condition without which we cannot ask the Lord acceptably for healing. We have nothing whatever to do with those who will not first receive Christ as their Saviour. Divine Healing is the Children's Bread, and it cannot be given to those who are willfully Children of the Devil, for these cannot exercise faith. We find in connection with this teaching that this is a very strong position. We show them the Beautiful Gate of Divine Healing; but we point them to Jesus, who has said, 'I AM THE DOOR OF THE SHEEP.' John 10:7. No goat can enter, much less any devouring wolf. Before they can reach the inner door of Healing, they must pass through the outer door of Salvation. They must receive Christ the Saviour ere they can partake of His blessing as Healer. We repeat it over and over again,

DIVINE HEALING IS THE CHILDREN'S BREAD

and it cannot be given to dogs. The Canaanitish woman must get beyond the recognition of Jesus as the son of David. She must see in Him the God of Israel. When she *worships* Him, and throws herself at his feet, with the cry, 'Lord, help me!' then He can say, 'O woman, great is thy faith; be it unto thee even as thou wilt.' Matthew 15:21–28. The Unitarians' creed, which denies Christ's power and Godhead, can never lead men to Salvation or to Healing. We teach that, in all the healings recorded in Scripture, where faith is not expressed it is always implied. Spiritual perception must come first; for '*without faith it is impossible to please God:*' for he that cometh to God must believe that He is, and that He is a rewarder of them that diligently seek Him.' Hebrews 11:6. How can one exercise a spiritual power, such as faith is, unless that person found that faith in Him who is its Author?

"Presenting that, we find too that Divine Healing points to

A STILL MORE BEAUTIFUL THING,—HOLINESS OF LIFE.

The thirty-fifth chapter of Isaiah presents first Salvation in Christ: 'He will come and save you.' Healing comes next: 'Then the eyes of the blind shall be opened, and the ears of the deaf shall be unstopped; than shall the lame man leap as an hart, and the tongue of the dumb sing; for in the wilderness shall waters break out, and streams in the desert. And the parched ground shall become a pool, and the thirsty land springs of water,' etc. Then HOLINESS follows: for the beautiful Redemption song continues: 'And an Highway shall be there, and a way, and it shall be called

THE WAY OF HOLINESS;

the unclean shall not pass over it, but it shall be for those: the wayfaring men, though fools, shall not err therein.' How blessed are those who walk therein: for this then there is

THE WAY OF LIFE;

the time of the singing of birds has come: 'And the ransomed of the Lord shall return and come to Zion with songs' (not with moanings), 'and everlasting joy upon their heads: they shall obtain joy and gladness, and sorrow and sighing shall flee away.'

"We do not strain the prophecy by applying it thus, for our Lord Himself applied it so in His answer to John the Baptist (Matthew 11: 4 and 5), and it is a glorious presentation of the good time when the whole being of the redeemed is perfected in Christ; and there is no perfection out of him.

"A great deal more might be said about this; but let me emphasize, that unless these points are first understood there is no progress; the way must be clear. By faith, the sinner must see Jesus as the Saviour. *Perceptive Faith* must be followed by *Receptive Faith;* for it is written, 'As many as *received Him*, to them gave He power to become the sons of God' (John 1 : 12). And receptive faith must be followed by a Retentive Faith, a faith that holds fast to Christ. That is followed by Active Faith; a true Christian must work for Christ. Active Faith must be followed by Passive Faith, the highest, and yet the lowliest form—a strong Christian calmly rests in the Lord. It is not in our seeing, our receiving, our holding fast, or our working, that Power lies; Power comes to him who is fully *resting in the Lord.* From that center all the rest proceed. Having taught these things you will see what the effect is; the effect is that we call upon the Church of God to live a higher life. We inquire at once, and firmly, from Christians who seek healing,

ARE YOU DEFILING YOUR BODY?

If you defile the body by any nicotine poison, by the filthy vice of smoking or chewing tobacco, then you sin against God and your own soul. You sow nicotine and reap cancer; you sow nicotine and you reap paralysis; you sow poison in the flesh, and you reap corruption. That is in exact accordance with the law of Sin and Death. For disease is the offspring of Father Satan and Mother Sin, just as much as Death. Let the words ring out in the ears of the Church of God—'Be not deceived; God is not mocked; for whatsoever a man soweth *that* [exactly that same thing, not something else] *shall he also reap;* for he that soweth to his flesh shall of the flesh *reap corruption;* but he that soweth to the Spirit shall of the Spirit *reap life everlasting.*' (Galatians 6 : 7, 8.) I talk plainly in this ministry, and affirm that the defilement willfully by a Christian of his body is sin, just as stealing or lying is sin; for it is written, 'Know ye not that ye are the temple of God, and that the Spirit of God dwelleth in you? If *any man* [be he minister, officer or church member] defile the Temple of God, him shall God destroy; for the Temple of God is holy, which Temple are ye?' (1 Cor. 3 : 16, 17.) No one can mistake God's word in this matter who has an honest mind. The human body of the believer is God's temple. It is written, 'What? Know ye not that your *Body* is the *Temple* of the Holy Ghost, which is in you, which ye have of God, and *ye are not your own!*' We are the Lord's purchased possession, and when He bought us, He did not only buy our Spirits, but He paid the price for the redemption of our souls and *bodies* too. Hence the apostle says, 'Ye are bought with a price [and, oh, what a price Jesus paid!] therefore, glorify God *in your body*, and in your spirit, *which are God's.*' (See 1 Corinthians 6 : 19, 20.) To disgrace God by defiling His temple is clearly to sin. To pollute the body with alcohol is sin, for it defiles and poisons the brain and all the body, and opens the door of God's Temple to many unclean devils. And so with every form of defilement. Novel readers are, for the most part, 'filthy dreamers who defile the flesh' (Jude 8); and the pernicious poison of fictitious literature of every kind excites the sensual desires of multitudes who pollute themselves continually. 'Abstain from all appearance [or every form] of Evil' (1 Thess. 5 : 22), is the absolute command of God, and every Christian must, by God's grace, obey it fully. Therefore, we have

MOTIVE POWER IN TEACHING THIS DOCTRINE,

which comes with great force to those who are sick, causing them to quit sin. They have to give up all secret as well as open sins. Excesses, also, in the conjugal relation, excesses in the exercise of any lawful power that God has given, must be abstained from. There must be a holding in subjection of the whole being. The body must be made the servant, and *never once the master.* [Amens.] Thus many are led to give up sin under the power of the teaching of the word of God in this ministry of Divine Healing, who otherwise would not do so.

"But, beloved friends, the Teaching comes first, as we have said—the elimination of truth from error. The minds of the people must first be delivered from the terrible thought that God can ever be the defiler of His people, and the glorious revelation must be made clear and plain that the hand of Christ is ever the hand of the Healer.

WE HAVE TO MEET AND ANSWER OBJECTIONS,

of course, and Old Testament difficulties are brought to bear especially upon this matter. We are confronted with the words of Job, which a good many people forget are not the words of God. The Book of Job is an inspired record of events in which God and Satan and men took part. The words of Job are not always the message of God. When Job said, 'Have pity upon me, have pity upon me, O ye my friends, for the hand of God hath touched me' (Job 19:21), it was not an inspired word, for the voice of God, reproving Job, rang out from the whirlwind, 'Who is this that darkeneth counsel by word without knowedge?' (Job 38:2). And Job had to confess that he had spoken things that he ought not to have spoken; uttered things he ought not to have uttered, that he had used words without divine wisdom; that he had sinned. He said, 'Behold, I am vile; what shall I answer thee? I will lay my hand upon my mouth' (Job 40:4). Again he said, 'I have uttered that I understood not; things too wonderful for me, which I knew not; . . . wherefore I abhor myself, and *repent in dust and ashes*' (Job 42:1-4). It was then that the hand of the Healer was manifested; for God healed Job, and delivered him also from the false accusations of his three friends who did not see that this was not the hand of God. They thought it was the hand of God, and Job was in the same position. But God revealed that drama which we see now, which Job did not see at the time and did not understand (and sometimes we do not), that while he permits the existence of sin and suffering, and other forms of evil, he never can be the author of evil. Therefore when Job said, 'What? shall we receive good at the hand of God, and shall we not receive evil?' Job was not sinning with his lips willfully, but he was sinning in his mind ignorantly, and he was speaking that which was not right. It is written, 'Let no man say when he is tempted, *I am tempted of God*, for God cannot be tempted with evil, neither tempteth he any man.' See James 1:13-16. Stealing is evil, disease is evil; and when Job said, 'The Lord gave and the Lord hath taken away; blessed be the name of the Lord,' Job was wrong. He did not sin willfully, nor charge God foolishly intentionally; but God proved to him that he had charged him wrongfully. Let us have the whole truth; the Lord gave, it is true; but it is equally positive that Satan took away; and poor Job ignorantly blessed God for what he afterward saw was Satan's work. You surely do not make God the author of the stealing of Job's sheep and camels and oxen and asses? You surely do not make God the author of the sin of Job's children, who in their sinful gluttony, drunkenness, and impenitence were in Satan's power and perished. The family was a sinful one, so sinful that Job daily offered sacrifice for them; 'For Job said, It may be that my sons have sinned, and cursed [the Revised Version reads *renounced*] God in their hearts.' Thus did Job continually.' See Job 1:4 and 5. They were a continuous sorrow to him, and had a foolish mother. He knew they were evil; they perished in their sin; for they despised their godly father. We say, then, what God's word says, that it was the hand of Satan that 'smote Job with sore boils from the sole of his foot unto his crown.' Job 2:7. It was not the hand of the Lord; and we should discern that while there is the divine permission, there is not the commission.

PERMISSION AND COMMISSION ARE POLES ASUNDER,

and must never be confounded. I would like to say a word just here, namely, that a great deal of error arises from confounding these two things. God permitted the Jews to blaspheme his own Son; permitted Judas Iscariot to betray him; permitted Satan to enter his heart and make him a thief, a betrayer, and a liar. But for anyone to say God committed these crimes would be to make God the author of perjury, of stealing, of brutality and blasphemy. Christ submitted; God, the eternal Father, permitted; but it was the temporary triumph of the Evil One; for Jesus himself said at that awful time to those servants of Satan who arrested him at Gethsemane, 'This is your hour, and the power of darkness.' Luke 22:53. He never once said it was the hand of God. There is a graet deal of error in our hymnology. For instance, a well-known hymn says:—

> "'Jehovah lifted up His rod,
> O Christ, it fell on thee;
> Thou wast sore stricken of God,
> There's not one stroke for me.'

That is based upon a misinterpretation of the Scriptures. A person once said to me that it was written in the word, 'He was stricken of God and afflicted.' I said, 'That is not true.' He said, 'That is what it says.' I said, 'It does not, and if you look at the word, you have seriously misquoted. In Isa. 53:4 it is written, 'Surely He hath borne our griefs [in the Revised Version instead of *griefs* the margin reads *sicknesses*] and carried our sorrows, yet WE DID ESTEEM HIM STRICKEN, smitten of God and afflicted.' We Jews, we, the people of God, said, 'Now, there you are on the cross; didn't we tell you that you were a blasphemer, and would come to a bad end?' And they reviled Him, derided Him, mocked Him, and wagged their head, and said, 'You are stricken of God, and afflicted of God, you are a bad man.' Oh, it is a bitter shame that the Church of God should take this false accusation as a truth, and fashion it into a hymn. It is not true. He was wounded for our transgressions, *He was bruised* for our iniquities;' but let us never forget what Peter said on the day of Pentecost to those who put him to death, 'Him, being delivered by the determinate counsel and foreknowledge of God, *ye have* taken, and BY WICKED HANDS have crucified and slain.' Acts 2:23. The hands which committed that crime were *'wicked hands,'* doing the devil's bidding. Christ with the Father agreed in the Divine Counsel, and with clear foreknowledge, to let Satan triumph for that bitter, awful hour; but it was that He might thereby provide for us salvation and healing, and every blessing we need, by that precious, atoning Sacrifice. The glorious words, therefore, follow, Isa. 53:5, 'The chastisement of our peace was upon Him, and with His stripes WE ARE HEALED.'

"You may say that further on the prophecy says, verse 10, 'Yet it pleased the Lord to bruise Him.' I read these words, 'to permit Him to be bruised;' and for many good and sufficient reasons I cannot enter into the matter now and here, but we have entered into it very largely in our teaching. There has been a good deal of difference of opinion amongst eminent scholars upon this subject. I hold that all through the Old Testament there is a mistranslation of the permissive into the causative. If what Peter says, namely, that He was crucified 'by the hands of wicked men,' be true, then his crucifixion could not be the Father's action in any sense, although it was his permission. But the awful guilt of that diabolical crime rests upon the Jews, for it was their sinful action, and Satan's work, of whom they were the blind slaves, through the 'envy' of their deceitful rulers.

"And so, throughout the whole of the Old Testament, I venture to say you can only rightly understand many passages by altering the causative into the permissive. For instance, 'Shall there be evil in the city and the Lord hath not done it?' Amos 3:6. Will any of you say that God creates, is the doer of, every iniquity in San Francisco? Again, 'I make peace, and create evil.' Isa. 45:7. If God creates evil, then where is our responsibility, should we fall into sin? Again, 'The Lord hath put a lying spirit in the mouth of the prophets.' 1 Kings 22:23. Does God put a lying spirit in the mouth of the prophet? Then he would be a father of lies, like the devil; and I want to see where the responsibility is, if we are led astray by a false revelation. Change the verb from causing to permitting, and the difficulties in these and hundreds of passages in the Old Testament vanish in a moment, and God justified from one of the foulest charges brought by infidelity, namely, that He is the author of innumerable crimes. He permits the existence of evil, but permission is not commission. On the contrary, does He not say, Isa. 5:20, 'Woe unto them that call evil good, and good evil, that put darkness for light, and light for darkness, that put bitter for sweet, and sweet for bitter?' The New Testament is abundantly clear upon the matter, and I think that we, as ministers of the New Testament, ought to interpret the Old by the New, and not the New by the Old. I lay it down as a canon of interpretation that when we are listening to the Christ we should say, 'A greater than Solomon is here.' And we are not going to Isaiah or Moses or David in preference to Christ. When he says, 'I say unto you,' it settles the question. He says, 'A good tree cannot bring forth evil fruit, neither can a corrupt tree bring forth good fruit.' Matt. 8:17. God is not a tree of good and evil. God is good, infinitely holy and infinitely pure, and nothing corrupt can ever come to us through His hands. Disease is evil, the product of Satan and sin, hence it can never come from God.

"So these are some of the points of the teaching.

AS TO THE PRACTICE,

we do not care that [indicating by gesture] in itself, about laying hands upon people or about anointing people. I should be very glad if everyone was healed as the Lord has graciously healed and kept me. For twenty-six years I have been delivered by Him alone in every time of trial, and kept in health and strength and in power of spirit, soul and body. I have been lecturing in your country continuously for six months, and before I left Australia had been for many years working up to my utmost strength. I have been speaking, I suppose, on an average about three times a day for more than one hundred and eighty odd days, and I do not feel any weakness. I have written much, conducting a vast correspondence, and had interviews with hundreds of persons. I had all the work of yesterday, and I did not take Saturday to rest, but was at work from an early hour of that day until 11 o'clock at night, preparing my mail for Australia. I seldom know what it is to absolutely rest, except in sleep and in a change of employment. I find rest and joy in continuous service. So I speak, and so it is, all of the grace of God.

"We do not teach that it is *essential* in Divine Healing to anoint with oil, or that there shall be laying on of hands. We say that all a true believer needs to do is to pray as the Centurion did, 'Lord, *speak the word only*, and Thy servant shall be healed.' Matt. 8:8. But then you must have faith it shall be done, not merely that it can be done. We have been largely used by the laying of hands in this ministry; but we believe in the ministry of anointing by the elders, as set forth in Jas. 5:14, 15: 'Is any sick among you? let him call for the elders of the church, and let them pray over him, anointing him with oil in the name of the Lord; and *the prayer of faith* shall save the sick, and the Lord shall raise him up; and if he have committed sins, they shall be forgiven him.' Look at the three *shalls* in that last verse. It is not *perhaps, may,* or *can,* but God says *shall*. Christ says, 'Ask, and it *shall* be given you; seek and ye *shall* find; knock and it *shall* be opened unto you.' Luke 11:9. He does not say these signs *may* follow them that believe, but He says clearly, 'These signs *shall* follow them that believe: in My Name . . . they *shall* lay hands on the sick and they *shall* recover.' Mark 16:17, 18.

"While we do not consider it *essential* in all cases to lay hands on the sick, yet we glorify God that He has used us in that wonderful ministry. In your city the blind have received their sight, the deaf have heard, the lame have walked, and their testimony is there [referring to 'American First-Fruits'], and many have been blessed. But

SUPPOSING THERE WAS NO HEALING IN THIS CITY,

it would not alter the fact that Christ is the Healer. Now, I ask you as ministers, suppose there was not one man *saved* in the city, would it not alter the fact that Christ is the Saviour? No; it would simply show there was no faith in San Francisco. That Christ is the Healer does not rest upon any human testimony, it rests upon the word of God, and not the testimony of man. We have not based it upon the testimony of men, and we shall never do so, God helping us. You do not base your belief that Jesus is the Saviour from sin upon the fact that somebody is saved, or says he is saved; but you base it upon the word of the living God; and there you stand. And there we stand, upon the Rock— resting on the God of Eternal Truth, whose Word we have.

"So this teaching is not new.

IF IT WERE NEW, IT WOULD NOT BE TRUE,

and what is true is not new. We want to get back to the old church lines, as laid down in the New Testament, to primitive lines; and if we are to get back primitive power, beloved, we will have to go a step further and get back primitive organization, primitive faith, primitive simplicity, primitive purity of life. PRIMITIVE POWER FOLLOWS ALL THAT.

"Well, beloved friends, I am very thankful for the opportunity of talking to you. I think I have taken up more than my time.'"

(The Chairman announced that "seven minutes remained.")

A member of the Club said they "would like to hear from the good lady," referring to Mrs. Dowie.

Mr. Dowie continued: "I thank you for your courtesy to Mrs. Dowie. Doubtless she will say a few words.

"It is also remarkable how my dear wife has been kept in connection with the whole of this ministry. I suppose it would almost savor of egotism if I spoke at length of what we have undertaken in this work for the Lord, and I will not. I don't want myself to be put in the front at all in this matter, yet to the glory of God let us say that during these last six years we have seen thousands and thousands of persons individually, and talked to hundreds of thousands, and through our pen to millions, and all in the strength which God supplies. We have had wondrous blessing. 'The Lord hath done great things for us, whereof we are glad.' Mrs. Dowie has worked with me continuously through all the toil of long journeys by land and by sea, followed by meetings lasting frequently all the day from ten o'clock in the morning until very late at night, and sometimes till far on in the following morning. So it has gone on from year to year, and we have had 'fresh oil' every day, new power has continually been given. I have never known for a single day what it has been to be unable to minister to my Lord in all these long years. And in this I greatly rejoice; for we live to do the will of God.

"I desire to say that I esteem it a privilege to talk to Congregational ministers; I was one of you; I am one of you in many things still. I was ordained nearly seventeen years ago as the pastor of a Congregational Church. I was born of the spirit in my native city, Edinburgh, Scotland, when I was a child seven years old, and was brought up in an Independent Church, as we used to call it. My father is a Congretionalist now, and most of my relatives are connected with Congregational Churches." A minister inquired,

"IS THAT WHAT YOU MEAN BY PRIMITIVE CHURCH ORGANIZATION?"

"No, sir, I do not think so by any manner of means. My views upon that subject have been expressed in a recent lecture, entitled, 'A Fact and a Question.' The Fact to which I refer is found in 1 Corinthians 12:28, 'And God hath set ($\varepsilon\theta\varepsilon\tau o$—*hath built into*) some in the Church, first Apostles, secondarily, Prophets, thirdly Teachers, after that, Miracles, then Gifts of Healings, Helps, Governments, Diversities of Tongues.' That is the fact according to the Holy Scriptures. The question is, 'Where are They?' and upon the right answer to that Question depends the whole truth as to the rightful organization of the Church of God.

"There is one more word I would like to add. I may say, brethren, I found it to be a very great blessing to myself to be able to keep very clearly in my own mind the primitive distinction between Spirit and Soul. I feel convinced that much error has crept into the Church, among which is the miserable doctrine of annihilation, in consequence of confounding the words Soul and Spirit. We have a lecture upon that subject, 'The Sanctification of Spirit, Soul and Body,' which we illustrate by a diagram. That diagram is not here; but perhaps you will be able to understand what it is after I have represented it to you. We present in this diagram four circles; the innermost to represent the indwelling of THE HOLY SPIRIT; the next circle is the SPIRIT ($\pi\nu\varepsilon\nu\mu\alpha$); the next the Soul ($\psi\nu\chi\eta$); and the outside circle the Body ($\sigma\omega\mu\alpha$). The triparte nature is not often preached, and man is too often represented as a duality instead of a trinity, made 'in the image of God.' We teach the doctrine largely from 1 Thess. 5:23, 24. The Holy Spirit is the sanctifier of spirit, soul and body. The difference between spirit and soul is essentially distinct, and is so shown in the Scriptures. The first chapter of Genesis shows that beasts have souls; and the same word is used concerning Adam's soul. But that expression has no reference to the spirit. Genesis 2:7 shows that man was constituted by God a triparte being—the Body of dust, the Spirit is the Breath of God's Life, and the Living Soul is identical with that of the animals, birds, fishes in Genesis 1:20 and 30, where the same word is used for their life. All our light on this matter must come from God's Word, which clearly points to a separation of Soul from Spirit. See Hebrews 4:12, 'The Word of God . . . piercing even to the dividing asunder of Soul and Spirit.' The soul can die, the spirit never. Christ 'poured out his SOUL unto death,' (Isaiah 53:12); but that was only His blood, not His Spirit, which could not die. The blood is the life. He poured it out (it was His soul) unto death. And so all the way through we have this distinction of Soul and Spirit in the testimony of God. It leads to many practical thoughts, and has a far-reaching importance not at first perceived—we have found it so in our ministry.

"As illustrating the rapidly growing interest in this ministry of Divine Healing, I may say that I have

RECEIVED FROM FIVE TO SIX THOUSAND PETITIONS FOR PRAYER

from all parts of your country, and also from many parts of the world during these six months. It is wonderful how God has guided the minds of the people to us from many lands, and the answers to prayer that have been given for many at great distances. It is needless that I should give instances of Divine Healing, for hundreds have publicly testified in our meetings in this State, and in this city. Many hundreds have also professed to find salvation in our meetings, and this is our highest joy. The Healings are going on all the time, and I glorify God for what he is doing. There is nothing done through my agency but what may be done through any of you.

I CLAIM NO EXCLUSIVE PRIVILEGES OR POWERS.

"We teach what is recorded in the 12th chapter of First Corinthians, that 'the gifts of healings' are in the Holy Spirit, like all the other gifts of God. They are not under the control of a body called the Church, they are not controlled by any person, call him by what office or title you may; *they are in the Holy Spirit;* and, if the Holy Spirit be in you, He will divide to you severally as He wills. ALL THE GIFTS are in the Holy Spirit, and, therefore, in the Church. The nine gifts of the Spirit mentioned in that chapter are a permanent possession of the Church, namely, the Word of Wisdom, the Word of Knowledge, Faith, Gifts of Healings, Working of Miracles, Prophecy, Discerning of Spirits, Tongues, and Interpretation of Tongues. 'All these worketh that one and the self-same Spirit, dividing to every man severally as he will.' The gifts are permanent, for it is written (Romans 11:29), 'For the GIFTS and calling of God are WITHOUT REPENTANCE.' They are not changed by the unbelief of men. Christ has bestowed the gifts, and they are a permanent possession. The Church is His Bride, and the BRIDEGROOM has endowed her with the gifts. He has not taken them away, and He does not mean to. Long have they lain in the Treasury of His Grace unused. May they be from henceforth fully exercised to bless humanity, and glorify God. May He grant a blessing on the word, and hasten the time when the Church will everywhere declare His 'SAVING HEALTH AMONG ALL NATIONS.' Amen."

The Club cordially invited Mrs. Dowie to say a few words to them, which she did as follows:—

"My Christian friends, I can simply confirm what Mr. Dowie has already told you about his doctrinal teaching; he has gone pretty well over the ground, in as short a space as he could get it into, and he has not missed many of the points. But there is just one passage I might mention which is often brought up by Christians, and that is the much misunderstood passage,

'WHOM THE LORD LOVETH HE CHASTENETH.'

That passage is taken right out of its connection, and many people do not know anything at all about its surroundings, and take it that the chastening means sickness, and, therefore, when they are sick they say the Lord is chastening them, and they cannot pray in faith to have it taken away. Our explanation is this: In the twelfth chapter of Hebrews it says: 'Wherefore seeing we also are compassed about with so great a cloud of witnesses, let us lay aside every weight, and the sin which doth so easily beset us, and let us run with patience the race that is set before us,' and so on. There the parallel is drawn between Christ and the Christian. Now our Lord Jesus never suffered from disease. We are to have the same sufferings as He suffered; we are to suffer just as He suffered; the parallel there is complete. If Jesus Christ had suffered from disease He could not have been the Messiah, because He had to be the spotless Lamb of God. Therefore, we can clearly see that it could not have been disease with which He was chastened. But the proof that this passage does not refer to disease as God's chastening is that the section closes with the words in the twelfth and thirteenth verses: 'Wherefore *lift up* the hands which hang down, and the feeble knees; and make straight paths for your feet, lest that which is lame be turned out of the way:

but LET IT RATHER BE HEALED.' Therefore Healing is God's purpose for us in running our race, and it cannot be a chastisement of disease that we recieve from the Lord.

"And, again, the parallel is also drawn between a child and his parents. When we chastise our children we would not give them disease. Our Lord asked (Luke 11 : 11, 12), 'If a son shall ask bread of any of you that is a father, will he give him a stone? or if he ask a fish, will he for a fish give him a serpent?' No father would do this, and no father would chasten his child with disease more cruel than serpents or scorpions. 'Like as a father pitieth his children, so the Lord pitieth them that fear him.' We cannot imagine a loving father chastising his children with deadly and painful disease.

"In regard to the practical working of this teaching, many Christians who come to our meetings tell us that when they receive this doctrine it brings them in touch with Jesus as if He stood before them. They now speak to Jesus as simply as a little child can speak to his earthly father; they feel Jesus is with them all the time, and they can bring all their little wants to Him and He sympathizes with them.

"We teach that

HE IS PRESENT WITH US ALWAYS,

and not an absent Lord. And so many thousands who have been suffering from every description of disease have been healed of the Lord. We have seen people come into our meetings bent with pain and scarcely able to drag themselves along; poor, suffering women who sometimes tell us they have not had a day's ease from pain for twenty or even thirty years, and in a moment they have seen the teaching, they understand it is not the Lord's will that they should suffer, and they just go to Him in simple faith and ask for healing, and they have gone away healed and well.

"We have preached this now for more than six years. People have come to us afflicted with almost every description of disease that you can mention. We have had many of those who have been healed with us day after day for six years in Australia, and we and hundreds of witnesses can testify that they have been perfectly healed; and the Lord has kept them; for he is not only our Saviour, and our Healer, but our Keeper."

The Chairman announced that fifteen minutes remained for questions. The Rev. Dr. Pond inquired: "I have been greatly interested—greatly interested, and I would like to ask Brother Dowie, not in the spirit of disputation at all, but to hear what he has to say about it, in reference to certain cases of sickness met with in the New Testament, mentioned just as we should mention them, as being the visitation of God's providence; take the case of Epaphroditus and others—I presume they are all familiar to him."

Answer—"In the case of Epaphroditus, nothing is said by Paul as to his sickness being God's providence. But his healing is joyfully recorded (Phil. 2 : 27): 'Indeed, he was sick nigh unto death, but *God had mercy on him;* and not on him only, but on me also, that I should not have sorrow upon sorrow.' Epaphroditus seems to me a good case of Divine Healing. As to the case of Trophemus, Paul simply says, 'I left him at Miletum sick' (2 Tim. 4 : 19). It does not say *why* he was left sick. He might not have been faithful; for at this time many of Paul's companions were failing him. Indeed, he says, only five verses before this, 'At my first answer, no man stood with me; for all men forsook me.' Of course Paul had many companions who were not faithful; Phygellus, Hermogenes, Demas, and others are named among those who forsook him. It does not follow that all of Paul's companions were capable of healing—just as some of you here might be incapable of receiving Divine Healing because of unbelief."

After many other questions by various ministers had been answered, the time having been extended for an additional fifteen minutes, the Club heartily gave a vote of thanks to Mr. and Mrs. Dowie for accepting their invitation to address them, and for presenting the subject of Divine Healing to them

"Christ Is All."

American Divine Healing Association,

PRESIDENT, REV. JOHN ALEX. DOWIE.

Weekly meetings of the following Branches of this Association (open to all) are held as follows:—

THE SAN FRANCISCO BRANCH,

Rev. C. F. Lane, M. D., President; Miss Laura F. Stone, 807 Leavenworth Street, San Francisco, Secretary; Mr. Geo. M. Wood, 211 Sutter Street, San Francisco, Treasurer.

MEETS IN THE CENTRAL PRESBYTERIAN CHURCH,

Corner Golden Gate Avenue and Polk Streets, every Monday evening at 7:30.

THE OAKLAND BRANCH,

Mr. Hugh Craig, 312 California Street, San Francisco, President; Mrs. Crawford, Atherton Street, Berkeley, Secretary; Mr. Arthur L. Thompson, Orange Street, Vermont Heights, Oakland, Treasurer.

MEETS IN THE SWEDISH LUTHERAN CHURCH,

Ninth Street, between Washington and Clay, every Tuesday evening at 7:30.

THE SAN JOSE BRANCH,

Mr. Geo. Harter, 336 North Second Street, San Jose, President; Mrs. M. E. H. Baird, 58 South Third Street, San Jose, Secretary; Mr. Chas. F. Bopp, P. O. Box 1144, San Jose, Treasurer.

MEETS IN THE FIRST METHODIST EPISCOPAL CHURCH,

Every Monday evening at 7:30.

THE BORDEN BRANCH,

FRESNO COUNTY, CAL.

Mr. Geo. Crowder, President; Mrs. Julia Dowda, Secretary; Mr. Geo. W. Dowda, Treasurer.

MEETS AT THE RESIDENCE OF MR. G. W. DOWDA,

Every Monday Evening at 7:30.

OTHER BRANCHES

At Los Angeles, Fresno, and Sacramento, Cal.; Portland, Or.; Tacoma and Seattle, Wash.; and Victoria, B. C., are expected to be formed during the year, and possibly in other places. Details of all Branch Meetings, and all information concerning the Association, can be obtained from the pages of "Leaves of Healing," a monthly magazine for the promotion of this work, published at the Office of "Leaves of Healing," 320 Sansome Street, San Francisco, and any other information required will be gladly given by the President, REV. J. A. DOWIE, on application, at the same address.

THE FOLLOWING PUBLICATIONS

CAN BE HAD AT THE OFFICE OF

"LEAVES OF HEALING,"

320 Sansome Street, San Francisco.

RECORD

OF THE

FIFTH ANNUAL COMMEMORATION

of the Rev. John Alexander Dowie and Mrs. Dowie's ministry of

HEALING THROUGH FAITH IN JESUS,

Held in the Free Christian Tabernacle, Fitzroy, Melbourne, on Lord's Day, Dec. 4th, and Monday, Dec. 5th, 1887, Containing Testimonies from those healed and Ebenezer Addresses.

MELBOURNE:
M. L. HUTCHINSON, 15 COLLINS STREET WEST.
188-.

39 pages 8vo. Price 10 cts. per copy, or 20 copies for $1.25, postage included.

Divine Healing Vindicated.

A REPLY BY THE

REV. JOHN ALEX. DOWIE,

TO AN ATTACK BY THE

REV. DR. CHAPMAN AND THE OAKLAND PASTORS' UNION.

Delivered in the First Baptist Church, Oakland, California, on Lord's Day afternoon, Jan. 27th, 1889.

REPORTED BY GEO. H. HAWES, 320 SANSOME St., S. F.

PUBLISHED BY THE AUTHOR,
SAN FRANCISCO,
1889.

28 pages 8vo. Price 10cts. per copy, or 20 copies for $1.25, postage included.

AMERICAN FIRST-FRUITS.

(New and Enlarged Edition.) Being a Record of 8 months'

DIVINE HEALING MISSIONS,

In the State of California, Conducted by the Rev. JOHN ALEX. DOWIE and MRS. DOWIE. With an appendix containing

TWO ADDRESSES ON DIVINE HEALING,

Delivered before the Congregational Ministers' Club of San Francisco.

PUBLISHED AT THE OFFICE OF "LEAVES OF HEALING,"
320 SANSOME ST., SAN FRANCISCO.

144 pages 8vo. Price 15 cts per copy, 10 copies for $1.25, postage included.

LEAVES OF HEALING,

A monthly International Magazine for the Promotion of the Kingdom of God. Edited by the Rev. JOHN ALEX. DOWIE.

PUBLISHED AT THE OFFICE OF "LEAVES OF HEALING,"
320 SANSOME ST., SAN FRANCISCO.

28 pages 4to. Price 15 cts. per copy, or $1.00 per annum.

Various Tracts and Pamphlets on Divine Healing will also be published from time to time at the above office—320 Sansome Street, San Francisco—where all information can be obtained concerning the work of the

AMERICAN DIVINE HEALING ASSOCIATION.

www.ingramcontent.com/pod-product-compliance
Lightning Source LLC
Chambersburg PA
CBHW030349170426
43202CB00010B/1308